ARMENIANS IN THE BYZANTINE EMPIRE

ARMENIANS IN THE BYZANTINE EMPIRE

Identity, Assimilation and Alienation from 867 to 1098

Toby Bromige

I.B.TAURIS
LONDON • NEW YORK • OXFORD • NEW DELHI • SYDNEY

I.B. TAURIS
Bloomsbury Publishing Plc, 50 Bedford Square, London, WC1B 3DP, UK
Bloomsbury Publishing Inc, 1385 Broadway, New York, NY 10018, USA
Bloomsbury Publishing Ireland, 29 Earlsfort Terrace, Dublin 2, D02 AY28, Ireland

BLOOMSBURY, I.B. TAURIS and the I.B. Tauris logo
are trademarks of Bloomsbury Publishing Plc

First published in Great Britain 2023
This paperback edition published 2025

Copyright © Toby Bromige, 2023

Toby Bromige has asserted his rights under the Copyright, Designs and Patents Act, 1988, to be identified as Author of this work.

For legal purposes the Acknowledgements on p. xi constitute an extension of this copyright page.

Cover design: Adriana Brioso
Cover image: *Synopsis historiarum* by Ioannes Scylitza (fl. 1081),
© Biblioteca Nacional De España

All rights reserved. No part of this publication may be: i) reproduced or transmitted in any form, electronic or mechanical, including photocopying, recording or by means of any information storage or retrieval system without prior permission in writing from the publishers; or ii) used or reproduced in any way for the training, development or operation of artificial intelligence (AI) technologies, including generative AI technologies. The rights holders expressly reserve this publication from the text and data mining exception as per Article 4(3) of the Digital Single Market Directive (EU) 2019/790.

Bloomsbury Publishing Inc does not have any control over, or responsibility for, any third-party websites referred to or in this book. All internet addresses given in this book were correct at the time of going to press. The author and publisher regret any inconvenience caused if addresses have changed or sites have ceased to exist, but can accept no responsibility for any such changes.

A catalogue record for this book is available from the British Library.

A catalog record for this book is available from the Library of Congress.

ISBN: HB: 978-0-7556-4242-7
PB: 978-0-7556-4246-5
ePDF: 978-0-7556-4243-4
eBook: 978-0-7556-4244-1

Typeset by Deanta Global Publishing Services, Chennai, India

For product safety related questions contact productsafety@bloomsbury.com.

To find out more about our authors and books visit www.bloomsbury.com and sign up for our newsletters.

CONTENTS

General maps	vii
Author's note	x
Acknowledgements	xi

BYZANTIUM AND ARMENIA: AN INTRODUCTION	1
The Armenians in the Byzantine Empire: A historiographical overview	6
Romanization: A process explained	9
Being Roman in Byzantium	13
Being Armenian in the early Middle Ages	17

Chapter 1

ARMENIAN ASSIMILATION IN ACTION, C. AD 867–1000	21
The areas of territorial settlement	22
Acceptance and adoption of 'Roman customs'	26
The army and the nobility	31
Religious conversion and conformity	36
Conclusion	43

Chapter 2

THE BYZANTINE ANNEXATIONS OF ARMENIA, 1000–64: IDEOLOGY AND OPPORTUNISM?	45
Basil II and his image	46
The context of the annexations	48
The subsequent annexations	56
Unforeseen consequences	63
Conclusion	70

Chapter 3

THE ALIENATION OF THE ARMENIANS, c.1020–71	73
The later annexations and settlements: Vaspurakan, Ani and Kars	75
Religious antagonism	80
The Royal Armenians in the empire	90
The 'rebellion' of 1040	91
Grigor Magistros	93
Gagik II of Ani	95
The first steps to separatism	96
Conclusion	99

Chapter 4
SEPARATISM, 1071–98 101
    Romanos IV, Manzikert and the Islamic world 103
    The separatism of the Armenian lords 109
    The Armenian Church 119
    From Philaretos to the First Crusade (1086–98) 124
    Conclusion 128

CLOSING REMARKS 131

Appendix I: The Harran Gate 137
Notes 138
Bibliography 168
Index 183

GENERAL MAPS

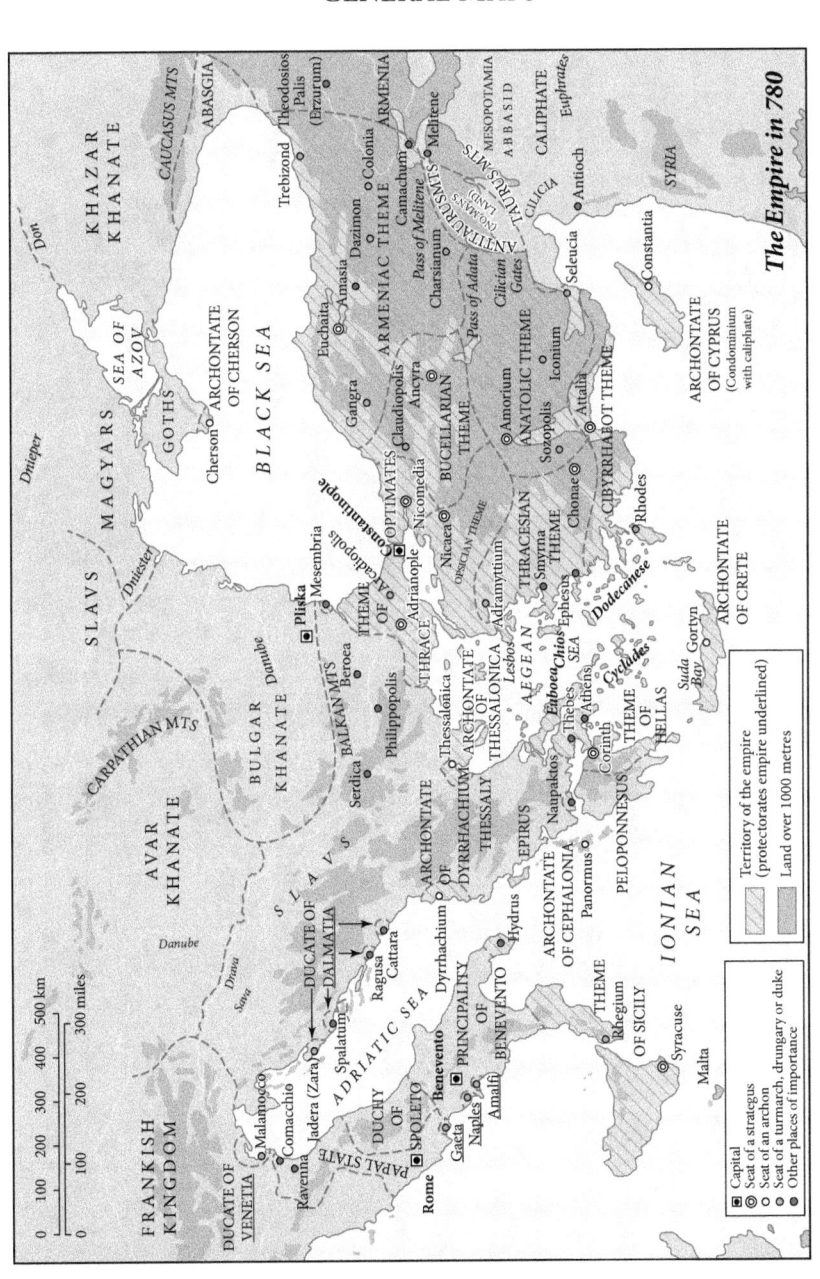

Map 1 Byzantium - 780 AD

Map 2 Byzantium - 1025 AD

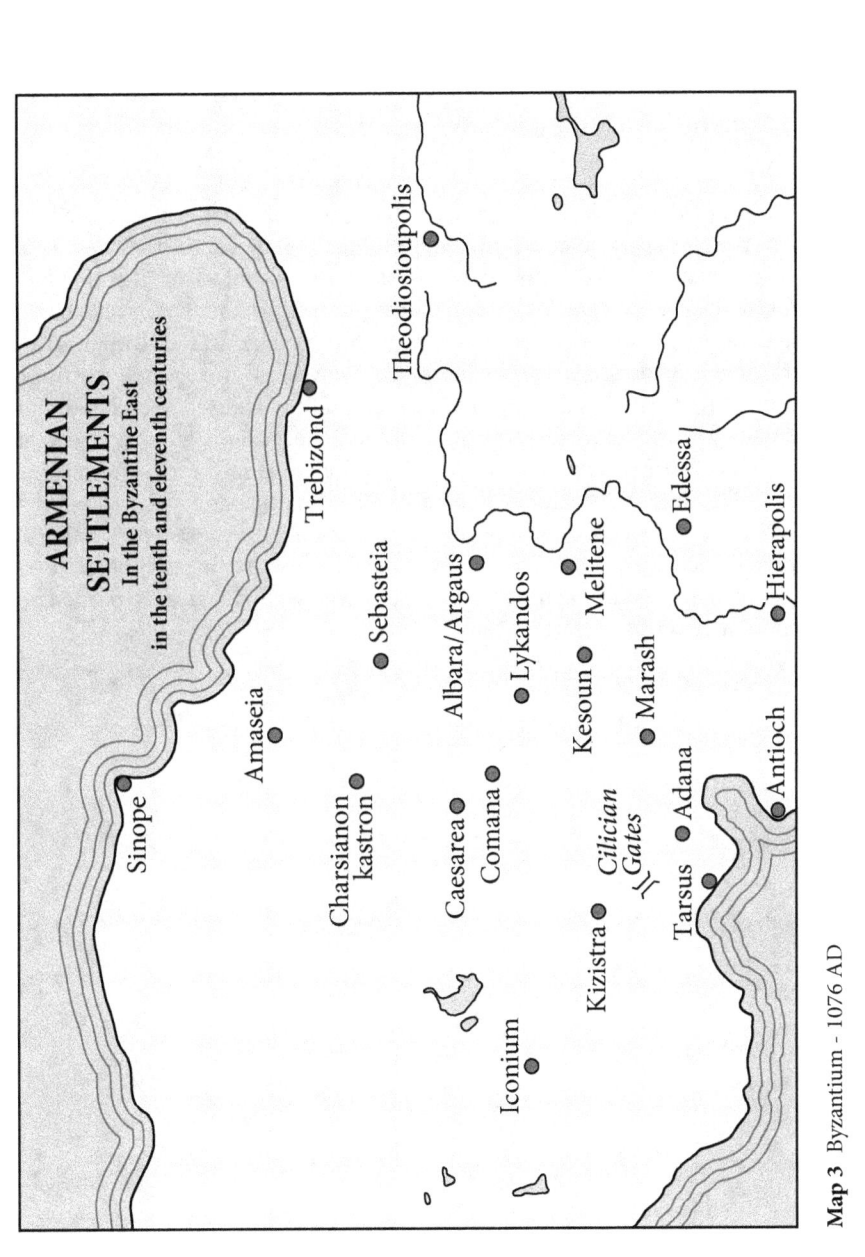

Map 3 Byzantium - 1076 AD

AUTHOR'S NOTE

The subject of this book deals directly with themes of identity in the medieval past. For the modern scholar, it is incredibly difficult to maintain strict consistency with identity labels, such as 'Roman', 'Armenian', 'Greek' and so on. This is in large part due to the inconsistencies that come from our medieval sources, which in turn highlights a certain fluidity when assessing themes of religious, social, political and cultural medieval identities. For the most part, I will clearly use either Byzantine or Roman to refer to the inhabitants of what is commonly referred to as Byzantium. Armenians will be plainly identified, as will their Georgian neighbours (who are sometimes called Iberians). Lastly, a group will emerge in the eleventh century whom I describe as Byzantine-Armenians. This particular label is an untidy but necessary term to group those of Armenian ancestry, sometimes only first generation from arriving in the empire, who are only partly assimilated. I will endeavour to address any confusion in the text where our sources are particularly troublesome in terms of clarity.

ACKNOWLEDGEMENTS

This book is a direct product of my PhD thesis, and as such I owe a great debt to my mentor and supervisor Professor Jonathan Harris for his guidance throughout my PhD studies, as well as advice on converting this into a monograph. A very special mention must go to my great friend and colleague Dr Niccolò Fattori who not only created the map for the Armenian settlements, but who I have shared many joyful memories as we studied for our PhDs together, and have continued to debate many aspects of migration and Byzantium whenever we have the chance. I would also like to pay my thanks to both Dr David Gwynn and Dr Hannes Kleineke for reading draft chapters and their sage advice.

Lastly, but equally importantly, I must thank all of those who have supported me outside of academia and on a personal level. I owe a massive debt to Matthew Williamson, for the advice he has given me through both pleasant and occasionally testing times. I must as ever mention my greatest friend Gregory Goss-Durant for his enthusiasm of pointing out my mistakes, both professional and personal. My love for Zosia Edwards who has been a rock from which this work has been built. A debt I doubt I will ever truly be able to repay. I reserve my great thanks to my parents Timothy and Fiona Bromige, who have supported me entirely through my academic study, and have also encouraged my pursuit of history from a very young age. Finally, I must thank my Grandfather Keith White for his ever sound advice and encouragement since I was a young boy – and to my Grandmother Patricia Ruth Venner White, who sadly passed during my PhD studies, as with the original thesis, I dedicate this book to her for she was always my greatest supporter.

Staines – March, 2023.
Toby Richard Timothy Bromige

BYZANTIUM AND ARMENIA

AN INTRODUCTION

In the reign of Nero (AD 54–68) a Roman general by the name of Gnaeus Domitius Corbulo was entrusted with legal powers to reorganize the eastern frontier and defend Rome's interests in Armenia against perceived Parthian aggression. The main cause of the dispute between the two imperial powers had been over the patronage of vassal kings who ruled the petty kingdoms along the Roman-Parthian border – in particular, the control over the Armenian crown. The kingdom of Armenia was integral to Roman foreign policy in the east: its people, history, language and customs were distinct from its surrounding neighbours, and crucially the location of the Armenian Plateau offered invasion routes for whichever power was able to exert its will over the region. As such, it was crucial for both the Romans and the Parthians to wield influence over the kingdom. The current occupant of the Armenian throne was Tiridates I, a member of the Parthian Arsacid house, who had ruled the country from AD 52 to AD 58, before being ousted by Corbulo in an earlier campaign.[1] A Roman client-king was installed by the name of Tigranes VI (58-61), but he was forced to flee when Tiridates returned a few years later with an army backed by his brother Vologases I of Parthia (AD 51–78). Tiridates was able to solidify his rule by defeating a Roman army at Rhandeia in 62, under the command of Lucius Caesennius Paetus, forcing a surrender and evacuation of all Roman troops from Armenia. The following year, Corbulo was reinstated as the supreme commander in the east, charged with restoring the reputation of Roman arms and bringing Armenia back under Roman influence. This Corbulo achieved and he was able to bring Tiridates back to the diplomatic table where a deal was reached. The Armenian king would travel to Rome, where he would surrender his crown for it to be placed back upon his brow by Nero's own hand.[2] Thus Armenia was to be ruled by the Arsacids but with the explicit blessing of the Roman emperor, establishing a precedence of ceremony and political legitimacy that would bring the two worlds closer together. Borders would fluctuate, dynasties rise and fall, but an inseparable link was established between Rome and Armenia that would last well into the medieval period.

* * *

The main aim of this book is to explore the development of the Byzantine-Armenian relationship during the period *c.*850–1100, mainly from an internal standpoint of Armenians operating within the Byzantine Empire. It will be argued that the most succinct way one can understand this relationship is by looking at it through four linked, chronological and at times overlapping phases: *assimilation, annexation, alienation* and *separatism*. Starting with *assimilation*, this book will argue that one must understand what was meant by custom (ἔθος), an ingredient of medieval Roman identity that is often highlighted in the source material, in order to successfully evaluate the motivation and success of Armenian assimilation in the centuries before the eleventh. In defining what was meant by customs it will be shown that during the ninth and tenth centuries particularly, Armenians did in fact adopt and practice those customs that made one inherently Roman, greatly contributing to the expansion of the Byzantine state in this very same period as soldiers, governors, priests and generals. Our attention will then turn to the next phase, *annexation*, which will come into focus with the study of the medieval Armenian kingdoms during the late tenth and eleventh centuries. These kingdoms were to eventually surrender themselves to Byzantium, most by the mid-eleventh century, although there were subtle differences in how these came about for each individual kingdom. Nevertheless, the result was the same: the exiled Armenian royalty and nobility were given estates in compensation for their ancestral lands in central Anatolia, where they were expected to become loyal Roman subjects. This policy was to have had unforeseen consequences. While Basil II, the emperor in whose reign many of the annexations were either planned or occurred, had worked hard to integrate the rulers of the annexed lands in estates in Cappadocia, after his death a number of events, notably the suspected Artsruni rebellion of 1040 and the annexation of Ani in 1045, undermined his original intentions. Rather, from the 1040s onwards the Armenians appear to have struggled in assimilating, and this is where we reach our third phase, *alienation*. It is in this period, largely the middle of the eleventh century onwards, that we start to see Armenians, now living across the eastern provinces, struggling to attach to the imperial centre with many coming to feel alienated from the empire that most had voluntarily opted to live in. Here, the analysis will turn to explain why this occurred, what tensions were exacerbated and which characters wielded influence in bringing about this souring of relations. Finally, in the years after the Byzantine defeat at Manzikert in 1071, one can witness the last phase of the relationship, *separatism*. It becomes increasingly obvious in the post-Manzikert world that many Armenians no longer looked to Byzantium for protection. Rather, many of the leading characters, of whom most had been formerly engaged in Byzantine service, sought out the creation of independent lordships separate from the Byzantine state, creating a vastly different world into which the First Crusaders arrived on their journey towards Jerusalem at the end of the eleventh century.

* * *

This book starts at the beginning of a crucial period in Byzantine history with the year AD 867, the date in which Basil I Makedon came to occupy the imperial throne. His coronation, in the September of that year, ushered in a new dynasty that would rule for the next 200 years and preside over the apogee of Byzantine civilization. Now Byzantium was no ordinary medieval state; it had a long tradition of continuous rulership from the first Roman emperor Augustus through to Basil's own time in the mid-ninth century. The regalia and reputation of the emperor were also firmly established on Roman terms, the emperor was considered to be above all other 'petty kings' with whom the imperial court treated, he was the secular guardian of the Christian Church and he presided as an autocrat over his Roman subjects, which constituted most of the population. These Roman subjects called themselves *Romaioi* and firmly identified themselves as the successors of the Romans of antiquity through political traditions and shared historical lineage reaching far back to the dawn of the Roman Republic. The *Romaioi* spoke Greek, which had long been the dominant language of the eastern Mediterranean since the time of the Alexander the Great in the fourth century BC, and by the ninth century it had long overtaken Latin as the language of the Roman people; the latter language began to fall out of use once the western half of the empire collapsed to the Germanic invasions of the fifth century AD. Latin was still used for a couple of centuries after the collapse in the west, most prominently in legal texts such as the *Corpus Juris Civilis*, a codification of Roman law by Justinian in the sixth century. Another crucial aspect of being Roman was to be a Christian, following the Orthodoxy of Chalcedonian Christianity as codified at the Fourth Ecumenical Council in 451. This was, however, the loosest aspect of being Roman. Christianity, in its many forms, had spread and been adopted by many of Byzantium's neighbours, who were no more Roman for having converted. Indeed, Christian practices in Byzantium were occasionally at odds with strict 'Orthodoxy', such as the period of Iconoclasm (726–843) which saw the *Romaioi* isolate themselves from the wider Christian world with the destruction of Holy Images. Of course, such religious divisions could be found throughout the medieval Christian world, but it certainly shows how the label of 'Christian' was at times a fluid and malleable construct.

By the mid-ninth century Byzantium found itself in a far smaller state than the Roman Empire of old; the rise of Islam in the seventh century had removed many of the lands of the eastern Mediterranean away from centuries of Roman governance; whereas some 200 years before that the Western Roman Empire had fallen, traditionally dated in AD 476, which again dispossessed the Romans of lands in Italy, Gaul, Spain and North Africa (though some of these would return under Roman control temporarily in the sixth century under Justinian's reconquests). As such, the Byzantine state in 867 consisted, geographically speaking, of Anatolia, the southern Balkans (which were hotly contested with the Bulgarian Empire), the Aegean Islands and a smattering of outposts in southern Italy and Sicily. Despite its smaller size Byzantium was still shaped by Roman attitudes that originated from antiquity; the empire saw its neighbours as inferior, whether through contrasting language, customs, religion or origin, which has led one prominent historian to suggest that it is possible to describe the Byzantines as xenophobic.[3] However, this superiority complex could not have practically worked when one considers that Byzantium was surrounded by 'barbarian' peoples with whom they had to treat, and historically the Roman state had assimilated foreign groups successfully into its polity for centuries, a process scholars have called *Romanization*. It is through this process that countless Armenians (and other non-Romans) came to assimilate into the empire in both an ancient and medieval context, with most coming to consider themselves Roman after a certain amount of time, possibly up to three generations after settling with the empire or attaining citizenship.[4] The Armenians, and their descendants who became Roman, played a particularly important role in the history of the medieval Roman state, rising to positions of authority in the church, military and government, with some attaining the highest office of state: that of the emperor. While there were some emperors before 867 who had Armenian ancestry, none became as important and influential as Basil I Makedon, who in turn would begin re-engaging with both Armenian peoples and states on a scale not seen since the sixth century.

In summary, the ninth-century Byzantine state was a relatively unified entity through its people, ideology and customs but flexible when it came to dealing with its numerous neighbours who were linguistically and religiously diverse. It had significantly contracted, geographically speaking, from the Roman state of antiquity but had lost very little of the Roman world view.

Armenia, on the other hand, was experiencing a revival of its own with Ashot I Bagratuni being crowned in AD 885 as the first independent ruler of the medieval Armenian kingdom, which had finally thrown off the Abbasid yoke after centuries of Islamic rule.[5] Armenia too had a long history stretching back into antiquity. As we have seen earlier the country sat between the two great powers of Rome and Parthia/Persia, serving as a crucial buffer state under the Arsacid dynasty (*c.*AD 52–428). In the fourth century Armenia became the first country in the world to convert to Christianity when St Gregory the Illuminator converted King Tiridates III (298–330) and his court in 301. This conversion was crucial in the future relationship that Armenia was to have with the Roman west, which in turn followed the conversion to Christianity en masse in the fourth and fifth centuries. Before the conversion, the Armenians had predominantly been Zoroastrians, heavily influenced by their Parthian/Persian neighbours, and this had shaped Armenia to be far more eastern-oriented when it came to geopolitical concerns. The Christianization of the country, and its people, later produced the creation of the Armenian alphabet by Mesrop Mashtots in *c.*AD 405, which in turn paved the way for a rich tradition of Armenian literature that was to develop over the centuries. Whereas the Byzantine state fought for its survival against the rise of Islam for much of the seventh through ninth centuries, the Armenian highlands had been conquered through simultaneous negotiations and campaigns by the caliphate and was gradually governed by powerful emirs after the elimination of the old native aristocracy that had stubbornly defended their homeland in the seventh and early eighth centuries.

The rise of the Bagratuni dynasty in the ninth century had as much to do with the declining power of the Abbasid caliphate as it did with the expansion of Byzantium's eastern borders to the threshold of western Armenia, the fates of these two polities and peoples were once again inexorably linked for the next two centuries. The medieval kingdom of Armenia struggled to maintain a coherent centralized structure for much of its existence, and this was largely down to two factors: geography and the Armenian nobility of *nakharars* and *azats*, the upper and lower class of landowners, respectively. The geographical circumstances feed directly into the role and behaviour of the nobility. Armenia's rugged geography in the Caucasus, dominated by mountains, narrow river valleys and high plateaus, made communication and centripetal processes difficult to maintain and enforce. Instead, local communities formed around local lords who held nominal allegiance to a regional leader, who in turn would recognize a wider/national ruler, which in ninth-century Armenia was the Bagratid king. Another problem that plagued the centripetal developments of medieval Armenia was the role of foreign powers, namely Byzantium and the Abbasid Caliphate. While the former would leave the newly crowned Bagratuni kingdom alone for some time, the Abbasids played a game of divide and conquer against their recent former subjects by recognizing Gagik I Artsruni of Vaspurakan (904–937/43) as king of Armenia in 908, rivalling the Bagratids of Ani. These two claims to kingship were never put to rest, with both claimants eventually coming to recognize each other as king, thereby dividing much of historical Armenia into two political entities.

Despite this geopolitical division, however, the medieval Armenian kingdoms were united in a common identity, strengthened by shared language and faith. Medieval Armenian identity was extraordinarily durable in the early Middle Ages, especially when considering the wider social and political context that Armenians faced within their own land. The inherent strength of this identity was drawn from its basic constructs: the land that was recognized as Armenian, the Armenian language, pride in and acceptance of Armenian Christianity (in a broad sense) and the shared history of the Armenian peoples from antiquity.[6] The Armenians were proud of their Christian heritage, being the first Christian nation, and their religion and church were crucial to their identity. The Armenian Apostolic Church was not in communion with the wider Roman Church, having come to disagreements over the conclusions reached at the Fourth Ecumenical Council in Chalcedon, thereby making the Armenian Church Miaphysite in doctrine; we will come back to the importance of this Christological difference later on. Yet a cautionary approach must be urged here, for all of our main Armenian narrative histories were written by men who had careers within the church and/or were writing history under the patronage of a particular princely house and saw the religious identity of the Armenians as the main paradigm of their shared identity. This is particularly prevalent from the ninth century onwards when correspondence between the Byzantine and Armenian churches increased, fluctuating between cordial relations and animosity over confessional differences. This complex relationship is often ignored by both our primary accounts and some secondary writers, who focus on a rigid dichotomy between Armenians and Romans, despite plenty of examples of when tolerance and accord are reached between the two sides. We will come back to this discussion in Chapter 2. In summary, the Armenians were a distinct people set in the disparate world of Caucasia and the wider Middle East, but for all of their prominent characteristics they were remarkably successful in assimilating into the wider sociopolitical milieus in the Christian west and the Islamic east – and especially the *Romanization* process they underwent when arriving in Byzantium.

The Armenians in the Byzantine Empire: A historiographical overview

It is crucial to recognize that from late antiquity Armenian migrants played an important role in both Roman and, later, Byzantine history, serving with particular distinction in the army as soldiers and generals. As one can expect, the topic of Armenians and the Byzantine Empire is not an entirely new enterprise; indeed, many eminent scholars have written on the subject with varying levels of success. The real difficulty when studying this interaction is answering the question: 'when do Armenian migrants lose their native identity and become Roman through a process of assimilation/Romanization?' Fundamentally, this book is going to answer this very question, but first it would be prudent to look at why attempts by previous secondary scholarship have not wholly answered this successfully and how some modern ideological factors have hindered previous historical investigation from analysing this process as objectively as possible.

One of the more prominent issues that scholars have struggled with is the use and consistency of identity labels used by our primary sources. Often terms such as Armenian, Iberian, Greek, Christian, Latin and Saracen can all be used loosely/broadly in different contexts to define different groups, as can vague references to genetical origins with phrases such as 'of Armenian stock/blood', loosely describing the ethnic origins of certain individuals. Without careful analysis this has led some secondary works to take surface-level labels as fact, without asking how we should attempt to understand the use of such labels, whether that be through linguistic, ethnic or religious characteristics. When it comes to the question of Armenians in the Byzantine Empire Anthony Kaldellis has recently tackled some of the issues of what he calls the 'Armenian fallacy' which he sees existing within Byzantine Studies. His definition is thus:

> [. . .] the assumption that Armenian identity was propagated genetically and could not be lost through cultural adaption and assimilation. Put it in the form of a syllogism: if x is an Armenian and y is descended from x, no matter how many generations have passed between them and no matter the admixture of any amount of what is called 'non-Armenian blood', then y is also 'an Armenian'.[7]

As such, no matter how Romanized an individual or family was, they are always seen to be Armenian in 'character' or 'origin', or even faith, and these misjudgements can be applied elsewhere to other ethnicities: for example, Bulgarians or Georgians or Arabs. Another crucial issue that Kaldellis has identified is how modern historians have been influenced by the horrors of the twentieth century where racial-ethnic groups were targeted and persecuted and so have attempted to paint modern concepts of ethnicity and heritage back onto the Middle Ages.[8] To accurately observe how ethnic groups operated and understood their own, and other, identities within the medieval context they lived in, the modern historian needs to tread carefully with the labels used by our primary sources and firmly analyse the language and descriptors of medieval identity – not to impose modern interpretations where they do not belong.

Returning to the case of Armenian assimilation into Byzantium, the precise nature and mechanics of *Romanization* are not universally agreed by Byzantinists to this day. Indeed, much of our previous understanding on the subject has been framed by works written decades ago. One such prominent author on this topic was Peter Charanis (1908–1985).[9] Central to his approach was his belief in the concept of medieval Hellenism and the negative impact which he believed the Armenian migrations had on this.[10] His understanding of what constituted Byzantium, and of what forms of acculturation the Armenians had to take in order to become fully Byzantine, was dictated by his strict division between what he saw as Greek and Armenian culture.[11] Charanis argued for viewing the Byzantines as essentially Greek: 'for those who passed under the ethnicity of "Romans" were in reality Greeks, i.e. Greeks in language and in culture': in one stroke applying his understanding of *Greekness* onto the medieval past and ignoring the very language the sources used to describe themselves, *Romaioi* or even their homeland, *Romania*. Despite these oversights, Charanis correctly identified the problems that arose between the *Romaioi* and the Armenian immigrants in central and eastern Anatolia, although his understanding of the causes is elementary and riddled with uncomfortable opinions:

> The discontent of the Armenians may have been justified but in the end it proved disastrous not only for the Greeks but also for themselves. But then it is in the nature of a minority, aware of its identity and with a sense of power, to be discontented.[12]

It is true that the Armenians in the eleventh century were indeed more resistant to the process of assimilation; however, the reasons for this are far more complex than a 'natural discontentment' found in ethnic minorities. The wide circulation of Charanis' works, particularly concerning the subjects of demography, migration and ethnicity, has strongly influenced how subsequent Byzantinists have understood Armenian assimilation, and his works are consistently cited to this day.

In contrast to Charanis, one of the most helpful works on Armenian assimilation is an article written by Nina Garsoïan, though much of the paper is a summary of where the various features of the assimilation process struggled, and it leaves open many areas where a wider enquiry is needed.[13] These include: a more thorough understanding of what the term 'Armenian' means in Byzantine terms, whether the term is a linguistic, religious or geographical indicator, or all wrapped up into one; removing the uniformity that has often been placed on Armenian minorities; and coming to a realistic understanding of the polemically charged religious tensions between the Byzantines and Armenians. Garsoïan's most pertinent point, however, is in highlighting the ever-problematic reliance on identity labels used by sources, whether that is in the material or literary record. These can often be confusing, interchangeable or attached to xenophobic clichés, all used by our medieval chroniclers on all sides and need careful unpicking to reach a clearer interpretation.

There have also been vital works on the social background of Armenian migrants, which is an important differential when it comes to measuring assimilation in the ninth and tenth centuries. The work of Alexander Kazhdan (1922–97) on the Armenian elite in Byzantium deserves credit for its informative survey on the Armenian origins of the Byzantine aristocracy, though he regards the existence of ethnic groups as a challenge to Byzantine uniformity and potentially falls into the aforementioned 'Armenian fallacy'.[14] Isabelle Brouselle has also investigated how Armenians integrated into the Byzantine nobility, but she parts company with Kazhdan by focusing on the ninth century. Brouselle's article offers some enlightening findings on the use of ethnic identification within family names. This phenomenon, she states, could be the result either of surnames not being common in the ninth century or of negative qualities attributed to persons of particular ethnic ancestry.[15] As mentioned earlier, Jean-Claude Cheynet is of the opinion that it took up to three generations for migrants to lose their ethnic identity, which may explain Brouselle's observation on the ethnic stereotypes surrounding the surnames of recent arrivals into the empire.[16] Cheynet's theory is actually rather durable, although there are examples of assimilation working more quickly, dependent on geographical settlement and direct input by the imperial court to amalgamate certain princely houses into the ruling elite, often facilitated by rapid appointments to governing or military commands. We will look more closely at examples of more rapid assimilation in the first chapter.

On the theme of assimilation there is the work of Angeliki Laiou (1941–2008) who attempted to understand what forms assimilation took in Byzantium. She concluded that the main mechanics of assimilation were 'Christianization, the use of the Greek language, service in the army or the administration, [and] intermarriage'.[17] There is little room to criticize this list; however, some were more important than others. We will return to many of these themes later when we define the process of *Romanization*. Lastly, Gilbert Dagron (1932–2015) provided a viable comparison for the assessment of migrating ethno-religious minorities in Byzantium with the case of the Syrians; S. Peter Cowe also deserves recognition for his work on the Syrian model of migration into Byzantium in the tenth century.[18] Not only were the Syrians who entered Byzantium largely followers of the Miaphysite Syrian Church, a doctrine largely shared with the Armenian Apostolic Church, they were also used by the Byzantines for the same purpose as the Armenians: to resettle depopulated areas after devastation or conquest to provide a Christian, albeit non-Chalcedonian, population which could be used as a buffer against a more hostile state.[19] We will come back to the example of the Syrians occasionally, as they provide useful illustrations to compare and contrast both imperial migration/settlement policies and a wider understanding on assimilation.

Romanization: A process explained

We have already touched on the term *Romanization*, which can be defined as the process by which Roman civilization and culture was spread among non-Roman subjects, through both direct and indirect means. Our attention will be turned to how Romanization worked in Byzantium shortly, but first we must understand how the process developed in antiquity. The Romans were well aware that the most practical way of controlling the vast lands and disparate peoples living under their rule was to provide a way in which newly conquered peoples could become Roman, or at the very least attached to its customs, and so less likely to rebel or cause problems. Indeed, in a speech given by the Emperor Claudius (41–54) in 48 where he argued for the elite of Lugdunum (Lyons) to be granted senatorial status, he further acknowledged the need to assimilate foreign peoples into the Roman state: 'What else proved fatal to Lacedaemon and Athens, in spite of their power in arms, but their policy of holding the conquered aloof as alien-born?'[20] Local elites all across the empire were seen as crucial in spreading Roman customs and culture, and in return they would remain in their position of privilege to which they had become accustomed. In this way, across the empire, temples, forums, schools, roads, aqueducts and other civic amenities were built to encourage the Roman style of life. These projects were often financed, wholly or in part, by local elites who sought to gain from citizenship and imperial patronage through collaboration with Roman governors and administrators.[21] Through this process Roman citizenship became a valued commodity that was sought throughout the Mediterranean, providing a bonding agent that recategorized some grand notions of identity. Such a view can be taken from the *Roman Oration* of Aristides:

> I mean your magnificent citizenship with its grand conception, because there is nothing like it in the records of mankind. Dividing into two groups all those in your Empire – and with this word I have indicated the entire civilised world – you have everywhere appointed to your citizenship, or even to kinship with you, the better part of the world's talent, courage, and leadership, while the rest you recognised as a league under your hegemony.[22]

The assimilation of foreign peoples became integral for how the Roman Empire maintained its control over its far-flung provinces over the centuries, and there are many instances that stand as testament to the successful nature of this process. Take for example the case of Marcus Valerius Severus, a native of Mauretania Tingitana, who successfully lobbied the Emperor Claudius for Roman citizenship and legal marriage rights for his city of Volubilis.[23] In this case, Severus was a member of the local elite who was able to gain patronage for the betterment of his community. Or another, Quintus Lollius Urbicus, a Numidian Berber and the son of a landowner, who was born in the early second century: a career as a soldier and politician saw him serve all around the empire, including Germania, Britain and Judea, revealing an incredible scope of free movement to rise up the social ladder. We know of this from a monument, standing in his native Tiddis (near Cirta, Numidia), which records his distinguished career and Roman credentials.[24] By 212, however, the draw of attaining citizenship had been removed by the *Constitutio Antoniniana* which granted citizenship to all free inhabitants within the Roman world, thereby creating a wide-ranging geographical-based citizenship that granted access to Roman law. Contemporary writers seem to suggest that the act was passed in order to increase the pool of soldiers/tax revenue at the emperor's disposal, but whatever the reasons were for such a move it created the largest body of citizens, sharing a broad civic and legal identity, that the Western world had ever seen.[25]

From the third century onwards, Roman citizenship was largely defined by two factors: the status of being a free man and residing within the confines of the empire. This definition permitted a continuation of the existing linguistic and religious diversity within the citizen body. The two main administrative languages of the Roman Empire were Latin and Greek, which were largely used in the western and eastern halves of the empire, respectively. Beneath the official languages, however, a wide array of tongues was spoken, with many of these languages and dialects lasting well into the fifth and sixth centuries, such as Neo-Punic or Isaurian, and others lasting down to the modern day, having become the main liturgical languages of various Christian churches such as Syriac and Coptic.[26] In terms of religion, one could find a plethora of religious and cultist worship, ranging from the traditional Greco-Roman Olympic Pantheon to foreign cults of Cybele, Isis, Mithras and the Dionysian mysteries. Judaism and Christianity could also be found in many cities across the empire, though the followers of these two religions were more populous in the eastern Mediterranean. The 'bizarre' (as the Romans saw it) nature of Jewish monotheism had been treated with reluctant tolerance by the Romans, but they had no time for Christianity and its followers. Seen as rebels, cannibals and the harbingers of bad fortune for the empire, the early followers of Christ's teachings found themselves subject to violent persecution at various stages in the first few centuries of the Roman Empire. There was one aspect that angered Roman officials towards Christians in particular, and that was their non-conformist attitude towards the Imperial Cult. Neither strictly a religion nor cult per se, what we call the Imperial Cult was a religiously focused statement of political loyalty towards the emperor-head, the leading figure of Rome who represented the body politic of the state and who had a connection with divine powers that watched over the earthly realm. It is important to recognize how inseparable religious and political life was in ancient Rome, with many important politicians holding religious offices concurrently with their political magistracies. For example, the position of emperor also held the religious office of Pontifex Maximus, head of the Roman state religion. From Augustus onwards, citizens and soldiers were expected by the state to make a profession of loyalty and give an offering to the emperor in shrines dotted across the provinces. These offerings and prayers were to bring about divine favour on the emperor who guided Rome and guarded her borders, while also showing their belief and acceptance of the political institutions and customs of Rome, that is, what a Roman is supposed to believe and do.

The Imperial Cult was to come under repudiation with the conversion of the imperial household to Christianity under the Emperor Constantine I (306–37), followed by many inhabitants of the empire through the rest of the fourth century. Any form of sacrifice to the emperor was excluded outright with an edict declaring such practices illegal in 324, although this did not mean that it entirely stopped.[27] This had a knock-on effect for the priesthood of the Imperial Cult with the religious dimension of the role now surplus to requirements; however, many did continue their political roles in city and provincial governance.[28] But as with many aspects of the Christianization of Rome, there were undoubtedly significant Roman influences on the development of the Church as a centralized institution. Constantine I was a great patron to the early church, granting tax exemptions and land for new religious buildings to be constructed, and this patronage allowed some forms of continuation for the ideology and practice of the Imperial Cult and specifically the role of the imperial office within the new religious hierarchy. The emperor was still seen by the church as God's representative on earth, and the imperial persons and institutions were held as sacred and part of the divine's plan. Whereas the Imperial Cult of old had held the person of the emperor as *divus* (divine), the position of emperor under the church was to slowly regain an element of sanctity, with the later Byzantine usage of *theios* to describe the imperial person.[29] As with the customs of the Romans of antiquity, the religious and political leadership of the emperor was inseparable, with prayers of safety and loyalty to the imperial title an expected part of every Roman's ideology and practice. Veneration of the Imperial Cult was not a mindless exercise or a simple declaration of loyalty. The purpose was to create a physical embodiment of the Roman state, allowing provincials in far-flung lands to hold and acknowledge the political entity that they inhabited. The prayers and offerings were part of a wider practical element which showed an engagement with the broader polity, and as such it was an important part of *Romanization* itself in bringing together diverse inhabitants, from Syria to Morocco, and Britain to Egypt, all gaining a sense of belonging: a shared 'Romanness'.

Another important aspect of *Romanization* was service in the imperial army – arguably the most common method of assimilation for barbarian and foreign peoples living in or on the frontiers of the empire. An assured way of attaining citizenship for the common, non-Roman man was to serve in the army for a period of twenty-five years, which upon completion gave them land and citizenship, along with any offspring that they might have. These auxiliary troops, often made up of ethnolinguistic units such as Syrians, Sarmatians and later Huns, Goths, Gepids and Alans, all fought alongside native Roman troops for the empire throughout the centuries. In the imperial period many of the auxiliary companies brought along a specialist skill, such as Syrian archers, Sarmatian cavalry or Rhodian slingers, thereby complementing the skilled heavy infantry that Rome and her Italian allies had been perfecting for centuries beforehand. Indeed, the very service of non-Roman peoples in the army had a knock-on effect on local languages such as in

Syriac where the word *r(h)ūmāyā* (Roman) could be defined as 'soldier' as well as an attachment to a 'Roman' identity.[30] This has led to some difficulties when scholars are unable to distinguish between the two meanings. As Tannous has argued, the Miaphysite patriarch Julian (687–707/9) was known as the 'Roman', either for his father's career as a soldier and Julian's subsequent upbringing around military life or that Julian had been given an education in a monastery in northern Syria and called 'the Roman' on account of his kinship.[31]

We have already talked through some examples of *Romanization* where service in the army granted provincials opportunities to rise through the imperial hierarchy, and this process was also used by the imperial court to pacify and convert hostile peoples on the frontiers. This process overlapped with diplomatic and foreign policy, with Rome taking noble hostages from neighbouring peoples so as to ensure good behaviour and spread Roman customs to barbarian peoples. One of the more famous examples of this comes with the disaster in the Teutoburg Forest in AD 9, where three Roman legions were destroyed by the Germanic prince Arminius who had been considered a trustworthy ally. Arminius was a prince of the Cherusci tribe, and it had been hoped that a Roman upbringing would bring about the slow *Romanization* of his tribe when he would return to rule. Alas, the opposite result came to fruition; however, while Arminius undoubtedly sought to use his knowledge gained from his childhood as a prisoner of Rome to gain the ultimate revenge, his younger brother despised his betrayal and held true to his new Roman identity, even fighting directly against his brother in the campaigns of Germanicus in AD 16.

It was not just foreign peoples whom Rome sought to pacify through service in the army, many provincials also came through the system to strengthen the ties between the centre and the periphery. For those who lived inside the empire's borders, a career in the army allowed significant social advancement for those capable enough to rise through the ranks. As the centuries wore on the main claimants to the imperial throne often came from the army. This was to reach its zenith during the period known as the 'Third-Century Crisis', which saw the rise of the 'barrack emperors' who between 235 and 284 produced fourteen different emperors with an average reign of two years apiece. For much of this period the soldier-emperors hailed from Illyria, a region in the western Balkans, and were to produce some of the more capable emperors in this period, such as Claudius II Gothicus, Aurelian and Diocletian whose reforms re-established solid imperial governance. While things were to calm down over subsequent centuries there was always an opportunity for a power-hungry general to use the army to push their political aims and seize the top job. As we will see later on in the Byzantine period usurpation and civil war came to be the most Roman of all pastimes, producing a quasi-meritocratic route to rule and allowing men of many origins to sit upon the imperial throne.

We have now explored the most important elements of the *Romanization* process in antiquity, showcasing diverse examples of becoming 'Roman' through the adoption of certain religious, linguistic and political identities. Our attention now needs to turn what it meant to be 'Roman' in a medieval context and how strong the links were between the identities that share the same origins, names and structures.

Being Roman in Byzantium

How the Romanization/assimilation process actually worked in Byzantium from the ninth century onwards will be the main subject of the next chapter. Here, I want to tackle a more basic issue: what did it mean to be 'Roman' in the Byzantine Empire? Obviously, the empire underwent significant contractions during the fifth and seventh centuries, and while this took many former 'Romans' away from imperial control it also brought about an ultimately more united Roman people than there had been since the Roman Republic. The Romans of Byzantium, especially from the 'Middle period' (*c.*800) onwards, had come to form an ethnic grouping, bound together by shared language, religion and identifying a native land that was their own and distinguishable from others. One can see the origins of such an understanding of the Roman 'homeland', in a geographical sense, with a sixth-century inscription found on a brick at Sirmium which says:

> Oh Lord, help the town and halt the Avar and protect the Romanía and the scribe. Amen.[32]

The claims of the Byzantines to their Roman identity and heritage have faced a whole series of responses, from outright rejection, scorn or patronizing explanations that they were in fact confused Greeks using the wrong terminology. Such views have ignored the very claims by primary accounts who talk openly about what made them and their fellow citizens Roman during the medieval period. As such, we need to look closely at how our sources described their 'Romanness' for want of a better word.

Investigating that issue is easier said than done since, when considering the Byzantine historiographical tradition, it begs the question as to whether the extant works contain any reliable indicators of contemporary identity at all.[33] Their authors were often merely compilers and copyists of now lost histories, and even when they were writing distinct histories of their own time, they studiously avoided originality and perpetuated archaic stereotypes from antiquity in order to maintain their link with a literary tradition that stretched back to Herodotus and Thucydides.[34] That being said, one can identify a common term that is used through a variety of sources to describe the main constructs of Roman identity in the medieval period, and that is the term 'custom' (ἔθος). So we find in the *De Administrando Imperio* a handbook produced by Constantine VII (913–59) to instruct his son Romanos II (959–63) on good governance, a series of extracts that reference said customs:

> [N]ever shall an emperor of the Romans ally himself in marriage with a nation whose customs differ from and are alien to those of the Roman order.[35]

Or defence against the precedent set by Romanos I Lekapenos (920–45) in allowing his daughter Maria (Irene) Lekapene to marry the Tsar of Bulgaria, Peter I (927–69):

> The lord Romanos, the emperor, was a common, illiterate fellow, and not from among those who have been bred up in the palace, and have followed the Roman *national* customs from the beginning.[36]

These passages are not, in fact, blanket proscriptions. Rather they belong to a particular political context. It is clear the claim that Romanos I was 'uncouth and poorly educated' was an attempt to discredit his reputation and point out his humble 'Armenian' origins by an embittered Constantine VII, who long dwelt in Romanos' shadow during the usurpation period which preceded his own sole rule. Furthermore, it is likely that he deeply resented the marriage that Romanos had brokered in 944 between Constantine's son, the future Romanos II, and Bertha of Provence, the illegitimate daughter of Hugh of Provence, the king of Italy.[37] Similar snobbery can be found over a century later when Anna Komnene made a similar retrospective criticism of Michael VII Doukas (1071–8) for agreeing to the marriage of his son Constantine to Helena, the daughter of Robert Guiscard, in 1074.[38] These two examples could be used to describe a closed system, impenetrable to outsiders, but this is simply not the case. After all, such marriages between Romans and non-Romans did take place and often without a word of protest being raised. The obvious example is that between Constantine VII's own granddaughter Anna and the Russian ruler Vladimir in 989, although the circumstances of the marriage were rather more desperate for the broker, Basil II, who exchanged his sister for a force of several thousand Varangians.[39]

Even if custom did not present any insuperable barrier to marriage alliances, it was nevertheless clearly important when it came to defining what a Roman actually was. If we turn to a slightly later period in the writings of Niketas Choniates we find an interesting reference to custom in the narrative of the campaigns of John II Komnenos (1118–43) in southern Anatolia. Here Choniates informs us that the emperor came across the descendants of those who had previously resided in the empire some few decades prior, who were still Christian but now lived under the rule of the Seljuk Sultan of Iconium. Rather than seeing themselves as under alien occupation, they on the contrary:

> viewed the Romans as their enemies. So much greater is custom, strengthened by time, than race or faith.[40]

It was the abandonment of custom, Choniates suggests, that marked the departure of these Christians from the Roman camp. Yet once again, the source here actually suggests that custom, though central to Byzantine identity, was not an insuperable barrier. After all, Choniates makes it absolutely clear that these 'former' Romans had remained Christian and had not converted to Islam to please their new masters. Thus, custom was apparently distinct from religion. This would suggest that the reverse was also true: just as the abandonment of Roman customs meant separation, by adopting them, a wide variety of people could be included.

In another instance that highlights the complex religious dimensions of the period, the twelfth-century Armenian chronicler Matthew of Edessa describes the Byzantine-Armenian warlord Philaretos Brachamios as:

> a superficial Christian . . . he professed the Roman faith and followed their customs.[41]

Let us unpack what is being said here. In the eyes of the Armenian Matthew of Edessa, Philaretos was 'a superficial Christian', meaning he followed the Chalcedonian Church of Constantinople, 'Roman faith', rather than the non-Chalcedonian Armenian Apostolic Church. This statement is made in the context of Philaretos' autonomous domain that ruled over large swathes of land with dominant Armenian populations such as Cilicia, Commagene and northern Syria during the late eleventh century. It also reveals Matthew's own prejudice towards the Byzantines and their attempts to impose imperial control over the Armenian Church in the 1060s and 1070s – a serious point of contention for Byzantine-Armenian relations in this period. Philaretos' family certainly had Armenian origins but they had been operating inside the empire for several generations and so held distinct Roman qualities, one being the Chalcedonian faith and the other 'their customs'.[42] Clearly Matthew is offering an indication of some other qualities/ideologies that made Philaretos Roman, at least in part.

Returning to the *DAI*, there is evidence to suggest that in the eyes of the imperial court a dividing line was presented by differing kinship and language:

> it is right that each nation should marry and cohabit not with those of another race and tongue but with those of the same tribe and speech.[43]

This is another clear statement by an elitist attitude towards outsiders that overlooks examples where outsiders were able to enter the charmed circle of the imperial court. The *Chronographia* of Theophanes describes the proposed engagement between Erytho/Rotrude, the second daughter of the Frankish king Charlemagne (768–814), and the Byzantine emperor Constantine VI (780–97) in 781. Theophanes informs us that the eunuch Elissaios was sent to the Frankish kingdom before the young woman travelled to Constantinople for her marriage, to teach her:

> the language and letters of the Greeks (Γραικῶν) and educate her in the customs of the Roman Empire.[44]

Both custom and language, Theophanes suggests, could be learned and adopted by an outsider through education and example. One assumes that the same could be said of the Arab Anemas, son of the last emir of Crete, who in 961 became a subject of the empire during the reign of Romanos II and fought bravely in the army, and of the Turk Prosouch who loyally served John II Komnenos after having a Roman upbringing and education.[45] It probably also applies to the Venetians whom Choniates says were adopted as 'natives and genuine Romans'.[46] Outsiders were able to become Romans, but again the issue remains, what exactly were these 'customs' that the sources spoke of?

There is an interesting section in Skylitzes' *Synopsis* that sheds some light on what these customs might have been. Within the chapter covering the reign of Basil I (867–86) events turn to the situation in southern Italy where Byzantine holdings were hard-pressed by the Lombards and the short-lived Emirate of Bari. We are told that the emir, Sawdan, destroyed the Italian city of Iontos in 871/2, and Basil I instructed a new city to be built to replace the lost settlement which would come to be called Kallipolis. It was settled by people from the town of Herakleia in Pontus in addition to those survivors from Iontos and the surrounding population of Apulia. It is at this point in the critical edition of the *Synopss* that an interpolation, found in several manuscripts, offers an insightful description of the characteristics of the city and its inhabitants. This interpolation does not appear to be a marginal note by Skylitzes himself but rather a later note by some unknown scribe, perhaps one who heralded from the city itself. In any case, the interpolation states: 'This explains why even today the inhabitants have the same customs, dress and political institutions as the Romans.'[47] Here were find once again the term custom but slightly elaborated upon by a contemporary voice. It is noted that the inhabitants of the city dress like Romans, although this could indeed refer to courtly dress worn by local elites, by which administrators, judges and governance officials mimicked the style worn in Constantinople. But what is far more important here is how the inhabitants of this city followed similar political practices and institutions as other Romans did, which one can assume to mean a shared ideological world view that places the Roman emperor, and his court, at the pinnacle.

This really is the missing piece of the puzzle. It is clear that 'custom' was not simply another way to describe either religious confession or native language; rather, the obvious conclusion is that these 'Roman customs' were in fact a subconscious, yet simultaneously active, belief, support and loyalty in the universality of Rome, her emperor, her Church and above all the sanctity of the empire and its institutions in contrast with those of its heterodox neighbours.[48] What made the people of Kallipolis, or so the interpolation attempts to portray, is a shared understanding of the world and how it should be ordered, noting the superiority of the emperor in Constantinople rather than the western claimants.

Indeed, returning to the previous examples we have covered, things appear a little clearer. In the case of marriages, the *DAI* is advising that foreign princesses should be educated in the Roman way so as to more easily understand and accept the political and ideological belief in the superiority of *Romania*. Indeed, the criticism of Romanos I for having not been raised with 'Roman customs' was to target his Armenian peasant background and insinuate that he may secretly harbour non-Roman views. When we turned to the twelfth century, and the example of those former Romans of Anatolia who are mentioned by Choniates, the key point borne out in the narrative was that these former imperial inhabitants now held their political loyalty to the Sultan not the emperor. Whereas in the case of Philaretos, he was seen as Roman by Matthew of Edessa for his service in the great institution of the Roman state: the army. Erytho/Rotrude was a Frank and would need to be re-educated to Roman values and ideology if she were to become the consort of the Roman emperor – as would be the case of Anemas of Crete or Prosouch the Turk. What made someone a Roman was fundamentally the acceptance of Roman customs, and this not only held together the peoples of *Romania* but also provided a pathway for foreigners to enter and assimilate into their new homeland.

Being Armenian in the early Middle Ages

Now that we have covered what it meant to be Roman in Byzantium it is only correct and proper to conduct the same exercise with our other main medieval identity: Armenian. It is imperative to understand how the Armenians themselves recognized and wrote about their identity through the primary accounts we have for the ninth through twelfth centuries. Medieval Armenian identity was without doubt the product of events from the conversion to Christianity in the fourth century to the formation of the medieval Armenian kingdoms in the late ninth century. We have already covered the basic constructs of Armenian identity earlier: the land that was recognized as Armenian, the Armenian language, pride in and acceptance of Armenian Christianity (in a broad sense) and the shared history of the Armenian peoples from antiquity.[49] The loudest of these constructs within our sources come from religious identity indicators, especially the independence of the 'true' Christianity of the Armenian Church and the perceived threats to this from both Islam and heretical Christian powers.

The manner in which religious identity indicators were viewed by our sources reveals how remarkably fluid they actually were in this period. We rely heavily on Stephen of Taron's *Universal History* for the Armenian perspective of events in the tenth century, but we must be cautious in how we treat Stephen's observations on Armenian identity. We must remain vigilant when using Stephen's account for study of increased engagement between the Byzantine and Armenian worlds, for Stephen placed great value on the religious aspect of identity, not simply because he was a churchman but more importantly because he believed it to be true.[50] Furthermore, with regard to the model of identity that Stephen of Taron followed, it has been argued that his inclusion of a theological letter, which dominates Book III of the *Universal History*, amounted to 'a defiant response to the Imperial Church as well as an assertion of Armenian parity with, and independence from, Byzantine intellectual and religious culture'.[51] Earlier Armenian historiography was dominated by an ever-present threat of religious annihilation by either the Persian or Arabic empires that surrounded the Armenian homeland. Yet in Stephen's lifetime there was no traditional Zoroastrian and Islamic power threatening the faith; rather, it was a Christian, albeit Chalcedonian, power that challenged the Armenians' religious independence. It is important to understand the motives behind Stephen's decision to give prominence to monastic communities and scholars in his history, for it offers some indication of Stephen's own view on his

Armenian identity, 'constructing it in terms of cultural memory and tradition as well as historic political and territorial expression'.[52] Greenwood goes further in expanding what this meant:

> This construction of Armenian identity, rooted in a simplified expression of the Armenian past onto which local traditions of sanctity and scholarship could be grafted, proved in the long term to be remarkably resilient, because identity, when expressed in terms of shared cultural memory, is able to transcend political and social upheaval.[53]

It is clear that the construction of Armenian identity, as enshrined by Stephen, was remarkably resilient. Yet the same identity indicators as viewed by Stephen are not consistently witnessed in the migrations into the Byzantine Empire during the ninth and tenth centuries. Indeed, our understanding of Armenian identity is severely limited in scope for the lives and feelings of everyone below the nobility. It cannot be overemphasized that it is nearly impossible to evaluate the factors of identity that the majority of Armenians held onto outside of the aristocracy, for our sources did not record their voices.

As such we can conclude from our tenth-century source that Armenians placed great emphasis on their Christianity as it underpinned their literary and linguistic heritage – in essence, their cultural significance in the world. This – coupled with the Miaphysite nature of the Armenian Apostolic Church – became the beacon around which Armenians viewed themselves in comparison with the other Christian peoples who lived around them. And it was this religiously themed identity that persisted through the main Armenian narrative sources stretching beyond the chronological scope of this study. The issue with using this understanding of Armenian identity is that it rarely appears in the Byzantine sources; in fact, it could be argued that it is entirely ignored. As we will see later, many of the Armenians who migrated into the empire in the ninth and tenth centuries seem to have had no difficulty in assimilating, despite the insistence on religious identity being held so dearly by our Armenian sources. This is not to claim that Armenian identity as viewed through Christianity was not real, merely that it was not the divisive and obstructive force towards the mechanics of assimilation that historians have usually assumed it to be.

Lastly, one must attempt to comprehend how the Armenian sources perceived Byzantine identity and their understanding of assimilation. Writing in the early- to mid-twelfth century, Matthew of Edessa was very liberal in his use of identity indicators for the Byzantines, at some points calling them 'Roman', at others 'Greek'.[54] Andrews argues that there is no discernible difference between these terms, and that the vitriol coming from Matthew at times only reflects his feeling of betrayal towards the Byzantines who were expected to be the guardians of the Armenian people. It is an oversight on Andrew's part to ignore the religious dimension of Matthew's critical depiction of the Byzantines, and one can see a link in Matthew's use of the word 'Greek' when discussing religious affiliation and the more positive (in his view) of the descriptor 'Roman' gradually fading from use. Furthermore, the arguments by modern scholars on the feeling of betrayal that Matthew reveals in his work distort our understanding of religiously fuelled identity politics and hinder our understanding of the previously positive relationship between Byzantines and Armenians.[55] While betrayal is a consistent theme in Matthew's work, it does not provide a stand-alone explanation for his dislike or mistrust of the Byzantines, whom he saw as a naturally perfidious and scheming people. Rather, it is through the paradigm of religious conflict and identity that Matthew saw the difference between the Byzantine and Armenian peoples, and this helps explain the variation in presentation of Byzantines within his text.

The Armenian sources only rarely comment on assimilated Armenians and on even more rare occasions criticize individuals for having undergone this process, either themselves or through subsequent generations.[56] Yet it is beyond doubt that the sources, both Byzantine and Armenian, did not see their identity as monolithic or immune to foreign influence; rather the fluidity of these two identities directly contributed to the success that brought an Armenian family to dominate the politics of the empire for nearly two centuries.

Concepts of identity were undeniably fluid in the eyes of our Armenian sources, as one would expect when utilizing sources from across three centuries in a comparative framework. Identity indicators such as religion, language and origin only mattered for an individual if they otherwise disturbed the political consensus within the empire. From our Byzantine sources one can see first-hand how the 'ethnic' background of an individual disappeared after a couple of generations, and a first-generation migrant was able to assimilate into the ruling elite smoothly. Unfortunately, one cannot apply these conclusions to the wider population of migrants, such as those who were forcibly moved by a series of emperors, as we simply do not have the evidence to do so. The social elite whom our sources were interested in documenting was intent on being considered Roman by their contemporaries, and this was largely based on the concept of Roman 'customs' coupled with an observation of Chalcedonian Christianity and command of Byzantine Greek. As argued earlier, these 'customs' revolved around the imperial court: court titles, salary, army commands, administrative and religious offices and active participation in the politics surrounding the position of emperor.

We have now seen examples from our primary sources where both Byzantines and Armenians contrasted themselves with the 'foreign' in their own context. What is clear is that despite some of the religiously charged polemics exchanged by Byzantine and Armenian churchmen, Armenian migrants were not disadvantaged by their Armenian faith in assimilating into the Byzantine Empire. Rather, as will be argued in full in the following chapter, Armenian migrants, by engaging with the empire through its institutions and shared political ideology, were willing and successful in assimilating into the Byzantine Empire.

Chapter 1

ARMENIAN ASSIMILATION IN ACTION, C. AD 867–1000

In the late ninth and tenth centuries Byzantium began to expand eastwards at the expense of its neighbours, the majority of whom held different religious beliefs, spoke different languages or subscribed to different political customs than the native *Romaioi* who lived inside the empire's borders. Consequently, it was also in this period that many Armenian people came to live under imperial rule with the expanding borders on the eastern frontier moving into western Caucasia. But this was not the only direction of expansion; the far more important area of foreign policy for Byzantium was in south-eastern Anatolia, specifically the lands in Cilicia and along the Taurus and Anti-Taurus Mountain ranges. These territories had formerly been controlled by Muslim emirates that had for centuries launched annual raids into central and western Anatolia. As these new lands fell to Roman arms, imperial policy saw to the resettlement of many Armenians as settlers in the newly conquered lands that had been vacated through war and conquest, viewing the Armenians as hardy and reliable Christians who could repopulate this crucial geographical area. The Byzantine emperors' recruitment of Armenians as settlers along frontier zones was not a new phenomenon; indeed, there are several examples predating the ninth century, which saw many Armenians forcibly moved to Byzantium's western frontier to bolster frontier populations. What made the ninth and tenth centuries distinctive, however, was that in this period the assimilation of Armenians was broadly successful and directly contributed to the success of Byzantium that would reach its apogee in the early eleventh century.

In the introduction we explored what it meant to be 'Roman' in a medieval context, with a particular focus on the importance of political customs, while also acknowledging the religious and linguistic components that contributed towards Byzantine identity. In order to comprehensively study and understand how assimilation worked it is important to establish an analytical framework or 'assimilation model' to determine the success of Armenians becoming *Romaioi*. This formulation has been divided into three constituent and interrelating parts that, I would argue, encapsulate the most important mechanics for successful assimilation for Armenian migrants:

1. The area of territorial settlement
2. The acceptance and adoption of 'Roman customs'
3. The religious conversion/conformity of the migrants

This chapter will therefore breakdown the experiences of Armenian migrants in the three predescribed categories and show how in all three areas Armenians adopted modes of behaviour that were expected for someone to qualify as a *Romaios*.

The areas of territorial settlement

The territorial distribution of Armenian settlers was one of the most influential factors to affect the degree of their assimilation into the Byzantine Empire during the ninth and tenth centuries. Although by the year 1000 Armenians had been settled throughout the empire, geographical differences between the areas of settlement in the west and east were to have a strong influence on the outcome of the process of assimilation. In the imperial capital of Constantinople, which was to have its own unique strengths in the assimilation process, it is possible to look at several 'encounters' between the *Romaioi* and Armenians, most often in the setting of the imperial court, and to assess what motivated Armenians to settle and assimilate into the Byzantine world. With this may be contrasted the settlements in the western provinces of Thrace and Macedonia on the one hand and the settlements found in the eastern provinces of Sebasteia and Lykandos on the other. It is clear from our evidence that the settlements in the eastern provinces of the empire were weaker in terms of assimilation, but this did not prevent the process altogether. Indeed, the active participation of Armenians in the army from the eastern provinces would suggest that the mechanics of assimilation were clearly in operation.

Our primary evidence does not reveal the Armenians settling in very large numbers in Constantinople, but we know that they were certainly active in the politics of the imperial court. It has been argued convincingly by other scholars that those who did find their way there tended to be from elite circles or at the very least made it into the upper echelons of society. For example, Manea Shirinian has argued that in the ninth century the Armenian presence in the capital had increased rapidly, though this would have predominantly been from the upper echelons of society, if the cases illustrated by the *Vita Basilii* or Genesios are anything to go by.[1] Shirinian identifies many influential Byzantines in the mid-ninth century, such as Photios, John the Grammarian and Leo the Mathematician, as Armenian in origin, but these claims have been challenged.[2] Charanis claims, 'It would be preposterous ... to call Photios ... anything but a Greek.'[3] This illustrates the problematic nature of the identity labels used by many modern historians, a problem best solved by using the contemporary nomenclature of the *Romaios*. More importantly, what Shirinian and Charanis agree on is that the ancestral background of an individual did not make anyone 'less' Byzantine, an essential prerequisite if successful assimilation was to take place. Thus, we are told in the *Vita Basilii* that the Emperor Basil hailed from Macedonia 'but traced his origins (γένος) to the nation (ἔθνος) of the Armenians'.[4]

While there were certainly prominent Byzantines of Armenian ancestry living in Constantinople in the ninth and tenth centuries, it has been claimed that there was also a wider community. Peter Charanis refers to an Armenian colony in the city during this period, but he provides no relevant evidence to support his assertion. He references the *Chronicon Paschale* for the presence of Armenian soldiers in the siege of 626 but presents no corroborative material for later centuries.[5] Nevertheless, there is indeed some evidence for the presence of non-elite Armenians. Those who are mentioned in Constantinople are most often encountered in the role of soldiers, for instance in 967 during the riot by the citizenry of the capital against the Armenians present in the city during the reign of Nikephoros II Phokas.[6] Such an example illustrates the importance of the Armenians in the Byzantine military, a theme that will be developed shortly. Sometime later in the eleventh century we are told by Michael the Syrian (who was writing in the twelfth) that there was an Armenian Church in Constantinople, implying a congregation and an Armenian presence.[7] While there is no support for this claim in either literary or material evidence, this does not necessarily make it untrue; rather, logic dictates that a place of worship must have existed to accommodate the Miaphysite Christian population who visited the city. Moreover, the numbers of Armenians living throughout the empire would make it nearly impossible to conclude that Armenians did not live in the capital at all.

The main focus when it comes to Constantinople nevertheless needs to be the evidence of the presence of the elites, for which we have far more information from our literary and material sources. There are several examples from the Armenian noble class settling in Constantinople during the ninth and tenth centuries. During the reign of Leo VI (886–912), Manuel, the local dynast of Tekis/Tephrike, ceded his lands in return for patronage in Constantinople. His four sons were given important positions and lands and they appear to have rapidly assimilated into the Byzantine elite, facilitated by their immediate placement in positions of military or administrative importance.[8] Another example dates from the reign of Nikephoros II Phokas, when the princes of Taron, Grigor and Bagrat, surrendered their lands in return for estates near Constantinople.[9] The brothers were to assimilate smoothly, receiving titles and positions within the administration of the empire. These examples are instructive. The very fact that the sources do not show the Armenian nobility forming a diasporic community within Constantinople suggests that they had speedily and successfully assimilated into their new surroundings. This was arguably facilitated by their immediate placement in key governmental or military positions in the empire, a theme explored later in this chapter. Constantinople thus played an influential role in the integration of both ninth- and tenth-century migrants, albeit predominantly for the nobility. The careers of this migrating nobility come to the fore again later when we look more closely at Armenian interactions with the main institutions of the empire.

Turning now to the second area of settlement, Thrace. On acquiring Armenian territory in 591, Emperor Maurice (582–602) is said to have removed Armenians from the eastern frontier to Thrace on a substantial scale, but there is some doubt to what extent this really happened.[10] Constantine V (741–75) oversaw a large transfer of Armenians, some of whom were Paulician heretics, like his predecessor choosing to settle many of them in Macedonia or Thrace.[11] There were also significant population transfers to the Balkans during the reign of Leo IV (775–80). We are told that Armenians and Syrians were removed from the eastern frontier, where they were suffering under attacks from the Abbasid Caliphate, and placed in Thrace.[12] According to the *Vita Basilii*, Maiktes the grandfather of Basil I:

> When he learned about [an Armenian called] Leo's origins and heard of the Arsacid community living in Adrianople, he chose a foreign country over his own.[13]

This example is, however, historically questionable. The *Vita Basilii* was written with the intention to create a more aggrandized history of the Macedonian house, and it is beyond any real doubt that the purported descent from the ancient dynasty of the Arsacids was entirely fictional. Yet this passage holds a greater significance than Constantine VII's wish to glorify his grandfather Basil I. It reveals the awareness at the imperial centre that assimilation was a normal and expected process for Armenian migrants.

Further population transfers and resettlement in the western provinces occurred in the reign of Basil I as a result of the emperor finally bringing about the destruction of the Paulician enclave on the upper Euphrates in 871.[14] While many of the survivors were relocated to Cilicia, some were later deported by John I Tzimiskes (969–76) to Bulgaria.[15] Yet another incidence of population transfer occurred in 988 during the reign of Basil II, when Armenians were moved to the Bulgarian frontier in order to provide a buffer against the resurgent power of the Bulgarian Empire under the Tsars Roman I (977–91) and Samuel (997–1014).[16]

The important element when it comes to the western provinces was the proximity of Constantinople, and the opportunity that it presented to the migrants and their descendants to travel there and improve their social standing was clearly a major force in the assimilation process. The most prominent of these aspirational migrants was the Emperor Basil I himself, referred to as the 'Macedonian' as a reflection of his birthplace.[17] In studying Basil's rise to the throne one can see that his Armenian peasant background did not block advancement; rather, it was Basil's close friendship with Michael III (842–67) that allowed him to rise through the ranks so quickly, in direct contradiction of Charanis' view that the hatred between Greeks and Armenians meant that interethnic friendships were unlikely.[18] In this context, the episode recorded in both the *Vita Basilii* and Skylitzes regarding the encounter between Basil's grandfather and an Armenian called Leo who had assimilated into the Byzantine court is also instructive. Unfortunately, the sources do not comment in any great detail on how the Armenians, who were settled in the west, assimilated. Were one to remove the exceptional experience of the Paulicians, who often gained the attention of Byzantine sources for their religious peculiarities, one finds that the majority of Armenians who were resettled on the Bulgarian border and served as a buffer against Bulgarian incursions appear to have quickly lost their Armenian characteristics.[19]

Finally, the eastern provinces of the empire need to be considered in terms of how significant the territorial settlement of migrants in this region was to the mechanics of assimilation. Throughout the late ninth and tenth centuries there was considerable expansion and settlement on the eastern border. We have already mentioned Manuel of Tekis, who settled in Constantinople, yet other Armenians also had similar interactions with the expanding empire. Skylitzes tells us of:

> Then there was Kourtikios, an Armenian by race, master of Lokana, who frequently sacked and devastated the Roman border regions; he delivered himself, his city and the people under him into the emperor's hands.[20]

We are not informed whether lands were offered in recompense for the surrender of Lokana,[21] though we do learn that in the following decade Kourtikios was actively serving in the Byzantine army.[22] Nor is there concrete evidence as to where Kourtikios was settled, but we have some clues. First, Kourtikios was to be found fighting on the Bulgarian frontier later during Leo VI's reign, which would suggest he was removed from the eastern frontier, in case he caused disturbances in the proximity of his former territories. Second, we have already seen in 886 that Basil preferred to move potentially troublesome figures to the capital, with Manuel of Tekis providing a comparable example. Yet, such individuals were not invariably settled in the west. We are informed in the *De Thematibus* of a certain Ashot 'the long armed', who journeyed to the capital to enter the emperor's service, bringing with him a certain Melias (the Great) *Magistros*.[23] Sometime after 896 Melias, or Mleh in Armenian,[24] returned to the eastern frontier in mysterious circumstances, operating in the same region where twenty years previously Kourtikios had thrown his lot in with the empire. Melias was arguably independent from the empire, although working in its interests, leading a group of fellow Armenians on raids against the Arabs around Lykandos.[25] Through Melias' efforts the area of Lykandos was to be incorporated into the empire as a new theme, with subsequent settlement of Armenians in order to provide a buffer on the upper Euphrates against Muslim counter-attacks. Areas such as Lykandos came to be so dominated by Armenians that later in the tenth century Leo the Deacon recognized the east as Armenian: 'when battle broke out on the plain of Lapara (this is on the boundary of Armenian territory)'.[26] It was Byzantine policy to repopulate the territories with eastern Christians to replace the newly converted Muslim population that most often moved with the frontier, normally being offered the choice between conversion and exile. The departure of the Muslim populations of Melitene, Tarsus and Antioch meant that the Byzantines needed to find a new population to stabilize the frontier, and in accordance with precedent, Armenians and Christian Syrians were utilized for this end.[27]

These examples demonstrate that while groups of Armenians were settled in both the eastern and western parts of the empire, it appears that Armenians could more successfully assimilate nearer the imperial heartlands and the capital, dropping their Armenian label. As to the Armenian migrants who were used to repopulate the lands in eastern Anatolia and Cilicia during the age of reconquest, the question remains as to what extent they underwent the process of assimilation. One must therefore turn to our primary evidence to examine levels of assimilation, and this evidence largely comes from Armenian involvement in the great institutions of the empire: the government and army.[28] The fact that later in the eleventh century, the Armenian elites settled not in Constantinople or Thrace but on their own estates in the east was to be a significant reason for their lack of integration.[29]

Acceptance and adoption of 'Roman customs'

A good starting point for the discussion of this element of our Assimilation Model is the visit of Basill's grandfather, Maiktes, to Constantinople 'when Constantine ruled together with his mother Irene', that is, during the 780s and 790s.[30] Maiktes, we are told:

> met a compatriot (ὁμογενεῖ) of his named Leo, and recognized from his outward appearance and distinctive apparel that he was no lowly and insignificant person, but rather a noble and prominent man.[31]

We can see that an Armenian (Leo), although recognized as a compatriot by a visiting foreign dignitary (Maiktes), was in actual fact a product of successful assimilation and therefore considered a *Romaios* – as explained through the narrative of his 'distinctive apparel', which one can assume to be the silk vestments of his rank or even his presence within the imperial court. Yet, the reason for why Maiktes migrated was not simply the result of this chance meeting. Rather, we are told that it was from hearing of an Armenian community living in the environs of Adrianople, and here we must return to the quotation already given:

> When he (Maiktes) learned about Leo's origins and heard of the Arsacid community living in Adrianople, he chose a foreign country over his own.[32]

We have another account of this story from Skylitzes, although the details are somewhat confused. Let us give it in full:

> Maiktes, a member of the Arsacid tribe, came into the capital for some reason or other. There he chanced to encounter a fellow tribesman called Leo. They became acquainted with each other and ended up being fast friends. When Leo realised that the other also had the blood of the Arsacides in his veins and was living in Adrianople, he held the stranger's land in higher esteem than his own.[33]

The two accounts share some characteristics in that both use the Greek word ὁμογενεῖ to describe the relationship between the two men, that is, their shared Armenian identity of varying degrees. Confusingly, however, the two published English translations offer different subjects and objects.[34] Yet of greater importance was how Maiktes was drawn into migrating to Byzantium through 'bonds of kinship' and the marriage to Leo's daughter. The presence of Armenians already living in the empire was clearly a draw for further Armenians to come and seek their fortunes.

This connection through 'bonds of kinship' also comes to the fore in an episode involving the young Basil I and a wrestling match, and here we are fortunate to have two independent accounts of the same event, from the *Vita Basilii* and Genesios' *On the Reigns of the Emperors*. Genesios tells us that an Armenian by the name of Constantine was sent during the reign of Theophilos (829–42) by 'his relatives and the rulers of his native land as a hostage and ambassador' to Constantinople. Within a short period of time Constantine had started to successfully climb the career ladder within the capital 'on account of the beauty of his soul and body and his noble disposition in all great affairs'.[35] The *Vita* tells us that this same Constantine was a patrician and father to the philosopher and logothete Thomas the patrician, who was well known at the court of Constantine VII, while Genesios tells us more about Constantine's career.[36] During the attempt to remove the Patriarch John VII Grammatikos (836–43) he is named as 'the commander of the tagma of the Exkoubitoi'. His career continued with the office of *Droungarios of the Arithmos*, then that of *Patrikios* and finally the *Logothetes of the Dromos*.[37] Here our accounts begin to diverge in their details. Both Genesios and the *Vita* tell the story of Basil's involvement in a wrestling match. Only Genesios states that this match was hosted by the Caesar Bardas, while the *Vita* adds that Basil's opponent was a Bulgarian champion. While Basil was victorious in both accounts, what is more intriguing is the description of Constantine the patrician. In both accounts Constantine comes to the aid of Basil by asking for sawdust (*Vita*) or straw (Genesios) to be laid upon the ground in which Basil was going to wrestle. The reason behind Constantine's aid to Basil, we are told by both, was their shared Armenian heritage. The *Vita* says:

> that Constantine the patrician whom we just mentioned, and who was a close friend of Basil (being himself of Armenian descent).[38]

While Genesios states:

> Constantine was favourably inclined toward him as they were related.[39]

Clearly, Basil had some bond with Constantine, although the *Vita*'s explanation of the relationship between Basil and Constantine is, on balance, the more plausible. The claim that the two were related was most probably an attempt by Genesios, who may have been the grandson of said Constantine, to claim a connexion with the Macedonian house.[40] As such, it is more likely that Constantine and Basil were close on the basis of their Armenian heritage. Yet, what these examples reveal for our present purposes is that an individual's Armenian origins did not prevent assimilation or even make it as slow as some historians have claimed.[41] The positions that were given to Constantine the Armenian show that assimilation was in fact a streamlined process when serving in an official position within the imperial hierarchy.

Both of these case studies provide invaluable commentary on how the imperial court understood, or at least viewed, assimilation in the tenth century. From the case of Maiktes it is clear that territorial movement was considered normal practice, abandoning patrimonial lands for new (and better) estates near the imperial centre. Furthermore, Maiktes is clearly identified as a member of the nobility – the only assimilation that the imperial court would be concerned with – and it is tacitly suggested that this was the social class that he would operate in. To Byzantine audiences his career path would be self-evident, a succession of offices of importance in the military or thematic governance. And yet there was no mention of the religious beliefs held by either Leo or Maiktes. A clear example that at least in the most immediate instance religious differences did not automatically prevent an Armenian from smooth assimilation into the empire. In the second case study, we have an Armenian (Constantine) who successfully embarked on a career of imperial-appointed offices. His Armenian identity (first generation, according to Genesios) only comes to the fore of the narrative in his interactions with the young Basil I. This was not to diminish his social or hierarchical status but rather demonstrate the quantity and expectation of Armenian assimilation into the Byzantine Empire to work.

Adoption of Byzantine customs may also have manifested itself in another, less constructive way. One common theme that repeatedly occurs when examining the careers of the newly arrived Armenian nobility was their penchant for engaging in the internal strife that was characteristic of Byzantine politics, and this might be viewed as evidence for the process of assimilation failing to produce *Romaioi*. The opposite is true. In effect, their participation in the internal politics of the empire reveals how quickly the Armenians had assimilated, sharing the behaviour of other Byzantine nobles involved in the politics surrounding on the occupant of the throne of Constantinople. What, then, was the Byzantine political ideology that the Armenians subscribed to when migrating into the empire in the tenth century?

The binding formula that held together the various peoples living within the empire's borders was the Byzantine political ideology, and this directly influenced the Armenian experience of serving in Byzantium's army during the age of reconquest. One of the key tenets of this political ideology was loyalty to the emperor and the Roman state which was strongly linked with Orthodox Christianity.[42] The exalted position of the Roman emperor combined both secular and spiritual authority. From the time of Constantine I, the emperor was God's anointed representative on earth who was seen to preside over an earthly kingdom that mirrored the kingdom of heaven. This unique ideology of governance was supported by the scriptures, specifically Mt. 22.21: 'Render unto Caesar the things that are Caesar's, and unto God the things that are God's.'[43] While the Roman emperors of late antiquity had in effect been the rulers over all Christians, as the vast majority of those confessing the faith lived in the empire, this ideological concept was still maintained in the territorially smaller state of Byzantium, meaning that in Byzantine eyes, all Christians still owed their secular allegiance to the emperor based in Constantinople. Loyalty to the emperor in practice related only to the office, rather than loyalty to the man (or woman) who occupied the throne, as is evident from the frequency of revolts, depositions, blindings and mutilations.[44]

It was this ideology that the Armenians had to come to terms with, so let us turn to some successful examples of assimilation from within the recently settled Armenian nobility in the tenth century and evaluate how they interacted with the Byzantine political ideology.

Our first example comes from the beginning of the tenth century with the career of Melias the Great. We have already seen how Melias entered imperial service with his lord Ashot 'the long armed'. Dédéyan believes that the relationship between Melias and Ashot was a feudal one, with Melias performing some military functions.[45] In any case, Ashot was killed by the Bulgars at the battle of Bulgarophygon in 896, a particularly heavy defeat for the Byzantines, as their army was at full strength, while Melias was able to escape. Melias returned to the borderlands of the south-eastern frontier and took up arms with fellow Armenian bandits, with whom Melias was said to have a natural affinity.[46] Melias was able to capture, fortify and hold the city of Lykandos and a short while later founded the city of Tzamandos, which ran against the grain of the defensive policy of Leo VI in the east.[47] Later, in 913, the region that Melias had been able to carve out for himself was recognized by the imperial centre and raised to the status of a full theme, with Melias as the *strategos* and subsequently gaining the rank of *magistros*. Previously, however, Melias seems to have been caught up with the revolt of Andronikos Doukas in 906/7 and is later found as a refugee with the Emir of Melitene.[48] Yet, his active participation in a plot does not provide sufficient evidence to suggest that Melias had no desire to operate within the Byzantine order. In fact, the entire coup was founded on an intense rivalry at court level between Andronikos and the eunuch Samonas. The general Eustathios Argyros, another who may have been caught up in the conspiracy, was soon recalled from exile and was responsible for setting up Armenian 'frontier wardens' on the south-eastern borderlands, of whom most were Armenians exiled for their involvement in the plot of Doukas.[49] And yet they were entrusted with military commands integral to the defence of the empire. It was through this service that the process of assimilation progressed; further titles being given in reward for the loyalty the Armenians showed the empire and the emperor of the Romans.[50]

Our next example comes from two brothers Grigor and Bagrat. Both were Taronite princes who in 967/8 exchanged their Armenian lands for estates in and around Constantinople. From the historical record the two brothers do not seem to have been entirely loyal to the Macedonian dynasty but rather found comradery within the powerful aristocracy that dominated the military commands in the east during the mid-tenth century. It would appear from our sources that the princes fought on the side of Bardas Skleros during his revolt of 976–9 against Basil II, as Stephen of Taron recounts. It is worth giving his account in full:

> Bardas, who was called by surname Skleros, rebelled and reigned as king in the regions of Jahan and Melitene. He was a valiant man and an expert in warfare. He rallied to his side the cavalry force of Armenia which served under the kingship of the Greeks. He divided the kingdom of the Greeks and advanced as far as Bithynia, fighting against king Basil for 4 years. They filled the whole country with rivers of blood.

> King Basil assembled the forces of Byzantium and those of Thrace and Macedonia, together with all the western peoples. He sent [them] into battle against the usurper Bardas. Bardas took up arms against him in battle. *The Armenian force fought valiantly in this; the sons of the prince of Tarōn, Grigor and Bagarat, and Zap'ranik prince of Mokk' terrified the forces of Greeks and confused them like a whirling tempest; some were slain by the sword and many were captured.* Here the eunuch Petranus was killed, the head of the force. Then, showing compassion and out of mercy on account of their Christian faith, they spared the lives of the survivors.[51]

This evidence is not straightforward, as it is not completely clear which side Grigor and Bagrat were fighting on. It would appear that the brothers initially supported the claim of Bardas Skleros: 'He rallied to his side the cavalry force of Armenia which served under the kingship of the Greeks.'[52] Yet one of the brothers appears after the revolt on the side of Basil, Grigor apparently being in command of imperial forces near Trebizond during the revolt of Bardas Phokas in 988/9.[53] Grigor eventually was to become *doux* of Thessalonica and was placed in charge of the defence of the Balkan frontier by Basil in the light of the resurgence of Bulgaria under Samuel.[54] It is thus evident that the Taronite brothers were not only successful in acquiring imperial titles and performing their duties in accordance with these positions but also participated in the most natural of aristocratic pastimes in Byzantium: civil war.

Our last example comes from the life and career of Ashot Taronites, the son of Grigor, *doux* of Thessalonica.[55] Ashot still used an Armenian name, although it seems likely that he was born after his father had migrated into the empire. His name is Hellenized in Skylitzes' account to 'Asotios', but this only serves as an example as to the audience Skylitzes was writing for in the early twelfth century.[56] The details of his career are useful in the assessment of the mechanics of assimilation. Ashot was captured in 995 by Tsar Samuel of Bulgaria while leading a reconnaissance force and falling into an ambush. This resulted in Grigor rushing to retrieve his son from captivity; the father perished fighting Samuel's troops.[57] We next hear of Ashot when he was released from captivity by Samuel so that he could marry Samuel's daughter, Miroslava. According to Skylitzes this came about when the distressed daughter threatened to kill herself, unless Samuel released Ashot. The newly wedded couple were then dispatched to govern Dyrrachium, where Ashot persuaded his wife to abandon her father and make for Constantinople on some passing Byzantine ships. Upon arrival at the capital, Ashot was given the title of *Magistros* and informed Basil that the leading citizens of Dyrrachium were willing to deliver the city into the emperor's hands.[58] From this point on we hear nothing further about Ashot's career, but his descendants were to occupy important roles under the Komnenos dynasty at the end of the eleventh century.[59] This rapid series of events, concerning a second-generation Armenian migrant, reveals remarkable loyalty towards the Byzantine state and suggests that assimilation could occur far quicker than scholars have previously allowed.[60]

It is clear from these examples that Armenian migrants subscribed to the political loyalties that were expected of them once they resided inside the empire.

Despite there being occurrences of disloyalty towards the occupant of the Byzantine throne, it was never disloyalty towards the political entity or institutions of the empire, and this will be an extremely important differential when we turn to the alienation of the eleventh century in Chapter 3. For the ninth and tenth centuries, the newly arrived Armenian aristocracy successfully settled into the roles expected of their class and their dominant role within the army.

The army and the nobility

Both a career in the army and the titles that were held through service were important and effective mechanics of assimilation, and those of Armenian stock came to dominate the high military offices in the ninth and tenth centuries. In evaluating the most dominant Armenian families and other selected figures within the Byzantine aristocracy and assessing how the granting of titles, offices and military positions contributed towards the process of assimilation, two distinct groups need to be analysed. The first are aristocratic families of Armenian stock whose ancestry is not reliably attested to in the primary sources, such as the Skleroi and the Phokades.[61] The second group are those who migrated in the time frame of this chapter (*c*.867–1000) and are documented in some form in our narrative accounts, such as the Lekapenoi and the Kourkouai.[62] These families are important not simply for rising to the pinnacle of the Anatolian aristocracy but also for assisting with further assimilation by surrounding themselves with newly arrived Armenians who received prominent positions within the army soon after their arrival.[63]

The claim of the Skleroi family to be Armenian may have originated from their origins in Sebasteia, the capital of the old Roman province of Armenia Minor. However, this is not conclusively proven by the primary sources, although the Skleroi's later affinity with the Iberian magnates on the eastern frontier insinuates some bond of kinship. The family first appeared on the scene in the early ninth century, when a Leon Skleros is recorded as the *strategos* of the Peloponnese in both 805 and 811.[64] The family's fortunes increased dramatically under the Macedonian dynasty, with a Theodoros Skleros holding the rank of *magistros* and *anthypatos*, while his two sons held military posts in Hellas and the office of *droungarios tou ploimou*, respectively.[65] Despite falling from favour during the reign of Leo VI, they may have supported the coup of the Lekapenoi, although this once again is a tentative suggestion.[66] It has been suggested that this support eventually resulted in a member of the family holding the office of *domestikos ton scholon*. John Kourkouas' replacement in 944 was styled the 'patrikios Pantherios' which leaves some room of interpretation to which military family he belonged.[67] Seibt identifies Pantherios as a member of the Skleroi on the basis of a lead seal that attests 'Patrikios Pantherios Skleros', which is most likely the answer to the question of his identification.[68] Pantherios' son Bardas had a long career, serving as *patrikios* and *strategos* of the frontier theme Kaloudia.[69] A significant achievement earlier in his career was his command of the eastern tagmata that were ordered over to Thrace to counter the Rus' threat and his defence of Arkadioupolis in 971, which helped cement his position as one of the leading magnates in the army.[70] His career in the years between his victory over the Rus' and his rebellion against Basil II is largely obscure. Skylitzes insinuates that Bardas was involved in a conspiracy against John I Tzimiskes and nearly lost his eyes for it, and Melias 'the younger' is found commanding the eastern armies in 972-3, which suggests that Bardas fell out of favour.[71] This, however, was not for long as Bardas at some point by 976 had resumed command over the eastern armies and posed a significant threat to Basil II.[72] While the Skleroi family were able to last well into the twelfth century, what they represent here is a classic example of the domination of the military commands by 'Armenian' families in the tenth century. There is no doubt that the Skleroi were assimilated, and their interactions with the other military families, most of whom were of Armenian stock, reveal how being assimilated was nothing more than expected.

The Phokas family was prominent among the Anatolian aristocracy for a substantial length of time and in that period arguably was the greatest threat to the ruling Macedonian house. Like those of the Skleroi, the origins of the Phokas family are obscure, for no contemporary source documents their arrival in the empire, and they most likely commissioned a forged genealogy.[73] In another parallel with the Skleroi, the frequent use of the *praenomen* 'Bardas' indicates a link to the Caucasus region, though this still offers no substantive evidence for their Armenian origin. The first member of the family to appear in the sources, in 872/3, was a certain Phokas, a Cappadocian soldier.[74] His career, as attested by sigillographic evidence, was modest but only in comparison with what his descendants were to achieve.[75] His son, known as Nikephoros the Elder, was the first to join the upper echelons of the aristocracy on the eastern frontier and was included within the *oikeioi* of Basil I.[76] He was further promoted to the post of *protostrator* and received a palace in the capital.[77] It has been suggested that after a remarkable career serving as *strategos* of Charsianon, and holding a command in southern Italy, Nikephoros was promoted to the office of *domestikos ton scholon* in 886 and actively involved in campaigns against the Arabs of Tarsus in 894. Nikephoros' sons, Leo and Bardas (both called the Elder), prospered further under Leo VI, although Leo the Elder was to fall from power with his failed coup attempt against Romanos I.[78] Consequently, Bardas' career was significantly curtailed, and he only appears in our sources with relatively minor military commands until Constantine VII overthrew the Lekapenoi in 945. At this point Bardas was apparently given the office of *domestikos ton scholon* for his loyalty, though most likely for not having tarnished himself by adherence to the previous regime.[79] Bardas' sons were also brought into the circle of senior officers, Nikephoros, Leo and Constantine receiving command of Anatolikon, Cappadocia and Seleucia, respectively: the army was thus entirely entrusted to the Phokades. The imperial patronage of the Phokas family in the 940s and 950s helps to explain how one of their own, Nikephoros, was able to seize the imperial crown following the premature death of Romanos II who died after only four years in power. Nikephoros, who had succeeded his father Bardas as *domestikos ton scholon*, had built an impressive military resumé during the campaigns across the Taurus Mountain range in the late 950s.[80] Nikephoros' career as a general, and later emperor, is distinctly relevant to Armenian assimilation in the second half of the tenth century.

In the manual on *Skirmishing*, a work commissioned by Nikephoros, though potentially written by his brother Leo, we have specific mention of Armenians and reference to their reputation.[81] We are informed that Armenians, particularly in the east, were exceptionally poor at sentry duty, a task that the author asserts is of the utmost importance, particularly when campaigning in enemy territory.[82] It is hard to hide the clear 'ethnic' tensions with this comment on the army, but this does not necessarily diminish the manpower or the 'fighting qualities' that the Armenian soldiers brought to the Byzantine army.[83] An examination of the actual number of Armenians in the service of the empire shows them to have been relied on to a surprising degree. Chapters 44/45 of the *De Ceremoniis* provide some figures for the strength of the Cretan expedition in 949. Armenians constituted a sizeable cavalry force with 1,000 coming from Sebasteia, 500 were recruited from Plantanion, and 500 from Prine, although in the event not all these forces sailed.[84] Furthermore, from the 'Armenian theme'[85] of Charpezikion we have figures for the military officers, along with ordinary soldiers, totalling 705. These include: 25 senior officers, 47 *tourmarchai*, 205 *droungaroi* and 428 soldiers.[86] The records for the expedition of 949 also inform us that 800 soldiers from the Thrakesion commuted their service at four *nomismata* each, which money was then used to pay 600 Armenians to stand sentry over the coastline of the theme.[87] It is thus clear that the Armenians were found throughout the Byzantine military and were also sought after for their prowess, since they – as troops stationed on the eastern frontier – were summoned for a campaign in the west. Throughout the campaigns of the 950s and 960s, Nikephoros relied heavily on both the Armenian element within his army and the Armenian settlers to consolidate the conquests in Cilicia. This reliance is captured once again with his preference for using Armenian soldiers as a garrison in Constantinople.[88] In addition, upon ascending the imperial throne, Nikephoros legislated specifically for Armenian settlers in the east, not only showing how important they were in their role of settling in newly conquered lands but also revealing the tensions that these settlers caused for administrative and legal processes.[89]

Yet, the rise of the Phokas family to the imperial throne must be viewed in the context of the previous Armenian family to have reached the heights of imperial rank, the Lekapenoi. For the Lekapenoi, their Armenian status is certainly not in doubt, while their lowly background further accentuates the importance of the imperial institutions as a mechanism of assimilation. The first member of the Lekapenoi family to be mentioned in the sources was Theophylaktos Abastakos, who was resettled in the late ninth century in Lakape, a region between Melitene and Samosata. Theophylaktos' career soared after he saved Basil I's life in Tephrike (Tekis) and was rewarded with lands and a place in the imperial guard.[90] The family took their name from the region where they were settled, and Theophylaktos' son, Romanos, was to radically change the fortunes of the family. We know very little about Romanos' background, and it may have been as lowly as that of Basil I, although, as noted by one of his modern biographers, 'he had no pious and literary grandson to give him a romantic history and royal pedigree'.[91] It may not be far-fetched to think that had Romanos II lived long enough, such a work might have been produced. Romanos Lekapenos' career is without doubt one of the more remarkable in the history of Byzantium and provides an excellent example of Armenian assimilation into the Byzantine Empire. Despite his father's imperial patronage, Romanos did not have access to the upbringing that was normal for the nobility who in turn dominated military commands. We have already noted the scathing comments of Constantine VII on Romanos' lack of culture, no doubt based in the resentment Constantine felt for being nothing more than Romanos' puppet for several decades.[92] Romanos held the position of *strategos* of the Samian theme in 911 before gaining a promotion to *droungarios tou ploimou* upon the fall of his predecessor Himerios in the reign of Alexander (912).[93] His coup d'état in 919 is not of great relevance here, but his patronage of other Armenians, particularly the Kourkouas family, was to bring about a resurgence of assimilated Armenians in military commands.

The Kourkouas family came to dominate the high military offices during the reign of Romanos I and can be viewed in comparison with the later domination of the same offices by the Phokas family after 945. The family had at least eight pre-eminent members between the second half of the ninth and the first half of the twelfth centuries. In the light of the prosopographical and sigillographic evidence from the tenth century, the Kourkouas family appears to have consistently exercised military and civilian commands on the eastern border. The earliest reference to a Kourkouas holding office was a certain John, found in the chronicle of Symeon, who held the position of *domestikos* of the Hikanatoi in *c.*886, indicating that the Kourkouai were already well established within the Byzantine elite even under the early Macedonian dynasty.[94] John was involved in a plot against Basil I and was possibly even the ringleader; however, the plot was foiled and John was blinded. This did not diminish the careers available to his descendants. Most prominent were the brothers John and Theophilos Kourkouas who held a succession of important offices in the mid-tenth century during the reign of Romanos I, which are attested by seals. A seal dated before *c.*927–30 has John as a *patrikios* and holding the office of *domestikos ton scholon*.[95] At some point after 930, John had gained the rank of *magistros*, possibly as a reward for his military successes involving the eventual capture of Melitene in 934, while Theophilos held the military governorship of Theodosioupolis[96] and was *strategos* of Chaldia and Mesopotamia.[97] Later in the century, Theophilos' grandson, John Tzimiskes, was even to take the throne itself. Unsurprisingly, the Kourkouai were to diminish in status with the overthrow of the Lekapenoi, despite the brief elevation to imperial status between 969 and 976.[98] John Kourkouas' son Romanos Kourkouas held the rank of *magistros* in 963 and was offered the office of *domestikos ton scholon* in the west, if he agreed to support Joseph Bringas, the *parakoimomenos*, against Nikephoros II Phokas.[99] A seal attesting a Romanos, imperial *protospatharios* and *strategos* of Mesopotamia may indeed be Romanos Kourkouas.[100] Romanos' son, John, appears later in 970 as commander of the army stationed in Macedonia and later as *magistros*. His 'immoderate insolence', most likely stemming from an alcohol problem, was noted by Leo the Deacon as the chief cause for the failure to prevent the Rus' invasion.[101] John was ultimately to pay with his life for failing to hold the Rus' threat at the siege of Dorostolon (971), where his first cousin once removed, Tzimiskes, was victorious over Svyatoslav.[102] The family reached its peak with the accession of John I Tzimiskes, but the minor role the family played in the rebellions of Bardas Phokas and Skleros in the early years of Basil II seems to illustrate their declining status.

There were other Armenian families of importance who migrated into Byzantium in the tenth century. The entirety of chapter 43 of the *DAI* details in full the delicate political balance in the region highlighting the difficulties faced by Romanos I in granting titles, gifts and properties in the capital. The internal factionalism in Taron resulted in the division of the country upon the death of Tornikios, as the sons of the *magistros* Krikorikios, Pankratios and Asotios took the country of Apoganem and the empire gained the region of Oulnoutin as provided in Tornikios' will.[103] The *DAI* suggests that Tornikios' wife and child moved to Constantinople upon his death, although later two Tornikioi are identified as Nicholas and Leo by Skylitzes.[104] If these two were the sons of Tornikios, it shows once again speedy assimilation, for they rallied to Constantine VII's cause in overthrowing the Lekapenoi in January 945. This episode has more value, however, than as just another example of assimilation. It provides a rare insight into the functions of languages in the diplomatic dealings between Byzantium and the Armenian magnates on the eastern frontier. In this episode the *DAI* refers to a man called Krinitis, the *protospatharios* and interpreter. It is the latter function that is of interest here. Krinitis was without doubt an Armenian who was serving the imperial court as a translator and held an appropriate rank within the court.[105] Yet it is worth noting that the ruling senior emperor, Romanos I, was of Armenian peasant stock and almost certainly had some command of his ancestral tongue.[106] While we have no definitive proof for Romanos' knowledge of Armenian, his use of an interpreter could indicate that even if he had been able to communicate in the Armenian tongue he would never have attempted to do so, for a Roman emperor could never be seen to conduct diplomatic exercises in any language other than Greek.

We have already seen how certain individuals, like Kourtikios and Melias 'the great', prospered in Byzantine service and through their careers assimilated into the Byzantine Empire. Kourtikios' descendants were highly active in Byzantine political life, a Manuel Kourtikios serving as *strategos* of Kibyrrhaiote for Bardas Skleros and commanding sizeable naval forces in the Aegean.[107] Melias may have been the grandfather of another Melias who we have seen earlier holding the office of *domestikos ton scholon* under John I Tzimiskes.[108] This same Melias is the most likely candidate for the figure painted on the northern wall of the Pigeon House Church at Cavuşin. Such rare imagery is naturally of considerable use for analysing both his career and his religious faith.[109] Melias' career was typical of the Byzantine-Armenian aristocrat serving on the eastern frontier. He operated in the highest circles of the officer class, holding the most important position after the emperor, *domestikos ton scholon*, and was without doubt a fully assimilated Armenian. Melias was left in command of significant forces in the east by Tzimiskes and subsequently defeated near Amida by the Hamdanids in 973 (his death and association with the Forty Martyrs of Sebasteia were to be commemorated in the Pigeon House Church).[110] Melias' appointment was not just a pragmatic choice by Tzimiskes; it represented the ideals behind Tzimiskes' campaigns against the Muslim world, uniting a wider Christian effort incorporating Byzantines, Armenians, Georgians and Syrians to fight the Muslim enemy. And it is in the context of religious unity among the various Christian peoples on the eastern frontier that we should turn the focus to assessing how Armenian migrants dealt with the confessional differences between the imperial and Armenian churches once they arrived in the empire.

Religious conversion and conformity

The imperial Orthodox Church, centred in Constantinople, and the ecumenical patriarchate, has often been seen as the most readily distinguishable form of Byzantine identity throughout the eastern empire' history and therefore held the potential to be the largest obstacle for Armenian migrants to fully assimilate. This is largely based upon a conservative reading of the primary evidence which often holds polemically charged insults in the main narrative prose. However, the nature of religious relations between the Byzantines and Armenians in the ninth and tenth centuries should not be misunderstood through the later perceptions of eleventh-century historians but rather approached through a cautious assessment of contemporary evidence which actually suggests a period of cooperation. While both Byzantine and Armenian sources viewed Christianity as an integral part of their respective identities, the claims of modern scholars that the Byzantines placed an ethno-national spin on the 'Greek Church of Constantinople' describe a development for later than the period under discussion here. In the ninth and tenth centuries there were no similar ethnic dimensions to the observation of the faith in Byzantium. An individual could be a Christian and not a *Romaios*, though in order to be considered a *Romaios* he had to be Christian. The only possible ethnic attachments to the observation of faith at this time were made by churches not in communion with the imperial church, such as the Syriac and Armenian churches, and the hostility between the Chalcedonian and Miaphysite churches expressed in the sources should be viewed as neither truly reflective of reality nor representative of the failure of Armenian migrants to assimilate into the Byzantine Empire.[111] What then were the differences between the churches from late antiquity through to the late ninth century? And second, in the light of some localized occurrences of religious hostilities on the eastern borderlands, to what extent, if any, were religious differences a significant barrier for Armenians to assimilate in the ninth and tenth centuries?

The Armenian Apostolic Church followed what is described as a Miaphysite form of Christianity. 'Miaphysite' churches, known collectively today as 'Oriental

Orthodoxy', had split from the main body of the Church after the Fourth Ecumenical Council of Chalcedon in AD 451, which lends its name to the label 'Chalcedonian' used by the Miaphysite sources to describe the adherents of the Church of Constantinople. The Miaphysite churches only recognize the acts of the first three ecumenical councils, namely First Nicaea (325), First Constantinople (381) and Ephesus (431). During these three councils the Church pronounced Christ to be divine – 'consubstantial' with the Father – and that although Christ was divine, as well as human, he had only one identity. It was at the Fourth Ecumenical Council at Chalcedon in 451 that the definition was revised to state that Christ, while being one person, had two distinct natures: divine *logos* and human *Jesus*. This view was criticized by the Miaphysites as too close to the Nestorian teachings that had been deemed heretical at Ephesus (431).

The rejection of the Council of Chalcedon was not a single clear-cut act from an Armenian perspective.[112] The exact nature of the conclusion of the council and how it had affected the correct Christological definition were thoroughly debated, not only between Armenians and Chalcedonians but also between the Chalcedonians and the Miaphysites of Syria and Egypt throughout late antiquity. It is in fact rather surprising that no Armenian representatives were at Chalcedon or were even invited to participate.[113] The actual date of the break between the Armenians from the Orthodox doctrine established at Chalcedon has thus been a hotly debated topic. Certain dates have been proposed: (AD) 488, 491, 527 and 544, or even later.[114] It should be noted that many years passed before the Armenians officially denounced Chalcedon, and that there is some question why it took so long for them to do so. There have been various theories, some interrelated, others not:

1. The Armenians were misled as to what Chalcedon actually stated, or that they were unable to understand the doctrine established at the council.
2. They were compelled by the (Sassanian) Persians who hoped to drive a wedge between the Roman Empire and the Armenian (ecclesiastical) hierarchy.
3. Their language was not able to express the Chalcedonian wording on the natures of Christ.
4. They were victims of false identification of the Chalcedonian doctrine with Nestorianism.[115]

It is likely that it was in fact a combination of these four factors that resulted in the Armenians eventually separating from the Chalcedonian Church. But the relationship between the two churches, from the fifth to the ninth century, is secondary to the present discussion, as the Islamic conquest of Armenia and the creation of Muslim emirates in the Taurus and anti-Taurus mountains in the middle of the seventh century created a buffer for circa 200 years between Byzantium and Greater Armenia. We have already seen that the territorial placement of Armenian migrants was a major differential for the process of assimilation and this was no less significant in the context of religion. Thus, for instance, those Armenians who were settled in the themes of Thrace and Macedonia experienced different religious assimilation by comparison with those who were used to repopulate the regions around Melitene and Tarsus in the tenth century.[116] What was significant, by contrast, was how the Armenians adapted to their new religious climate upon arrival in the empire.

The most commonly cited barrier to successful assimilation was the religious hostility between Armenians and Orthodox Byzantines and vice versa. Garsoïan is of the opinion that the relationship between the two religious groups was fundamentally hostile throughout the period from Chalcedon to the ninth century, despite her acknowledgement that the religious polemic of the sources is not truly representative of relations in this period.[117] Bartikyan has gone further and identified a deliberate anti-Miaphysite policy, stating that 'the intrigues of Armenian-Chalcedonians have a history of many centuries, and the Byzantine state and church were their instigators'.[118] However, Garsoïan's point about the polemic has a great deal to recommend it. So, for example, in a poem the ninth-century nun Kasia denounced Armenians as deceitful, evil, mad, capricious and slanderous, but nowhere did she suggest that they were not true Christians.[119] Kasia was, however, based in Constantinople. Tensions between Chalcedonian and Miaphysite adherents might be expected to have been more strained on the frontier if the report of the late-tenth-century historian Stephen of Taron is to be believed. Talking about David III of Tao, Stephen wrote about the religious animosity between the Chalcedonian and Miaphysite inhabitants on the eastern frontier:

> [the Chalcedonian Iberians] harassed the city with the sword and famine. And the church of the [Miaphysite] Armenians outside the circuit wall; which had become a bishop's residence and monastery – previously it had been an Armenian complex [dedicated] to the Holy Cross and St Gamałiēl – they converted it into stables and billets for the forces of Iberia. The Arabs shouted from the wall, 'Why are you Christians treating the sanctuary of Christians in that way?' And the Vracʻikʻ replied, 'We shall be occupying the Armenian church and your mosque in the same way.' For this reason, the wrath of God was provoked against them.[120]

Incidents like this, however, are encountered only very rarely and cannot be used as a kind of benchmark for Miaphysite-Chalcedonian relations.[121] If one looks to evidence from earlier in the tenth century, certain leading figures in the Apostolic Church seem to have held pro-Chalcedonian tendencies, particularly the *Katholikos* Yovhannes Drasxanakertcʻi, also known as John V the Historian (898–929). It is through the comparative use of both the history of Yovhannes and the letters of Patriarch Nicholas I Mystikos that we can glean some evidence of cordial relations between the two churches.[122] In fact, it is extraordinary that in a direct exchange of letters between the religious leaders of the Byzantine and Armenian churches there is barely a mention of the Christological differences. A letter, copied in Yovhannes' *History*, highlights how the political situation in the Caucasus overrode the religious differences that so often dominate the narrative sources.[123] It should be noted that the Patriarch Nicholas I Mystikos was acting as part of the regency council for the infant Constantine VII, and this may possibly explain why he focused on political issues between the two polities, rather than theological differences. At the head of the letter we can see that Nicholas addresses Yovhannes, 'To the most holy, God-loving spiritual Father [Yovhannes], Katholikos of Greater Armenia', highlighting the Byzantine acknowledgement of his position as head of all Christians in the Caucasus.[124] The letter from Constantinople also insinuates the Byzantine desire for a Christian alliance against the Muslim enemy, something that can be directly compared to the correspondence between John I Tzimiskes and Ashot III (953–77) in 971.[125] One must be cautious, though, of treating this episode as fully representative of this period. Yovhannes' pro-Chalcedonian tendencies are clear and in a later letter from Nicholas I to the *Shahanshah* Ashot II the Iron written in 924/5 we are informed that the imperial court had been contacted about ordaining the next *Katholikos*. Indeed, as Nicholas noted:

> On this matter my Father – I mean Photios . . . – spent much pains, partly by letters, partly by dispatch of envoys, although circumstances denied his efforts a successful issue.[126]

What these letters tell us is that the dealings between Byzantium and Armenia were concerned not solely with the issue of Christian unity, although it was certainly an underlying point, even when not discussed directly. We do not have, however, the expected insults or aggression from either side on the religious differences, and while one must acknowledge the unusual circumstance of Yovhannes holding pro-Chalcedonian tendencies, this does not diminish the underlying statement that this period was one of toleration. One cannot, however, just look at the external relations to understand how Armenians dealt with the religious aspect of assimilation. Instead, one must follow the obscure path provided by our sources for information about the experience of Armenian migrants when they first settled in the empire.

As we have seen, the geographical setting of Armenian migrants was a defining factor in the assimilation process, and the same was true in terms of religion. In the west, proximity to the capital and detachment from the roots of their native church probably helped to ensure that the migrants simply merged with the Orthodox majority. The only evidence of an Armenian Church existing in Constantinople is from Michael the Syrian, who claims it stood until the time of Alexios I Komnenos (1081–1181) when it was burnt to the ground, but he does not tell us when it was built or where it was situated.[127] The complete lack of ecclesiastical infrastructure for the Armenian migrants who were settled in Macedonia and Thrace would have slowly eroded their independence as a religious unit, and many were probably unaware of the differences in Christological doctrine, or church identity, and therefore were unlikely to resist strongly the acceptance of the Orthodox rite. While it is hard to determine the rate of the adoption of the Chalcedonian rite by those migrants who were settled in Thrace, a particularly famous figure rose from the ethnic group in the mid-tenth century in the person of Basil I, the founder of the

Macedonian dynasty. Basil showed all the signs of being an active member of the imperial church, with nothing to indicate his Armenian religious heritage. The issue with regarding the adoption of the Chalcedonian rite as evidence of assimilation into the Byzantine state is the lack of explicit accounts and examples of this. The sources are dominated by events concerning the nobility or upper echelons of society within the capital itself and do not preserve writings from migrant communities in the provinces. As discussed earlier, many influential members of the Constantinopolitan elite had Armenian ancestry, but there is no evidence that any of them held to the Miaphysite doctrine of their ancestors. The vast majority of the Armenian aristocracy who migrated to Byzantium, whether in the tenth century or in earlier periods, embraced Orthodoxy within a generation of settling within the empire.[128] This was largely motivated by a desire to increase their social standing through marriage or to gain access to the higher positions within the Byzantine state, in either the civil or military administration. The willingness of the Armenian elite to 'convert' to Byzantine Orthodoxy only supports further the re-evaluation of confessional identity in this period. Rather than viewing it in terms of a dichotomy of the Miaphysite and the Chalcedonian, it can be argued that the differences were sufficiently surmountable not to bar assimilation. Returning to the example of Melias (the younger) who appears in the Pigeon House Church at Cavuşin, Melias was most certainly of Armenian origin, yet his depiction in an Orthodox Church suggests that he was a Chalcedonian. Matthew of Edessa's account omits the religious and ethnic background of Melias and his subsequent death, though he designates him as a Roman.[129] While the absence of polemical language from Matthew in this regard is fascinating, what is more important is that Melias, a man of Armenian origin, was now fully Roman and probably a Chalcedonian Christian.

The Armenian migrants who were settled in the eastern themes of the empire were to have an experience different from those of the nobility or migrants who were settled in the west. The Byzantine policy of using Armenians to settle on the depopulated borderlands that had been taken by conquest from local Muslim dynasties brought about an expansion of the Armenian Church into Byzantium. Stephen of Taron informs us of a wave of newly established bishoprics in Byzantine cities in the east:

> In the days of lord Xačʻik (973-992), patriarch of Armenia, this people of Armenia spread and extended across the regions of the west, to the extent that he consecrated bishops for it in Antioch of Syria, in Tarsus of Cilicia and in Sulind, and in all these districts.[130]

Furthermore, Stephen tells us that bishops from Armenia and 'from the side of the Greeks' were present at the election of the Katholikos Sarkis I (992–1019) in 992.[131] This would indicate that cordial relations between the Byzantine and Armenian clergy existed on the eastern frontier, where localized tensions were just that: localized. The pattern of religious tolerance seems to have mirrored that of political comradery, as we have seen in the correspondence between Yovhannes

Drasxanakertcʻi and Nicholas I in the early tenth century – and later in the relationship of John I Tzimiskes and Ashot III.

The reliance on settling eastern Christians, be they Syrian or Armenian, in the newly conquered territories suggests that the religious differences were downplayed to achieve wider political goals. There are still examples, however, of religious antagonism between Byzantine churchmen and the Miaphysite Eastern churches. In the reign of Nikephoros II Phokas, the emperor encouraged the Syrian Jacobite Patriarch, John VI Sarigta (965–85), to relocate to northern Mesopotamia in order to escape from the persecution that Miaphysite Christians were suffering under the newly installed Chalcedonian Patriarch of Antioch.[132] This in turn led to a migration of Syrians to the lands around Melitene. We are informed by Michael the Syrian that Nikephoros had promised to come to terms with the Miaphysite Christians so that they would be free from persecution. Yet, a little further on the same source tells us that this promise was immediately rescinded and the members of the ecclesiastical hierarchy of the Syrian Church were brought to Constantinople and threatened with imprisonment if they did not accept the Acts of Chalcedon.[133] The Syrian Patriarch and bishops were subsequently thrown in prison for refusing to agree to these terms and were only released upon the accession of John I Tzimiskes in 969. This, Cowe suggests, was a 'means of regularizing and homogenizing [Cappadocia] in order to tie it closely to the centre and reduce the effect of centrifugal forces among the recent immigrants', which, he further argues, was an intentional policy to reduce a Miaphysite religious group to subservience to the empire.[134]

Remarkably there were no recorded attempts at this stage to enforce the same policy on the Armenian migrants who had likewise settled in the regions around Melitene, and there is even evidence that some within the Armenian ecclesiastical leadership desired to bring about a reconciliation between the two churches. The short reign of Vahan I (968–9) was a result of the newly elected *Katholikos*' attempt 'to foster closer relations and achieve agreement with the Chalcedonians'; he was promptly forced to flee to Vaspurakan for protection and a successor, Stephen III (969–72), was elected.[135] There then followed a bitter dispute between the two men, which seems to have divided the Armenian Church, and it is with some relief that Stephen of Taron reports that '[Vahan] and [Stephen] died in the same year (972) and disorder was removed from this country of Armenia'.[136] One cannot ignore the attempts by the Byzantines to bring about religious unity, yet it would be wrong to exaggerate local tensions, as found, for instance, in Sebasteia, to argue that the Byzantines were completely intolerant towards eastern Christians living on the frontiers.[137] Such a policy, had it existed, would have not only alienated large swathes of the population who were relied upon for the security of the empire but also severely damaged the military capabilities provided by the Armenians.

Moreover, it would be wrong to categorize all Armenians as Miaphysites; in fact, a substantial minority of Armenians followed a Chalcedonian Armenian Church, and a discussion of this group is essential when dealing with religious assimilation. The group referred to as Armenian Chalcedonians, or sometimes

Cat͑/Tzatoi – following the Chalcedonian rite – had a large following in Taron and Tayk.[138] Their liturgical language was not Greek but Armenian, even when residing in monasteries of the imperial church.[139] Unfortunately there is a trend in modern scholarship to view this group as 'un-Armenian', something that uncritically echoes partisan sources originating in times of religious tension. Bartikyan goes further than most in claiming that the Byzantine government and church were the main supporters of Armenian Chalcedonians, which encouraged Armenians to abandon the Apostolic Church and allow themselves to be used as Byzantine agents in Armenia.[140] The origins of the hostilities between Chalcedonians and Miaphysites in the Caucasus can be found in the sources. In the example earlier, from Stephen of Taron, we find the soldiers of David III of Tao using a Miaphysite church as a stable, an action which confused even the Muslim garrison that they were besieging. The region of Tayk was strongly Chalcedonian in profession, despite its geographical location being surrounded by Armenians who were not. The actions of the soldiers, however, are not wholly typical of relations between the two groups. The value of this example is realistically only that it highlights the existence of localized religious tensions. The Armenian Chalcedonians are incredibly hard to identify in our primary sources. We will see in later chapters how difficult it is to demonstrate whether those of Armenian origin had adopted the Chalcedonian rites or came from an Armenian Chalcedonian family. Suffice it to say that to claim Armenian Chalcedonians were a 'horrible non-phenomenon which emerged under external pressure' is at very least both misinformed and insensitive.[141] One of the key issues here is the use of identity labels by the contemporary sources. In the medieval Armenian sources, the Armenian Chalcedonians were often grouped with their Iberian (Georgian) or Byzantine neighbours.[142] This difficulty is compounded by both Byzantine and Georgian sources using their own identity labels which do not obviously correspond with one another, thereby making it extraordinarily difficult to assess the true size and nature of the Armenian Chalcedonian population.

There is one further issue that needs to be considered regarding the relationship between the Byzantine and Armenian churches and the categorization of individuals in a religious context. Nina Garsoïan has stated that 'neither side could be anything but fundamentally hostile to those whom each reciprocally viewed as heretics'. Yet, this raises the question of the application of Byzantine law particularly in the context of Armenian assimilation. While in Christological terms the Armenians fell into the Miaphysite definition by the church in Constantinople, to state that the Armenians were seen by the Byzantines as heretics in a legal framework would be contrary to the evidence at hand. We have seen previously that Nikephoros II Phokas promulgated laws specifically targeting Armenian settlers on the eastern frontier, thereby acknowledging their non-heretical status. In addition, the consistent granting of high offices and titles to Armenians throughout the ninth and tenth centuries dispels any sense of the Armenians being seen as 'alien'. Indeed, the granting of titles legally made the recipient subject to Roman laws, ignoring the religious and also ethnic differences entirely. One clear example can be found in the career of Eustathios Romaios, a Constantinopolitan judge who ended his career as *droungarios tes viglas* (chief justice). One such case that Eustathios dealt with was the matter of the inheritance of a man of Georgian origin.[143] In this case the court refused to recognize the ethnic origins of the man, which could possibly have entitled him to special treatment under the law, and the reasoning behind this is very relevant to the process of assimilation. As the man in question had held imperial office, and therefore imperial gifts, possibly through a salary or stipend that was attached to his position, it was the opinion of the court that this 'makes it necessary for him to follow the laws of the Romans'.[144] Therefore, if an individual held Roman titles he was recognized legally under Roman law. This is incompatible with the argument of Garsoïan that Armenians were viewed as heretics. There is simply no evidence to support this claim. After all, many held imperial titles whether they lived within the boundaries of the empire or outside of it. While hyperbolic rhetoric was used by people on both sides of the divide to describe the other, fundamentally the religious background of an Armenian migrant did not prevent assimilation, and even if it was an issue, it was one that was overlooked on account of the important role the Armenians played in the Byzantine military and government.

Cheynet has argued that it usually took three generations for assimilation to be complete, and yet there is simply no evidence to allow us to assess the rate of 'conversion' for the Armenian migrants from the Christianity of their ancestors to the Christianity they found within the empire.[145] What we can see, however, is that the religious tensions only rarely flared up at a local level. The evidence of the sheer number of Byzantine-Armenians in imperial service during the eleventh century, and the lack of evidence for those continuing to practise the Armenian liturgy, suggests that many did indeed 'convert'. But the only thing that can be said with any certainty is that religious differences had no real effect on the ability of Armenians to assimilate in the ninth and tenth centuries: the eleventh century was to be an entirely different scenario.

Conclusion

It is clear that in the period *c.* 867–1000 Armenians were successfully able to assimilate into the Byzantine Empire. By analysing Armenian assimilation through the pre-established Assimilation Model, we can witness the transformation of Armenian migrants into *Romaioi*. The examples cited document the assimilation process in action. The population transfers from the eighth through to the tenth centuries meant that Armenian settlements were placed in different areas, and this factor produced varying results in terms of assimilation. Those settled in the west, most specifically in Constantinople, rapidly transformed into *Romaioi*, as they were closest to the imperial institutions that facilitated interaction with the Byzantine state. Our sources concentrate on the aristocratic interaction with this process, with many examples that they integrated best when involved in the institutions of the Byzantine state: imperial administration and the army. We have traced a number of the main Anatolian families in the late ninth and tenth centuries, assessing their 'Armenian background'. Some families, such as the Phokades, had debatable heritage, but many of the families that were to dominate the army commands in the middle and late tenth centuries were almost certainly of Armenian stock. There are some surprising instances of rapid assimilation, such as the Taronite princes and brothers Grigor and Bagrat. Nevertheless, the background and career of Basil I demonstrates that even the non-elite Armenian migrants eventually assimilated.

Chapter 2

THE BYZANTINE ANNEXATIONS OF ARMENIA, 1000–64

IDEOLOGY AND OPPORTUNISM?

I mentioned in the introduction that the Byzantine-Armenian relationship progressed through four interconnected, and occasionally overlapping phases: *assimilation, annexation, alienation* and *separatism*. In this chapter we are going to explore the first change between these phases, that of successful assimilation of Armenian migrants within Byzantium, to the period of annexations that saw the western Armenian kingdoms annexed and their exiled ruling classes migrate to vast estates in central and eastern Anatolia. There are many important questions to be answered here, such as: what was the motivation behind Armenian kings and princes to surrender their lands? And those of the Byzantine emperors, primarily Basil II, to acquire them? We will also need to understand why external relations changed between Byzantium and Armenia. This will involve tracing the way in which internal factionalism within the Byzantine Empire led to its intervening in Caucasia as never before and analysing the factors that dictated where the displaced Armenian rulers were to be settled. In truth, the annexations proper were a direct result of the Byzantine-Georgian conflict that broke out in the final years of Basil's reign, a conflict that went on to produce unforeseen consequences which ultimately undermined the process of assimilation and produced the alienation of the Armenians in Byzantium. However, we have already seen that in the tenth century some Armenian princes were willing to give up their ancestral lands for estates and careers within the empire, and so the phase of *annexation* has some overlap with the events we have discussed in the previous chapter. What becomes increasingly clear is that Basil's reign did not represent the definitive change in the Byzantine-Armenian relationship but rather gathered the ingredients for the recipe of alienation of the Armenians that was to come in the mid-eleventh century.

As we move into events during the eleventh century our main sources of evidence that we were familiar with in the first chapter fade and are replaced with new authors. Strangely, from a Byzantine perspective, we have no contemporary history of the early eleventh century that has come down to us to the present day and so must rely on the *Synopsis* of Skylitzes. This raises pertinent questions regarding the sources Skylitzes used when writing his work, and it has been supposed that he relied on an unidentified, but debated, source for the years

976–1025. Warren Treadgold has argued that the source was in fact one written by Theodore of Sebasteia, who is identified in Skylitzes' introduction, with a possible title being *History of the Lord Basil the Porphyrogennetos*. This is challenged by Catherine Holmes who argues that the evidence is too insubstantial to draw definite conclusions, but with no offer at an alternative Treadgold's identification seems the more likely.[1]

Skylitzes' *Synopsis* returns to relevance in this chapter when his narrative turns to Armenian affairs in the early 1040s. His grasp of detail (and even interest) mirrors that of his probable sources Demetrius of Cyzicus and John the Monk of Lydia. One must, however, acknowledge that Skylitzes' account of Armenian affairs dramatically increases in both length and details from the 1040s onwards and this is most likely down to his use of a biography of Katakalon Kekaumenos who was active in the Byzantine governance of Ani.[2] Thankfully we have a series of adequate sources from the eastern provinces that make up the shortfalls in the Byzantine historical record. From the Armenian tradition we lose Stephen of Taron, although fortunately he continues to the death of David III of Tao in 1002. Stephen's narrative is resumed almost immediately with Aristakes Lastivertc'i, our most reliable Armenian source for the next two chapters, taking the Armenian narrative up to August 1071. Matthew of Edessa is also writing on this period, but his remoteness from events, at least up until c.1050, makes his work less valuable. As this chapter focuses mainly on the events in the Caucasus during Basil's reign, we are able to access Georgian sources which supplement the historical details we get from their Armenian counterparts. The source known as *The Book of K'art'li* augments our knowledge of Basil's campaigns against the Kingdom of Georgia during 1020–2, offering a sometimes-balanced account of the motivations behind the key characters Basil II and Giorgi I (998/1002–1027). There is also further evidence to help our understanding of the apparent Armenian willingness to voluntarily offer their kingdoms upon the death of the reigning monarch – something that will be explored in full later. Our last contemporary account, and arguably the most valuable for studying events on Byzantium's eastern frontier in the late tenth and early eleventh centuries, is Yahya of Antioch. Here, we are given invaluable details of the actions and motivations of many of the key characters on Byzantium's eastern frontier.

Basil II and his image

Before we move on to the annexations there is one last issue arising from the primary sources that needs to be explored: why did Basil II not come under significant criticism from our Armenian sources, despite the fact that it was under his rule that the independence of the western Armenian kingdoms reached their final phase? It is indeed unusual that both Basil and his brother/successor Constantine VIII receive constant praise from Armenian sources despite their religious convictions. A clear example of this appears in Grigor Narerkac'i's *History of the Holy Cross at*

Aparank, the first quarter of which is dedicated to praising the two emperors for their gift of a relic from the True Cross to the monastery:

> And these two brothers, Basil and Constantine . . . were elevated to the magnificent honour (and) glory of the golden (and) ornate imperial throne. And they occupied it with dignity, peace, and tranquillity, extending their own most-trusted progeny, high and marvellous branches stemming from the lordly, royal, and well-rooted tree.[3]

One can observe similar positive descriptions in the account of Aristakes who firmly presents Basil as the righteous party in the Byzantine-Georgian conflict over Tao,[4] while even the less than favourable account from Matthew of Edessa describes Basil as 'the saintly Roman emperor'.[5]

The attitude towards the Byzantines does indeed harden in the writings of Matthew of Edessa and Aristakes as they continue their narratives towards their present day (early twelfth and late eleventh centuries, respectively), but despite the fact that they were writing with the benefit of hindsight, they do not apportion blame to Basil from the seizure of Armenia, when they might have done so. It should also be noted that the later religious issues that came to dominate the Byzantine-Armenian relationship from the mid-eleventh century onwards were also not levelled against Basil. The explanation for this is actually quite simple. Basil was remembered, by Armenian sources, for his policy of religious tolerance that had existed in the ninth and tenth centuries, and so the contrast with later emperors who attempted to impose Orthodoxy on their Armenian subjects is made even greater by our sources writing at the end of the eleventh century.

A revealing episode that demonstrates existing religious tolerance can be found when the *Katholikos* Peter I (1019–58) visited Basil in Trebizond during the winter of 1021. Peter, the spiritual head of the Armenian Church, was in reality a heretic in the eyes of the Byzantines and yet this did not prevent diplomatic dialogue between the two parties.[6] Furthermore, it would be illogical for the Artsruni settlement to have gone ahead had there been pre-existing tensions or intolerance of religious differences; in fact, we see an active expansion of Miaphysite religious houses and places of worship in Cappadocia from the mid-1020s onwards. The events leading to the persecution of the Armenian Church by Basil's successors cannot be projected back upon this period in order to emphasize the fundamental religious differences between the Byzantines and Armenians. Rather, the works of Matthew and Aristakes suggest that the writers themselves saw that the later problem was exactly that: later. Indeed, the antagonism that the Byzantines and Armenians were to develop towards one another later in the eleventh century was the product of unforeseen circumstances that arose from the annexation and settlement of the Armenians in the 1020s as well as the arrival of Gagik II of Ani in Cappadocia in the mid-1040s.

When one observes Basil's actions in terms of the area of settlement, or even his religious policy, it becomes apparent that he chose to continue the policy of cooperation and tolerance with the empire's eastern heterodox neighbours.

We will see shortly that during Basil's campaign against David III of Tao, it was reported that the emperor freed the Armenian priests of Sebasteia from the authority of the Greek metropolitan, easing the religious tensions that had the potential to encourage discord in the eastern themes.[7] In so doing, Basil ensured that the social and religious framework so established mirrored that to which the Armenian migrants had been accustomed in their own lands, something that would potentially aid assimilation as long as the religious differences were not exacerbated by the imperial centre.

The deterioration of Byzantium's status in our Armenian sources reflects the growing hostility between the Byzantine and Armenian churches during the mid-eleventh century, which involved series of debates on the differing theologies of the two churches and in some cases threats of forced conversions of the Armenians living within the empire or even the complete destruction of the Armenian Church.[8] A full analysis of the relations between the Byzantine and Armenian churches in the eleventh century is found in Chapter 3; the question to keep under consideration is: why did the religious differences not interfere with the diplomatic relations between Byzantium and Armenia at the time of the annexations?

The context of the annexations

External relations

The annexation of the Armenian kingdoms in the eleventh century was a seismic event in the history of Byzantine-Armenian relations, although not without precedent. We have seen in the previous chapter that once the Armenians arrived in the empire they quickly engaged with the process of assimilation and contributed to Byzantine society, most commonly through military service. On a geopolitical scale, the strength of the Byzantine-Armenian relationship can be seen in the evidence of friendships existing between Caucasian magnates, both Armenian and Georgian, and their Byzantine counterparts on the other side of the frontier. Our task here is to understand the context of the relationship between the polities of Byzantium and Armenia up until the annexations; in so doing, we shall witness the shared comradery of fighting a common Muslim enemy, which in turn brought a closer Christian bond, despite the theological differences.

There have been claims that Byzantine policy towards Armenia revolved around the aim to incorporate the Christian realms in Caucasia, as they did not sit comfortably with Byzantine imperial ideology.[9] This is simply not the case. Imperial policy towards Caucasia was driven by local cooperation set against the Islamic powers that had previously dominated the Taurus and Anti-Taurus Mountain ranges. It is of great importance to challenge previous views that have seen the period of the Macedonian dynasty as one of 'the systematic advance ... [of Byzantium's] eastern frontiers', which suggests a continuous foreign policy on the eastern frontier for nearly 300 years – painting Byzantium as a typical expansionist imperialist state.[10] Obviously there has been a great deal of revisionism concerning the nature of the Byzantine Empire in the past couple of decades, with some scholars specifically tackling the question for the period of reconquest, 842–1025. Yet the study of Byzantine foreign policy, and its trajectory, must be based on solid primary source evidence, and the works of Constantine VII provide a logical starting point.[11] We have already seen that both Basil I and his son and successor Leo VI oversee expansion and settlement along a revitalized frontier in the east, with many instances of Armenians taking the most prominent roles as governors, generals, soldiers and settlers. It was during the reign of Romanos I, and led by his highly able *domestikos ton scholon*, John Kourkouas, that strategic areas such as Theodosioupolis and Melitene were permanently seized by the empire. Both cities had been outposts for Muslim raiding parties to launch into the Anatolian heartland for centuries, and the acquisition of key strongholds was more favoured by imperial policy than the direct occupation of large swathes of territory.

One can ascertain from the primary evidence that a pragmatic approach to annexation was often taken by the imperial court, although this did not always guarantee successful results. In chapter forty-six of the *DAI* Constantine VII records the attempted annexation of Artanuj (Ardanoutzin), when its ruler, Ashot Kiskasis (Asotios), in 923 offered control of the city peacefully, and the episode shares many themes with Basil's annexations in the eleventh century.[12] We are informed that a monk by the name of Agapios of Kyminas was entrusted to treat with Romanos I with regard to the surrender of the Artanuj, with Constantine VII informing us of Agapios' instructions:

> I adjure you, by God and by the power of the honourable and life-giving Cross, to go to Constantinople and tell the emperor to send and take over my city, and have it beneath his dominion.[13]

It would seem that internal disputes in Iberia were the cause for Asotios to turn towards surrendering his lands; unfortunately for the Byzantines those Iberian magnates with whom Asotios was in conflict wrote to the emperor in the following manner:

> If your imperial majesty approves this and enters our country, then we put off our servitude to your imperial majesty and make common cause with the Saracens, since we shall have fighting and hostilities with the Romans and shall, perforce, move an army against the city of Ardanoutzin and its country, and against Romania itself.[14]

Constantine VII noted with glee the panicked reaction from Romanos, who was especially fearful of a potential Iberian-Muslim alliance that would be a serious test for the border defences, resulting in the emperor immediately backtracking from his attempt to take the city. One should note that the likelihood of an alliance between the Iberians and Muslim emirates was more reflective of the time when Constantine was writing (948–52), rather than in the 920s when the episode occurred.[15] The lessons learnt, however, on this occasion seem to warn against direct annexation, unless it was entirely necessary and had the full support of the neighbouring powers. We will see shortly that this lesson was not entirely heeded by Basil II when dealing with the annexation of Tao in 1000/1. On that occasion the Iberian princes, Gurgen and Bagrat, attempted to thwart any annexation of Iberian lands, despite the legal claims and treaties that had previously been made between the emperor and the previous ruler, David III.

There are other passages in the works of Constantine VII that resemble potential plans for annexation. In his description on the environs of Lake Van, Constantine states:

> If these three cities, Chliat and Arzes and Perkri, are in the possession of the emperor, a Persian army cannot come out against Romania, because they are between Romania and Armenia, and serve as a barrier and as military halts for armies.[16]

One must, however, put this statement within its proper context. The specific mention of Byzantine control over three important cities in the region of Vaspurakan highlights the recognition of their strategic value in terms of defence of the Byzantines against Muslim raiders who had plagued the empire in the previous centuries.[17] Those who see this as a 'future initiative' for annexation nevertheless fail to recognize the nuances of the statement 'in possession of the emperor'. The control of key territories through allies, normally local magnates, was common policy in the early to mid-tenth century. This passage highlights the lack of trust between the imperial court and the Artsruni princes who had recently declared themselves 'Kings of Armenia' in direct competition with the Bagratids of Ani. Furthermore, Constantine's comment on the natural defensibility of Armenia is simply a pragmatic observation, and it would be fanciful to read this as an imperial-sanctioned annexation plan of western Armenia that future emperors were to heed and which indeed was never put into practice.

Even during the reigns of Nikephoros II Phokas and John I Tzimiskes, the Byzantines never made any serious aggressive claims to Armenian or Iberian territories.[18] Rather, the period represented a new phase of rapid expansion through aggressive military operations on the south-eastern frontier, aiming to eliminate the fractured remnants of Muslim control over the Cilician plain, as well as the environs of Antioch and northern Syria. We have already noted the correspondence between John I Tzimiskes and the King of Armenia, Ashot III, with a letter preserved in Matthew of Edessa's chronicle that contains a running narrative of the exploits during John's campaigns and the language used is cordial and relates to the shared Christian glory attained by the defeat of the Muslims in Syria and Palestine.[19] Bizarrely this particular episode has been portrayed by some as an example of Byzantium threatening Armenian independence, even though Matthew's account specifically mentions that Tzimiskes was seeking to avenge the defeat of an imperial army under the command of Melias, the *domestikos* of the east, outside the walls of Amida in July 973.[20] Despite the geographical proximity of Tzimiskes' campaigning to Armenia, the events actually show remarkable levels of comradery between the Byzantines and the Armenians, to the extent that they fought together against the common enemy of the region, the fractured emirates of the Abbasid Empire. At no time does there appear to be a serious contemplation of annexation of Armenia on the part of Byzantium, nor did the imperial ideology or recognition of foreign princes justify the use of aggressive seizure of Armenian lands. As Jonathan Shepard commented, 'Imperial recognition of a prince as "prince of princes" . . . did not betoken plans for formal annexation. Bestowal or withdrawal of the title served as a bargaining chip';[21] in other words, Byzantine foreign policy considered diplomacy rather than direct military action as its preferred method in its dealings with its eastern Christian neighbours in Caucasia.

One must also recognize how the Byzantine-Armenian relationship, in an external context, constantly transcended the political boundary that existed – as is evident from the blend of ethnolinguistic groups cohabiting on either side of the frontier, the diplomatic and religious exchanges and importantly the distribution of imperial titles from Constantinople to neighbouring rulers.[22] As mentioned earlier, the Armenian king was referred to as 'our spiritual son' in official forms of address by the imperial court,[23] while the Taronite princes, Grigor II and his brother Bagrat III, were both given the titles *magistros* and estates in the empire in return for the annexation of their inheritance in 967. David III of Tao held the title of *kouropalates*, as he was the most prominent Iberian prince – a title which in turn was given to Bagrat of Iberia upon David's death, while Bagrat's father, Gurgen, was accorded the title of *magistros*, with the aim to pacify the Iberian princes' ambitions on the frontier after David's death in 1001.[24] The granting of imperial titles was a significant feature of Byzantine diplomacy, in that it brought powerful neighbouring magnates within the Byzantine sphere of influence. The titles also brought with them an imperial stipend which was valued by foreign rulers, as set out in the *DAI*.[25] The relationship created by this practice brought Byzantium and Caucasia closer together politically and shows that the concept of the frontier was far looser than has often been interpreted.[26]

It becomes clear, however, that during Basil's reign the policy towards Caucasia changed. The context surrounding Basil's direct interference in Caucasia is important – that being how David III of Tao supported Bardas Phokas in his rebellion of 987–9 and Basil's desire to punish a neighbouring magnate for involving themselves with internal affairs. These events do not support the theory of preconceived annexation; rather, it seems to be a pragmatic decision to neutralize the most powerful magnate on Byzantium's eastern frontier in order to prevent similar situations from occurring. Let us look more closely at these events that brought Basil into direct interference in Caucasian affairs.

Tao/Tayk and the rebellions of Skleros and Phokas

In many ways the annexations were a product of their own time, although previous interpretations have interpreted selective primary evidence to show a long-term desire of Byzantium, and the Macedonian dynasty, to bring about the absorption of the Armenian kingdoms. Such historiographical discussion can be found earlier in the introduction. The most immediately pressing task is to establish a clear chronological history of the annexations, their context, historical causes and effects on the politics of Caucasia. Once this study is completed, the focus will turn to analysing how Basil II's reign represented a dramatic shift in Byzantine policy for both foreign and internal relations with the Armenians. To reiterate, it will be argued that Basil's reign was not the moment of change in the Byzantine-Armenian relationship, but it represents the period in which the seeds of alienation were sown for the Armenian settlements in the mid-eleventh century.

Strictly speaking, the region of Tao/Tayk is not Armenian but Iberian (or later Georgian). Its people recognized themselves as Iberian, they were Chalcedonian Christians and spoke/wrote in the Georgian script. The princes of Tao most often held the Byzantine title of *kouropalates* in recognition of their primacy over the other Iberian potentates and held significant influence over their Iberian and Armenian neighbours alike.[27] In many ways the princes of Tao, perhaps reflecting their geographical proximity to Byzantium, were the readiest to accept Byzantine titles and imagery. One can see in the depictions of David III of Tao and his brother Bagrat in the complex at Ošk′i that their crowns are adorned with Byzantine *pendila* which suggests that their political authority was now drawn from Constantinople rather than Baghdad.[28] Yet, it was the very fact of Tao's primacy and closeness in cultural spheres that brought Tao into conflict with Byzantium. For David was to become embroiled in the struggle for power between the Macedonian dynasty, ruling in Constantinople, and the military officer class whose base of support came from the Anatolian heartlands. It is therefore necessary to turn our attention briefly to these revolts and assess how David became entangled in the internal politics of Byzantium which would draw Byzantium into direct interference in the Caucasian geopolitical scene.

In the previous chapter we saw the rise and eventual dominance of the Byzantine military by a series of families of Armenian origin, who by 963 had come to occupy the imperial throne to 'protect' the Macedonian princes Basil and Constantine. The murder of Nikephoros II Phokas and accession of John I Tzimiskes split the fragile coalition of competing families between the Phokades, supported by such families as the Melissenos, and the Kourkouai with the Skleroi as close allies of the new emperor.[29] Tzimiskes immediately removed the Phokades from the highest military commands, ending a monopoly that had existed since Constantine VII's coup against the Lekapenoi in 945.[30] The response was as expected: revolt. Bardas Phokas, a nephew of Nikephoros II, had originally been banished to Amaseia but secretly made his way to Caesarea where he was able to raise the banner of rebellion.[31] Ultimately Phokas' struggle was in vain, his support quickly slipped away with bribes and promises from Bardas Skleros on behalf of Tzimiskes, and Phokas himself was eventually tonsured and sent to the island of Chios. The rest of Tzimiskes reign is not strictly relevant here, but upon the emperor's death it was Bardas Skleros who expected to assume the 'protection' of the imperial princes Basil and Constantine.[32]

Basil the Chamberlain had other plans.[33] Immediately the military commands were reshuffled again; Bardas Skleros was dismissed from his position as *domestikos* of the east and demoted to *doux* of the soldiers in Mesopotamia. His response was just as predictable: revolt.[34] Skleros' revolt lasted some three years, and the imperial court was forced to recall a general who could match Skleros' experience and ability: Bardas Phokas. The revolt was finally crushed in March 979 when Phokas defeated Skleros in battle. Importantly, however, David III of Tao is said to have provided a cavalry force for the imperial armies.[35] There are multiple sources attesting David's military assistance. From the later materials from hagiographical accounts and the book of *K'art'li*, we find a Georgian man identified as T'ornik,[36] a man who lived in the Great Lavra of the Holy Mountain, who received a request from the imperial court to deliver a message to David III of Tao. T'ornik was sent by the imperial court to David to seek aid and was successful in his task. T'ornik himself was given the command of 12,000 'elite cavalry' and successfully routed Skleros in battle, in return for which David was granted the 'Upper lands of the Greek Empire for him to hold during his lifetime'.[37] Skleros was to take refuge with the ruler of Iraq, Emir Adud al-Daula, and remained an external threat to Byzantium for nearly a decade. Yet Skleros' revolt had shifted the power balance in Byzantium, with the Phokades regaining primacy among the Anatolian military aristocracy.

One can find the narrative of the years intervening between the end of Skleros' revolt and the revolts of 986–9 elsewhere; we will skip ahead to the revolt of Phokas.[38] By the time Phokas had raised his standard in 987, Basil II had overthrown Basil the Chamberlain and embarked on a less-than-spectacular campaign in Bulgaria.[39] Despite aiding the imperial forces in 979, strangely David sided with the rebel forces of Phokas some eight years later, possibly indicating that David assisted Bardas Phokas personally, rather than the Macedonian dynasty, in 979. Apparently David maintained cordial relations with Bardas Phokas from the time when the latter was *doux* of Chaldia and so was happy to provide a force that attacked Grigor Taronites, who had been sent to Trebizond on the orders of the emperor.[40] We are informed that the force of David immediately withdrew after they heard of Basil's victory at the Battle of Chrysopolis, in which the emperor was able to capture Phokas' brother Nikephoros.[41] The revolt of Phokas was put down a short while later with the imperial victory at Abydos. It is no surprise that Basil turned to deal with those who had assisted the rebels, particularly one as inconsistent in their support as David III of Tao.

It is clear that David's involvement in the internal affairs of the empire had worried Basil, and with his focus firmly upon the hostilities with Bulgaria in the west the threat posed by David on the eastern frontier was potentially too great to ignore. As it happened, Basil chose to deal with David directly because of his troublesome interference with the internal politics of the empire, which threatened the stability of the eastern frontier, and certainly offended Byzantine political theory that the emperor should not tolerate such behaviour from an inferior Christian prince. Basil, we are told, sent a force into Tao under the command of the Patrician Djakrous in 990, and according to Yahya's account:

As to David, king of the Georgians, he asked the emperor Basil pardon and grace, promising him obedience and submission and that after his death his estates would be annexed to his Empire because he was very advanced in age.[42]

Yahya is the only source to report this event in 990, and within a decade of David's death a new crisis began to brew in the east.[43] Yet, the details surrounding David's death also need unpicking, as our primary sources are divided on the method by which he died and whether there was any foul play. The Armenian chronicler Aristakes, who starts his account with the *Kouropalates*' death, claims that David was killed by his *azats*,[44] and that '[this was] because they had wearied of him, and were interested in promises [made to them] earlier by the emperor'.[45] Sadly, Aristakes does not expand on what these promises were, while Matthew of Edessa gives a similar account but emphasizes the role of the archbishop of Georgia, Hilarion, as the chief conspirator in the murder of David.[46] The differences in our primary account need to be addressed. What were the promises that Basil allegedly made to David's vassals, and why does Matthew accuse the archbishop of Georgia? With regard to the *azats* we are lacking specific evidence in this particular instance, but one can look back, or ahead, to establish whether there was a trend in the diplomatic interactions between Byzantium and the political entities of Caucasia that may have been tempting enough for the *azats* of David to commit treason. We have discussed in detail in the previous chapter how certain Armenian lords were tempted to voluntarily hand over their lands and receive estates and titles within the empire. For example, the principality of Taron, to the south of Tao/Tayk, was annexed by Nikephoros II Phokas where the emperor 'raised them (the heirs [Grigor] and [Bagrat] Bagratuni) to the rank of patrician and granted them estates which provided good revenues'.[47] The issuing of imperial titles and lands to foreign magnates on the frontier of Byzantium was an intrinsic part of Caucasian foreign policy, and one can expect that a similar offer had been made to the nobles of Tao. While we do not know the exact terms of the deal struck between Basil and David in 990, we can presume that the landed aristocracy were aware of what they would gain after the annexation. Stephen of Taron does indeed confirm the settlement of the *azats* of Tao on lands inside Byzantium, but he does not specify where.[48] Returning to the implication of the archbishop of Georgia, the fact that it appears only in Matthew's account makes it somewhat unlikely, although Yahya gives us some further details regarding the treaty of 990 that provide an explanation. It would appear that the archbishop of Georgia was sent in 990, along with 'high-ranking officers', to agree to the terms set by Basil and we are told they were 'conferred with dignities and overwhelmed with favours'.[49] Sadly, the events surrounding David's death were not recorded in detail by Yahya, who is without doubt one of our most important sources for events in the east, but we can see that the association of the archbishop of Georgia with the *azats* of David may well correspond with Aristakes' account of David's death. It should be noted that Matthew misdated this event to 985–6, rather than 1000–1, although the question regarding dating issues does not necessarily reduce the historical value of Matthew's account.[50] Moreover, his anti-

Chalcedonian views may have prompted his explicit inclusion of Hilarion as a conspirator in the plot against David's life. Interestingly, however, Basil himself was not accused of being involved by any of the sources, despite having the most to gain from David's death.[51]

In the aftermath of the annexation, in 1001, Basil was faced with opposition from the Iberian magnates on the northern border of Tao. David had no natural heirs and so had previously adopted Bagrat (960–1014), king of Abkhazia, and heir to the kingdom of Iberia as the inheritor to his lands. The settlement of 990, however, had technically removed Bagrat from his inheritance. Bagrat and his father, Gurgen of Iberia (958–1008), met with Basil upon the annexation in 1001 but were unable to prevent the Byzantine incorporation of Tao. As had become a recurring theme in Byzantine foreign policy, Basil bestowed upon Bagrat and Gurgen the titles of *kouropalates* and *magistros*, respectively.[52] This move had an interesting twist; the title of *magistros* was lower than that of *kouropalates* in rank within the Byzantine hierarchy, thus Basil chose to give Bagrat, the son, the higher title. The ploy ultimately failed to create a division between the two, but it did anger Gurgen to the extent that he attempted an invasion of Tao.[53] He was frustrated by Nikephoros Ouranos, the recently installed *doux* of Antioch, through what would seem to have been negotiations rather than fighting.[54]

While Basil spent most of the early years of the eleventh century occupied in the west with the subjugation of Bulgaria, events on the eastern border began to challenge the status quo in Caucasia. The fusion of the kingdoms of Abkhazia and Iberia into the unified Kingdom of Georgia in 1008 by Bagrat disturbed the balance of power in the region, and upon the accession of Bagrat's son Giorgi, Byzantine policy on the eastern frontier was forced to change dramatically. According to Aristakes, Bagrat was given land in the region of Tao that was attached to his title of *Kouropalates*. Basil demanded the restoration of the lands to Byzantine control upon Bagrat's death in 1014, which he saw as his legal right. Basil wrote to Giorgi reminding him to '[a]bandon [those territories] which I gave to your father out of the Curopalate's portion as a gift, and be prince solely over your patrimony'.[55] Aristakes reports further that '[Georgi] did not consent to this; rather, taking pride in his youth, he wrote a contrary reply: "I shall not give anyone even one single House [from the territory] over which my father held sway."'[56] At this time Basil was reaching the climax of his campaigns in Bulgaria, the decisive battle of the Kleidion Pass taking place in the same year. The emperor was therefore unable to venture east personally to settle the matter. Our sources are divided on the manner in which Basil responded to the stubbornness of Giorgi. Aristakes claims that Basil sent a force eastwards that was defeated by Giorgi.[57] Skylitzes states that '[w]hen George ... broke his treaty with the Romans by invading the frontier regions, the emperor campaigned against him in full force'.[58] As is common when dealing with Skylitzes, the chronology can be problematic, and it is most likely that he was talking about Basil's campaign in Iberia during 1021 and has omitted the seven-year gap between the two events, whether by choice or ignorance.[59] In any case, the actions of Giorgi forced Basil into military action on his eastern frontier, at a time when he was unable to give the situation his full attention, and therefore we must now look to his campaign in 1021.

Basil launched his eastern offensive in 1021 with the intention of dealing with his troublesome neighbour and regaining the lands in the region of Tao that Giorgi had been occupying since 1014. According to the account of Aristakes, Basil came eastwards with the intention of settling the dispute peacefully – testifying that 'he greatly desired that his journey end in peace and that the land remain in a flourishing state'.[60] The book of K'art'li offers no context for the hostilities between Giorgi and Basil. However, further information is provided by Yahya. He mentions correspondence between Giorgi and al-Hakim (996–1021), the Fatimid Caliph of Egypt, offering a joint enterprise in making war upon the emperor, which immediately brought about preparations by Basil for a new campaign in Syria, a clear indication of the importance of the frontiers under threat.[61] Yet it was during his preparations at Philomelion that the emperor learnt of the death of al-Hakim. Released from the need to reassert Byzantine interests in Syria, Basil turned to the north-eastern frontier and was able to bring about a show of Byzantine power that Giorgi had never expected. The war between Byzantium and Georgia is neither significant nor relevant for this study, but to put it simply Giorgi was unable to withstand concentrated Byzantine military power and sued for peace in 1022. More significant, however, than Basil's victory over Giorgi was how the powers of Caucasia had reacted to the show of force by Byzantium. For it was during Basil's journey and stay in the east over the winter of 1021/2 that the kingdom of Ani was offered to Byzantium.

The subsequent annexations

Ani (I): Background and the Treaty of Trebizond

The annexation of the kingdom of Ani is a long and confusing episode in the narrative history of Byzantium and Armenia, and this is largely a result of the inconsistencies in our sources when used comparatively. So, let us start from what we know with relative certainty. While Basil was wintering in Trebizond during the winter of 1021, after his first year of campaigning against the Georgian King Giorgi, we are informed that he was approached by the Armenian *Katholikos* Peter I and we have three different accounts of the meeting from our Armenian sources, Matthew of Edessa and Aristakes, and the Armenian version of the book of K'art'li.[62]

The sources state that Peter was granted the honour of presiding over the feast of Epiphany. The *Katholikos* carried out the blessing of the Holy water in accordance with the Armenian tradition, and it resulted in some sort of mirage, whether of fire or rays of light.[63] Aristakes tells us in his account that the Byzantine bishops who were present followed the canons of the imperial church; this is an important side note, for this was not the first occasion that Basil had shown religious tolerance while he was present in the east. Matthew goes further in his account, claiming after the celebration of Epiphany:

Basil in turn secretly went to Antioch [. . .] Going up the Black Mountain to a place called Paghakdziak, he received the Christian baptism from the superior and spiritual leader of the place and henceforth became like an adopted father of the Armenian nation.[64]

This event is most likely apocryphal, although it offers an insight into the twelfth-century Armenian image of Basil, not as a conqueror but a paternal protector of the Armenian peoples.[65] Yet, we must try and contextualize why Peter was in Trebizond in the first place. Aristakes states that the king of Ani, Yovhannes-Smbat III (1020–40), had told Peter to 'give the emperor a written will so that after my death he shall inherit my city and country', which Aristakes explains was because the king had no royal heir.[66] Matthew's account on the other hand claims that Basil

> went forth to the East with innumerable forces, demanding Ani and Kars from the Armenian king. [Yovhannes III], the son of Gagik I [989–c.1020], resolved to hand them over since he was a cowardly person.[67]

We do have some information regarding the annexation of Ani from a Byzantine perspective. Skylitzes, who does not mention the incident in his work on Basil, instead refers to it later in his chapter on Constantine IX Monomachos (1042–55), where he recounts that:

> [w]hen George, the chieftain of the Iberians, raised arms against the Romans, Iovanesikes (Yovhannes), ruler of the country of Ani, fought alongside him. Then when the emperor Basil went into Iberia and fought against George . . . Iovanesikes was afraid that the emperor (Basil), enraged by his alliance with George, would do him some severe damage. So he took the keys of the city, deserted to the emperor, surrendered himself voluntarily into his hands and gave him the keys.[68]

Forced with such conflicting information, we must attempt to ascertain the truth behind these events and determine the background to Yovhannes-Smbat's decision to grant his kingdom to Basil. The sources offer two explanations. One was that Yovhannes-Smbat had no natural heir and so desired his powerful neighbour to protect his lands after he died. The other was that he had fought in alliance with Giorgi against Basil, during the Byzantine-Georgian war, and so was forced into a similar position as David III of Tao back in 990, when he in turn had made Basil the legal inheritor of his lands upon his death. In this instance, the first option does not seem logical, nor does it accurately reflect the internal situation within the kingdom of Ani. On the death of Gagik I in 1020 a quarrel broke out between his two sons, Yovhannes-Smbat and Ashot IV. Yovhannes was the elder, being described as both 'wise and very intelligent' and 'uneducated', whereas his brother, Ashot, was seen as 'courageous, brave and mighty'.[69] The two brothers fought each other for the throne and were eventually brought together by a compromise brokered by the leading families of the kingdom. Yovhannes-

Smbat was to be king in Ani only, while Ashot was to rule over the rest of the kingdom.[70] Conversely, Aristakes offers a different narrative in which Giorgi of Georgia plays the leading role in bringing about the compromise, and he adds further context for the internal factionalism within the kingdom.[71] Giorgi, it appears, was by far the most powerful magnate in Caucasia, possessing the ability to settle disputes in neighbouring kingdoms, while at the same time following through with force, if it were required. Furthermore, Giorgi appears to have imprisoned Yovhannes-Smbat for a claim by one of Ashot's *azats* that his lands had been unjustly held by Yovhannes-Smbat, but the king of Ani was released after Giorgi took three fortresses from the kingdom.[72] In a further significant episode reported by Aristakes we are told how Ashot travelled to Constantinople in order to receive support in the form of auxiliaries so that he might press his claims to the lands granted to him by the aforementioned treaty. As to who these 'grandees in the environs [of Ashot's holdings]'[73] were is hard to guess, but what this example reveals is how willing the Byzantines, and in particular Basil, were to interfere with the internal affairs of the kingdom of Ani even before the annexations. It would appear that these events occurred in 1021 and thus can provide the contextual background to the meeting between the *Katholikos* and Basil in Trebizond that winter. Moreover, it is entirely plausible that Yovhannes-Smbat wished to ensure that his brother would never gain the city of Ani and so made the foresaid agreement out of spite.

In terms of the second factor, the alleged alliance between Yovhannes-Smbat and Giorgi, it is only Skylitzes who refers to this directly. He comments that Yovhannes-Smbat was worried about his alliance and the wrath of Basil who was currently campaigning against the Georgians.[74] There are, however, details from Matthew (which are out of chronological order in his work) and Aristakes that can offer an alternative approach. Matthew mentioned Georgian support for Yovhannes in the civil war with his brother Ashot which, as has been mentioned previously, occurred in 1021. Aristakes, whose account is more reliable for the internal events of Armenian in the early eleventh century, does not corroborate Matthew on this point, however. It is entirely plausible that this is the alliance to which Skylitzes was referring, but this still does not seem likely. The comment by Matthew that Yovhannes-Smbat was 'a cowardly person' may tip the scales; Yovhannes-Smbat may have been regarded a 'coward' for having lost much of his power to his brother, Ashot, and so sought to gain a powerful ally who would help sustain his rule during his lifetime. Yovhannes-Smbat was, after all, according to Skylitzes, 'honoured with the title of magister and [Basil] appointed him ruler for life of Ani and of the so-called Great Armenia'.[75] It is almost impossible to be certain of the exact sequence of events here, but it seems unlikely that Yovhannes-Smbat actively campaigned against Basil, as only Skylitzes refers to it. The main point is that there is very little substantial evidence to paint Basil as an aggressive imperialist towards Ani in the primary sources, and, as argued earlier, it would appear that the move was driven by the internal factionalism within Ani itself. We will return to the eventual annexation of Ani during the reign of Constantine IX Monomachos later.

Vaspurakan
The southern Armenian kingdom of Vaspurakan, ruled by the Artsruni family since 908, also came to be annexed by Byzantium during the reign of Basil II, with the actual event taking place sometime around 1019.[76] The narrative of the annexation of Vaspurakan is complicated by the inconsistency in our primary sources, alongside the claim of some secondary works that Vaspurakan was an example of a 'forced annexation', like the annexation of Tao. One must analyse the realities of the annexation of Vaspurakan in light of previous annexations, alongside the reasons, as given by the primary sources, for its ruler, Senek'erim-Yovhannes (1003–21), to seek a deal with Byzantium, and the internal and external factors behind this decision.

There is extensive debate over the date of when the annexation of Vaspurakan actually occurred, and the confusion found within the primary accounts is further reflected in the main secondary works. One example of this is can be found with Garsoïan who believes the date of the offer to Basil by Senek'erim was made in 1016, while also claiming that Byzantine troops from the Balkans had already been sent to Vaspurakan and had reduced the kingdom to the theme of Vaspurakan.[77] A short while later, however, Garsoïan states that Senek'erim moved with his household to Cappadocia in 1021: overall her dates are thoroughly confused and at points contradictory.[78] We also have Cheynet who comments in his notes on Skylitzes that the annexation took place during the winter of 1021–2, while referring to Dostourian's translation of Matthew of Edessa as evidence.[79] This is a misreading, as the translation specifically mentions the year 1018–19, and the events in Matthew's narrative do not match Cheynet's claims. To gain the most accurate date of the annexation we must revisit the primary sources and carefully evaluate the information they provide on the reasons behind the annexation and place these reasons within their historical context.

The account by Matthew of Edessa does not place any precise date on the correspondence between the emperor and Senek'erim, nor the visit by David, son of Senek'erim, to Constantinople to ratify the agreement. We are told, however, that David was honoured by Basil who adopted him as a son.[80] This would suggest that the agreement could not have taken place in the winter of 1021/2, as Basil was wintering in Trebizond, not in Constantinople. Even though Matthew places the trip of David Artsruni before Basil's eastern campaign, we have seen countless examples of why we cannot rely on Matthew's account for chronological accuracy. Yahya places the annexation of Vaspurakan in the same period as the climax of the Byzantine-Georgian war (1021/2) but importantly before his account of the revolt of Nikephoros Phokas and Nikephoros Xiphias in 1022.[81] One cannot ignore Yahya's high degree of reliability, but perhaps exploring the stated motivations for Senek'erim giving up his kingdom could shed further light as to when the annexation occurred.

Once again, our secondary sources offer unsubstantiated opinions on the nature of the annexation. Garsoïan is of the opinion that Basil was able to apply pressure on Senek'erim who was completely willing to cede his lands in return for lucrative estates in the empire. This line of argument is further supported by

Ara Dostourian, who states, 'It is more likely that Basil pressured the Armenian king to give up his lands to Byzantium'.[82] Furthermore, Cheynet states that '[t]he first attacks of the Turks may have unnerved him [Senek'erim], but there was probably a certain amount of pressure from Basil who was campaigning against the Georgians at that time and wintered over in Trebizond'.[83] These interpretations do not have the support of the primary sources, all of which say that Vaspurakan was given willingly and give reasons beyond that of imperialist expansion for the peaceful annexation of the kingdom. Indeed, Holmes offers a different perspective, arguing that 'the surrender of the Artsruni lands may have been the culmination of a long, symbiotic diplomatic courtship', citing the evidence provided by Grigor of Narek and the work of Mahé.[84] Here one can witness close interactions with the Artsruni ruling house and Basil II's regime, particularly with the transfer of certain relics from Constantinople to the monastery at Aparank. This was achieved by a minor lord by the name of Zapranik from the principality of Mokk, who not only actively engaged in the political upheavals of Basil's early reign but, after receiving pardon from Basil for supporting Skleros, went on to serve in the military.[85] This closeness, coupled with the Artsruni's audience with Basil in 1000, highlights the cooperative and fluid relationship that characterized Byzantium's eastern frontier.

The length of this relationship helps contextualize how a voluntary annexation took place, but the direct causes were undoubtedly brought about by contemporary events. Indeed, our main primary accounts date the origins of Senek'erim's motivation to seek a voluntary settlement at some point towards the end of the second decade of the eleventh century. Aristakes suggests that Senek'erim, whom he also confusingly calls David (the same name as his son and heir), was being harassed by the Persians (Turks) at some point in the late 1010s and so gave his 'patrimonial inheritance' to Basil and gained security on new estates away from the frontier.[86] Matthew of Edessa supports this version of events, giving further details of David, the son of Senek'erim, being defeated in battle against the invading Turkomans, stating:

> After this Senek'erim resolved to hand over the land of his ancestors to the Greek emperor Basil and in its stead to obtain Sebastia; so he immediately wrote to the emperor.[87]

Skylitzes' account is in line with other primary sources, stating that '[i]t was because he had been under great pressure from the Hagarenes [Muslims] and was unable to withstand them that he took refuge with the emperor and handed over his own lands'.[88] None of these sources imply external pressure from Basil on Senek'erim, and while it is fair to observe that Basil was applying military pressure in Caucasia throughout his conflict with Giorgi, it would appear that Senek'erim had kept out of the conflict, unlike his northern neighbour Yovhannes-Smbat of Ani. It is impossible to place a firm date of Senek'erim's arrival on his estates in Sebasteia, though we can be sure that it occurred before 1022 when the Artsruni were caught up in the revolt of Nikephoros Phokas and Xiphias.[89]

The later annexations: Edessa and Kars

Before we can embark on a comparative investigation of the initial settlement of the Armenians in the Byzantine Empire during the eleventh century, we need to complete the chronological sweep of external relations between Byzantium and the Armenian kingdoms. The case concerning the annexation of the ancient city of Edessa offers us the chance to see whether Basil established a new policy in removing cooperation with local magnates in favour of direct rule and whether this policy was intentionally continued by his immediate successors.

Basil II died on 20 December 1025, but the annexations of Armenian lands continued well after his death. Not only were the treaties which he had made with Yovhannes-Smbat III of Ani still legally binding, something which his successor Constantine IX Monomachos would address later during his reign, but there were also two further annexations of Armenian territories independent of Basil's legacy – the city of Edessa and the Kingdom of Kars. As discussed earlier, Ani had been promised to Basil in 1021 by its ruler Yovhannes for debatable reasons and the annexation in 1045 will be addressed shortly. In the intervening period we can now turn to the Byzantine annexation of the city of Edessa, which lies outside of Greater Armenia but which had a sizeable Armenian population, as reported and exemplified by one of our main primary sources, Matthew of Edessa.

The annexation of Edessa took place in 1028, with our sources depicting a city divided between two competing internal groups. Aristakes gives us an account of the factionalism within Edessa:

> [Salamay], afraid that the chief [men] of the city would not obey him, sent one of his loyal servants to Maneak [George Maniakes], who at that time held sway over the borders of the Byzantine district and resided in the city called Samusat (which they say was built by Sampson). [Salamay] had done this so that [Maniakes] would inform the emperor to give [Salamay] princedom and eternal inheritance in the Byzantines' land [confirmed] by writ and the royal seal. 'And,' [Salamay] said, 'I shall give him the city, without warfare'. When emperor Romanus [III] heard this, he wrote [to Salamay] a document of consent, making him an *antipatos* patrician, and subsequently exalting him with great and prominent honour.[90]

Conversely, both Matthew and Skylitzes paint a different picture of the event. Matthew's account recognizes the character of Salamay, whom Matthew calls Salman, was engaged in the bitter power struggle in Edessa:

> Finally Salman, exhausted by her assaults,[91] sent to Samosata, to the Roman commander Maniaces, also called George. Salman wrote to him and said: 'If you obtain from the Roman emperor a high position and the command of a district for me, I will deliver Edessa into your hand'.[92]

Skylitzes' account does not contain information on the exchange of the city for estates in the empire; rather, it paints Maniakes as acting independently from the Emperor Romanos III:

> George Maniakes ... the commander of the cities on the Euphrates who resided at Samosata, attempted to take the city of Edessa in Osroene. This city was controlled by Salaman the Turk ... bribed with gifts, promises and honours, he surrendered it [Edessa] to Maniakes in the middle of the night.[93]

Here we have three sources that more or less recount the same event and in general agree on the details of the internal situation within Edessa. None of the accounts demonstrate Byzantine aggression; rather, the sources show that Salman (or Salaman) took the initiative in contacting the Byzantines in order to gain estates in the empire. It is important to recognize that Maniakes was not holding a high-ranking office. His rank of *protospatharios*, held alongside his office as *strategos* of the cities on the Euphrates, was certainly not high enough to direct foreign policy at his own discretion.[94] And yet Maniakes proceeded with the occupation of Edessa, and only Michael Psellos informs us that Maniakes was punished for overstepping his authority by a jealous Romanos.[95] One can certainly spot the similarity in the exchange, that is, an agreement to annexation in return for estates within Byzantium; however, in this case the similarity must be questioned for Basil's reasons for his settlement of Armenian princes in Cappadocia were very different from those that were given to Salman for Edessa, and it would appear that Salman was settled in Samosata.[96] In summary, we have an extraordinary situation where direct annexation was achieved without any consultation with the emperor in Constantinople. One thing is for certain: had Basil still lived he would most certainly been involved in the annexation of lands and the settlement of foreign rulers on estates inside the empire: either his successors pursued a different policy or they did not have the ability to maintain strong imperial foreign policy.

The final Byzantine annexation of Armenian lands came with the Kingdom of Kars several decades later in 1064. Situated to the west of Ani, Kars had been an autonomous kingdom from the time of Ashot III (953–77) who appointed his brother Mushegh (963–84) to have royal authority over his domains.[97] At the time of its annexation by Byzantium, the political and military situation of Caucasia had changed dramatically from that which we saw during the earlier annexations, as the growing power of the Seljuk Turks started to apply ever-increasing pressure on the borders of Byzantium and the Kingdom of Kars. This does place a strain on the relevance of this annexation for our present purposes; however, the context is still required, for the placement of the court of Kars within Cappadocia will need further attention in the following chapter.

It is suspected that the ruler of Kars, Gagik-Abas II (1029–64), had been under pressure from the Seljuk Sultan – in what manner, our sources are unwilling to tell us. We do know from Matthew of Edessa that the Seljuk Sultan had demanded fealty from Gagik-Abas, although he was able to avoid doing this formally by showing the Sultan sycophantic friendship. Following what is now a familiar trend, we are informed by that Gagik-Abas 'abandoned Kars and went over to the Romans. The Emperor Ducas [Constantine X Doukas, 1059–67] gave [Tzamandos, Larissa, Amasia and Comana] to Gagik, and the Armenian king settled there, together with his noblemen, thus abandoning his ancestral home'.[98] All told, the annexation of Kars was a minor affair within the broader analysis of the annexation of the Armenian kingdoms and it took the form of a peaceful exchange between the two parties. It is not far-fetched to suggest that Gagik-Abas merely followed the precedent set by his fellow Armenian rulers, and it was an attractive alternative in the face of increasing Seljuk activity in the area. In fact, the Byzantines were barely capable in holding on to their newly acquired territories, with the lands of Kars falling to the Seljuk Turks before the year was out. As the earlier quote shows, Matthew of Edessa lamented the loss of Armenian land to the Byzantines and subsequently the Turks, but in recognizing the mostly voluntary nature of the annexations he blamed the Armenian kings and nobles as much as the Byzantines for abandoning their ancestral home for comfortable estates in the empire.

In summary, the largely voluntary nature of the annexations of the Armenian kingdoms goes against the claims of a preconceived agenda of the Macedonian dynasty to subjugate to Christian polities of Caucasia. We have seen that the campaign which drew Basil eastwards in 1021 was a result of Georgian aggression and the occupation of lands in Tao that legally belonged to the empire as a result of David *Kouropalates*' will that came into effect in 1000/1. It was in this context, we are told, that the annexations of Ani and Vaspurakan were brokered. As demonstrated earlier, there is no substantial evidence of aggressive force being used to persuade either Senek'erim Artsruni or Yovhannes-Smbat to surrender their patrimonial lands; rather, both had their own reasons to seek a deal with the Byzantine emperor, Basil II.

Unforeseen consequences

The annexations of the western Armenian kingdoms by Basil II were to have untold consequences for the Byzantine-Armenian relationship in the later eleventh century. Certain commentators on the subject of the annexations, like George Ostrogorsky, have seen Basil's annexations in Armenia as part of a triumphant expansion of the empire, whereas others have argued against this view, with Michael Angold openly criticizing Basil for passing his successors a 'poisoned chalice' by destroying the buffer states and opening the frontiers of the empire to new aggressive neighbours.[99] Indeed, this has produced a further response from Catherine Holmes who argues:

> That in the middle of the eleventh century new adversaries appeared and challenged these structures cannot be blamed on those who developed them much earlier for entirely different situations.[100]

This formulation is very much applicable to the alienation of the Armenians from the Byzantine Empire in the mid-eleventh century. Basil could not have foreseen the breakdown in the Byzantine-Armenian relationship during his own lifetime; rather, he still very much relied on the mechanics of assimilation that had successfully transformed previous Armenian migrants into *Romaioi*. Yet there are two problematic episodes which helped produce the ingredients of the later alienation that had their origins in the decisions made by Basil during his eastern campaigns of 1021–2. The first of these came from the choice of Basil to settle the Artsruni of Vaspurakan in Cappadocia. The intention of Basil was to counteract the aristocratic forces that had troubled his rule from the very beginning, which ultimately backfired with the Artsruni siding with the rebels during the Rebellion of 1022. While the Artsruni were to switch back to Basil's side at the pivotal moment, the actual outcome was to produce an unforeseen problem: the Artsruni's personal loyalty to the occupant of the Byzantine throne, not the position in itself. This will have later consequences in the 1040s. The second decision by Basil that was to have unforeseen consequences was the decision to allow Yovhannes-Smbat III to retain his throne until his death. Whatever the underlying motives were for Yovhannes-Smbat's submission to Basil in the winter of 1021 it had one key element: it was voluntary. This aspect was crucially important for Yovhannes' heir, Gagik II of Ani, did not wish to give up his patrimonial lands that his uncle had so willingly agreed to some twenty years before. Instead, Gagik witnessed how his lands were claimed by Byzantium, unjustly in the young king's eyes, and thus sowing the seeds of alienation in Gagik that were to sprout in the following decades. We will look at each of these episodes in turn.

The Rebellion of 1022

To understand the first of these episodes, it has to be borne in mind that internal considerations partly dictated Basil's policy towards Armenia. For example, he most likely decided to settle the Artsruni on crown lands in Cappadocia in order to counter the challenge of the Anatolian aristocracy, and the Phokas family in particular, against the ruling dynasty and its right to rule.[101] James Howard-Johnston suggests that the fractured and constantly competing *azats* would have been completely familiar within their new social circumstance as they would have experienced similar interfamily competition in their homeland.[102] Basil thus could not foresee the difficulties that were to come and had expected that a similar path of assimilation would await the newly arrived Armenians as it had their forebears.

What Basil had not expected was for the loyalty of the recently arrived Artsruni to be tested so quickly by a rebellion originating in the very region in which they had been settled. A short while after the settlement of Senek'erim and his court in Cappadocia, a member of the Phokas family, called Nikephoros, started a rebellion against Basil, which at the outset the Artsruni appear to have supported, echoing similarities with the intervention of David III of Tao in the rebellion of 987–9.[103] We have several accounts of the 1022 rebellion, all of which differ in content to varying degrees. Skylitzes' record of the rebellion is remarkably brief, leading us to rely on the account of Yahya of Antioch, which in all fairness is the stronger account for events occurring in central and eastern Anatolia. Our Armenian sources, on the other hand, produced similar accounts of the events, albeit with different leading characters.[104] According to Aristakes, Senek'erim, the exiled king of Vaspurakan, initially took a leading part in the rebellion but had a sudden change of heart:

But then suddenly, as a person awakening from sleep, or as a mighty man coming to himself after drunkenness, he realized the impropriety of the deed. And because there was no other way of disrupting the wicked union, one day, at an unexpected hour, he took the one whom they had styled king and went away from the army as if to advise him. Suddenly, pulling out his sword he killed [Nikephoros Phokas], beheaded him, gave the head to his servants and had it speedily taken to the emperor.[105]

In the account of Skylitzes the participation of the Artsruni is entirely omitted, and the role of Senek'erim is ascribed to a patrician named Nikephoros Xiphias, who after killing Phokas was imprisoned and tonsured on the island of Antigonos.[106] This is corroborated by Yahya, who provides the most detailed narrative of the rebellion and does not identify any of the member of the Artsruni being involved.[107] There is further confusion in Aristakes' account in that he names Senek'erim as the man who killed Phokas, although it would appear that it was actually Senek'erim's son, David, who Aristakes was actually referring to, which is corroborated in Matthew of Edessa's account of the rebellion.[108] It is hard to reconcile the two versions of events; Yahya has so far been the most reliable account, and it is unusual that he would have missed such a crucial role played by the Artsruni, had they indeed been present and involved. Yet our sources are not infallible, and it is not unreasonable to assume that the Artsruni would have had some interaction with the rebellion, as it occurred right on their 'new' doorstep. Our Armenian sources record that the alleged actions of the Artsruni in apparently ending the rebellion were richly rewarded by a grateful Basil, who granted them further lands and the towns of Caesarea, Camndaw and Khawatanēk.[109]

There is some contention within our secondary scholarship as to how these events actually unfolded, in a similar fashion to the debates discussed earlier around the date in which the Artsruni first approached the Byzantines to offer Vaspurakan in return for estates in Cappadocia. Holmes argues that the granting of lands to the Artsruni was 'merely a circumstantial reward rather than the prime motive of the Artsrunik migration', which does not seem chronologically correct, as the migration of the Artsruni and settlement on their original estates occurred before the rebellion.[110] What appears more likely is that the lands the Artsruni controlled were expanded in return for their assistance against Phokas and Xiphias. Yahya reports that in the aftermath of the rebellion:

> After the murder of Phocas, the emperor had all those who had openly participated in the revolt arrested; he took their wealth; he killed a certain number, blinded some, and imprisoned others.[111]

If we are to believe the scale of the revolt, the number that were implicated and punished would have been considerable, especially in and around Cappadocia from where many of the supporters of the Phokas family originated. It is perhaps from these confiscations that the Artsruni were entrusted with further territories by Basil, as recorded earlier by Matthew; either way, the Artsruni were clearly placed in a prominent position in the very region from which the Anatolian families had traditionally sourced their support and directly owed their position to the emperor.

Depending on how we observe the events during the Rebellion of 1022, we either witness the last attempts by the Anatolian aristocracy to overthrow an ageing Basil or some form of ethnic tension arising with the newly settled Armenian nobility in Cappadocia. To some historians the differences between the two groups were one of considerable substance, as one has argued:

> [The] cultural divide formed a formidable barrier between the two aristocratic worlds. Reinforced by geographical separation, it was likely, in most circumstances, to prevent a general coalescence of interests.[112]

Such an idea is not without its merits. It would be sensible policy to settle large numbers of non-Romans in the very lands where rebellion had been rife, creating a solid base of loyal supporters for the emperor in Constantinople for the foreseeable future. But the 'formidable barrier' seems a little far-fetched or at least a reading of history with the benefit of hindsight. As demonstrated in the previous chapter, there is insufficient evidence to suggest that such a barrier did exist in the tenth and early eleventh centuries and would have been an unlikely active consideration when forming imperial policy of settlement.

Rather, Howard-Johnston argues that the cultural differences between the Armenians and the existing inhabitants were artificially perpetuated by the capital, as it prevented any form of alliance between the princely houses and the 'Powerful' Anatolian magnates against the imperial centre. And yet we have just seen that the Artsruni initially supported the rebellion of the forces they were intended to counterbalance: not a strong start to this theory. And even if this were indeed the intended policy of Basil, then this would suggest that attempts at assimilation had been abandoned, or to a lesser extent ignored, so as to sustain the cultural divide in the east for the sake of stability. In the final analysis this argument does not engage with the primary source materials that highlight the successful rate of assimilation in the tenth century, nor does it offer a reasonable explanation as to why the process of assimilation should have been so readily abandoned by Basil.[113] On the contrary, our evidence indicates that Basil was still relying on the mechanics of assimilation to work; otherwise why else would he have placed Senek'erim Artsruni as *strategos* of Cappadocia?[114] What this episode in reality shows is how well suited the Armenian nobles were to Byzantine society, and that the expectation to assimilate in due course was still held by the emperor. Much like the other noble houses of Anatolia, the Artsruni were willing to play the political game, and most importantly play it well, just as many of the Armenian families that arrived in the ninth and tenth centuries had done before them.[115] The Artsruni were able to benefit by switching sides at the correct time and were rewarded for it. It is possible that they may have been aware of Basil's actions towards David III of Tao who backed the wrong man in a rebellion and was forced to hand over his lands upon his death. Furthermore, they could also have learnt of the leniency granted towards the Taronites for having originally supported the revolt of Bardas Skleros and so took the opportunity to back the emperor when the timing was right. Basil had made a mistake but one that would not be revealed until nearly fifteen years after his death. In order to accelerate the loyalty aspect of the assimilation model, that being the acknowledgement of the universality of Rome, her emperor and its institutions, Basil created a personal tie of loyalty between himself and the Artsruni. This would be something that his successors could neither replicate nor reciprocate.

Ultimately Basil had brought together internal and external policy to solve a variety of problems, the most important being the realignment of the Anatolian aristocracy with one that would never challenge imperial rule, and in this Basil was able to place the Armenians on crown lands in Cappadocia to neutralize the threat posed by the 'Powerful'.[116] In terms of the policy's success, in the short term it appears to have been a near disaster, for the revolt of 1022 in Cappadocia developed to the rear of Basil while he was campaigning against the Kingdom of Georgia.[117] Cheynet offers a plausible explanation for the outbreak of this insurrection: when the emperor made Senek'erim the *strategos* of Cappadocia the Anatolian aristocracy recognized what Basil was attempting to do and so tried to dispose of the ageing emperor before it was too late.[118] Yet, when one considers that the Artsruni originally joined with the conspirators against Basil, before apparently seeing the errors of their ways, it is unlikely that this was anything but a minor factor. In any case, later events, as will be discussed in the next chapter, reveal that the original alliance between the Crown and the Armenians, which was to diffuse and counteract the power of the Anatolian magnates, broke down on account of a rising belligerence and persecution by the capital that turned the Armenians into a very similar problem to the one they were originally intended to prevent.

While the causes of the revolt of 1022 are indeed interesting it is the results from it that are far more influential for this study. For afterwards, the Artsruni held a loyalty to Basil II himself rather than to the Byzantium state. That loyalty would be put under significant stain with Basil's death and subsequently exacerbated by the actions of his successors that directly weakened the tenuous loyalty structures of the Artsruni to Byzantium. We will return to these difficulties shortly when the issue of loyalty came to a head in 1040. Indeed, it was the response of the imperial centre to the issue of Artsruni loyalty that contributed to their biggest mistake: the placement of Gagik II of Ani as the overlord of the Armenian estates in the east.[119]

Ani (II)

We have already covered the background and binding treaty that bequeathed the kingdom of Ani to Byzantium earlier; in this section, there are two aims. First, to construct a summary narrative of events from when the Treaty of Trebizond was agreed in the winter of 1021/2 through to the ascension of Gagik II of Ani some twenty years later in 1042. The second aim will be to show that the very nature of the annexation of Ani, in 1042 rather than 1021, was a significant problem.

The agreement made in 1021 was (largely) voluntary. Whereas the events and actions committed by the Byzantines in the early 1040s to press their claim to Ani produced a dramatic deterioration in Byzantine-Armenian relations and ultimately sowed the seeds of Armenian alienation with Gagik II, who in turn brought such resentment with him when he was eventually settled on estates in Cappadocia.

Returning to 1021/2, the Treaty of Trebizond was quite simple in its contents. Yovhannes-Smbat, the king of Ani, agreed to handover his patrimonial lands to Byzantium upon his death. The reason behind Yovhannes-Smbat's submission is not entirely clear, but our sources hint at two potential, if not mutual, reasons. First, Yovhannes-Smbat may have allied himself with Giorgi which in turn enraged Basil; but seeing as Basil made no claims at annexing Giorgi's lands it seems out of place that he insisted on Yovhannes-Smbat's surrender of Ani. The second reason is linked to the internal conflict between Yovhannes-Smbat and his brother Ashot, both of whom claimed the throne of Ani. Yovhannes-Smbat's domain was largely limited to the city of Ani itself, while Ashot held the rest of the country. It is more likely, therefore, that in order to gain external assurances against his more powerful brother, Yovhannes-Smbat approached Basil in order to gain Byzantine assurances over his rule, though on the condition that he passed his domain to Byzantium when he died, in direct similarity to the agreement Basil forced David III of Tao to agree to in 989. In any case, the deal was agreed by both parties and the status quo was maintained until the 1040s, by which point the major characters concerned were all dead.

During the intervening period from the Treaty of Trebizond through to the ascension of Gagik II we have some information from the Armenian tradition that reports on the existence of the treaty after it was made. According to Aristakes, Constantine VIII, the brother of Basil II, decided on his deathbed to renounce the claim to Ani and asked an Armenian elder by the name of Kiwrakos to

> [t]ake this document and give it to the king of Armenia and say, 'Since that invitation for death which is sent to all mortal beings has also come to me, take your letter and give your realm to your son, and let your son give it to his sons, for all time!'[120]

According to Aristakes, Kiwrakos did no such thing but held on to the document and sold it later on to Michael IV (1034–41) for 'much treasure'. This episode is not found elsewhere and should most likely be discarded as apocryphal; however, this element of betrayal and self-destruction of Armenia is a common theme running through Armenian historiography of this period, as exemplified by Aristakes' work. Much like with Basil, we have here the Armenian tradition absolving Constantine VIII of any blame over the later Byzantine claim to Ani, rather focusing on the character of Kiwrakos and his ultimate betrayal of his homeland. There is a theme occurring where our Armenian sources, for the eleventh century especially, hold the Macedonian dynasty in high regard. Nevertheless, we must turn to the events of the early 1040s and assess the motives and characters behind the annexation of Ani.

By the beginning of 1042 both claimants to the throne of Ani were dead. There are many frustrating inaccuracies around the dates of the deaths of Ashot and Yovhannes. Matthew gives 1039 and 1041, respectively, for the deaths of the two brothers, while Aristakes states that they both died in the same year.[121] Nevertheless, their deaths gave rise to the enforcement by the Byzantines of the deal made between Basil and Yovhannes. In Armenia, however, there were no attempts to fulfil the treaty on the part of the leading lords of Ani with the *azats* quickly choosing to place Yovhannes-Smbat's nephew, and Ashot's son, Gagik II on the throne. These events were not going to be ignored in Constantinople. We are told by Matthew that Michael IV launched two successive campaigns into Ani to seize the kingdom, while Aristakes speaks of four successive campaigns, but either way they were both eventually defeated outside of Ani by Vahram Pahlavuni.[122] It was to take a new emperor and a different strategy to bring about the successful enforcement of the treaty.

Constantine IX Monomachos was selected by the daughters of Constantine VIII, Zoe and Theodora, to become the figurehead of the Macedonian dynasty after the deposition of the unpopular Michael V (1041–2).[123] Before Constantine was able to turn his attention towards the annexation of Ani, he almost immediately had to deal with the rebellion of George Maniakes and the Russian attack on Constantinople in 1043.[124] George Maniakes was the same general who had conquered the city of Edessa back in 1031 and over the following decade came to be one of the empire's leading generals. Maniakes was responsible for the successfully campaigning in Sicily, a target that Basil II had been planning towards the end of his reign. Amongst Maniakes' forces were Normans, Lombards and a contingent of the Varangian guard, including Harald Hardrada, the future claimant to the English throne and ultimate loser at Stamford Bridge in the famous year of 1066. The attack by the Rus' on Constantinople was an ultimate failure but one that certainly caught the attention of the emperor in the capital. Michael Psellos, who was an eye-witness account of the attack, records the defeat of the Russian fleet in dramatic detail, with the secret weapon of Greek fire once again delivering the city from a naval threat.[125]

With Byzantium distracted by more immediate problems the Armenians in Ani found time and space to prepare for the next attempt by the empire to bring about the annexation. Unfortunately, the kingdom found itself in the throes of civil war once more, with the royal court being split between pro-Byzantine and pro-Bagratid factions. Gagik himself expected to maintain the status quo and may not have even been aware what his uncle had agreed in Trebizond nearly two decades beforehand. It is possible that in Gagik's eyes the previous division of the kingdom, with Yovhannes ruling in the city of Ani while Ashot ruled over the rest of the kingdom, had made his predecessor's treaty invalid, as he did not control the territory that he had offered to Basil in the first place. Skylitzes goes so far as to claim:

> As Kakikios (Gagik) was willing to confess himself a Roman subject but *not* to renounce his father's lands, the emperor thought war should be declared on him.[126]

Our Armenian sources have a slightly different perspective on the events from Skylitzes, which could be attributed to the accessibility of more reliable information closer to the events at hand. Aristakes and Matthew of Edessa both inform us of a division within the kingdom of Ani itself, between pro-Byzantine and pro-Armenian forces. The leader of the former party was a man named Sargis, whom Aristakes identifies as the executor of the late Yovhannes' will. Sargis, it appears, was willing to hand over Ani in return for titles and estates in the empire, thereby putting him in direct opposition to the newly installed Gagik who sought to maintain his kingdom.[127] The internal division did not last for long, with Gagik capturing Sargis and defeating the subsequent Byzantine forces sent to seize Ani. With imperial foreign policy having thus far failed to acquire Ani, Constantine decided to change tack and use a trick out of the old Byzantine playbook: bribery.

Unusually our two main Armenian sources are in agreement as to what happened next with both levelling the blame for the annexation on the deceitful noblemen of Ani, as the recipients of the bribes, rather than the perfidious Byzantines.[128] The emperor, we are told, wrote to Gagik, stating, 'I need but to see you, then shall return your kingdom to you and shall write a document giving you your land and city in perpetual inheritance'.[129] Despite some initial hesitation Gagik was eventually encouraged to journey to the imperial capital by the *Katholikos* Peter I, along with some of his court, where unsurprisingly upon his arrival he was immediately placed under house arrest until he agreed to give up his lands in return for estates in Anatolia. After some thirty days of resistance, Gagik was forced to agree to the terms and began his exile on his new estates.[130]

Clearly the manner in which Byzantium annexed Ani was decisively different to that of the earlier annexations, and this can be explained by two points. Firstly, the internal divisions in Ani did not help settle the matter, and this was a direct result of the previous division of the kingdom between Yovhannes-Smbat and Ashot in 1021.[131] Secondly, the processes by which the earlier annexations had been conducted by Basil and his predecessors were no longer maintained. As far as we can tell, the earlier annexations had a common current running through: they were consensual. As we will see in the next chapter, it was the behaviour of Gagik in the subsequent decades and the thoughtless placement of Gagik's new estates among his compatriots in Cappadocia and Sebasteia, who were themselves having difficulties with the imperial centre, that brought together the key ingredients for the alienation of the Armenians in the Byzantine Empire. It is from this point that the relationship between the Byzantines and Armenians fundamentally changed. We will return in the next chapter to explore the root causes of said alienation and evaluate whether Gagik's personality was the driving force behind Armenian alienation or more subtle, long-term, forces were at work.

Conclusion

There is no doubt that for this book, and more importantly the study of the Byzantine-Armenian relationship, the events of the early eleventh century were

2. The Byzantine Annexations of Armenia

a pivotal moment. The direct intervention by Basil in Caucasia in the late tenth century ultimately laid the groundwork for the later annexations of the western Armenian kingdoms towards the end of his reign. The annexations were in themselves to have unintended consequences, and the repercussions would ultimately take the form of alienation, as we shall shortly see. There is no doubt that Basil II sort to establish a more loyal class of nobility on the very lands from which both the Skleroi and Phokades had been able to draw support for the numerous rebellions against the crown. But it was to be these new loyalty structures between Basil and the first wave of Armenian migration in the early 1020s that were to later cause trouble and very much went against the precedents of successful assimilation. The original thinking on Basil's part should be lauded; he dealt with a very much short-term problem as he saw it. The irony being that it was from this very class that the soldier emperors of his infancy came from, and he personally did nothing to establish smooth transitional succession plans after his death from which his policies would eventually take fruit. It is an important consideration to ask whether the successors of Basil, in particular Constantine IX Monomachos, had any awareness of what Basil intended to do with the newly settled Armenians. As thing turned out, Gagik's imprisonment in Constantinople in 1045, followed by the establishment of the hot-head young king among his kin in Cappadocia, was a very stupid move. The annexations of the Armenian kingdoms were certainly a turning point in the Byzantine-Armenian relationship, but the causes of the alienation of the 'Royal Armenians' were ultimately the product of the mid-eleventh century, not of Basil II's own time.

Chapter 3

THE ALIENATION OF THE ARMENIANS, c.1020–71

We have now arrived at our third phase in the Byzantine-Armenian relationship: alienation. This chapter will seek to establish the process by which the Armenians, a people who we have seen successfully settling and assimilating back in Chapter 1, came to feel alienated within the Byzantine Empire by the mid-eleventh century. Our main concentration of focus for this section will be on the experiences of the exiled 'Royal Armenians' who now lived and ruled over large estates in Cappadocia and around Sebasteia, although we will address some of the more important events within Armenia itself. The first task will be to trace the growth of the Armenian settlements in eastern-central themes of the empire from the 1020s onwards. The initial granting of lands to the exiled Armenians was accompanied by issuing administrative and military titles by the court to the leading figures within the newly arrived Armenian community, at first concentrated on the exiled royal Artsruni and accompanying nobles. This policy of title-giving was an intentional policy to draw the newly arrived elites into service of the imperial institutions which had been so successful in furthering Armenian assimilation in the preceding centuries. At some point, however, roughly around the same time that Gagik II of Ani came to be settled in Cappadocia, the Byzantine-Armenian relationship seems to have altered. It is hard to determine exactly when this change took place. The reasons as to why it happened are also a matter of debate. Some historians have linked it to a demographic change in Cappadocia and the area around Sebasteia that allowed the Armenians to dominate the landscape across these important themes, while others point to the effects of religious antagonism between the Imperial and Apostolic churches, which came to influence internal relations within the provinces, and this ecclesiastical deterioration certainly grew at alarming speed in the 1050s. What becomes increasingly apparent when studying these crucial decades before Manzikert (1071) is that the religious tensions were not, in of itself, a direct cause for the alienation of the Armenians living within the empire, although it certainly compounded the deteriorating relations between the imperial centre and the 'Royal Armenians' out in the provinces. Rather, the leading cause for the dramatic arrival at alienation came through the actions and ideologies held by the leading Armenians themselves, notably the Artsruni brothers, Atom and Abusahl, and Gagik II of Ani. These men, who formerly held kingly rank within their native lands, came to distrust the policies and goodwill of both successive emperors and the imperial court, bearing witness to their interactions and policies towards their Armenian subjects which hardened the line of separation between the native *Romaioi* and wider ethnolinguistic communities.[1]

As we have done at the start of previous chapters, it is worth addressing the change in our primary evidence, for their scope and style of historical record alters our understanding of these crucial decades before the collapse of the Byzantine eastern frontier in the 1070s. Of the Byzantine sources, our main narrative account, Skylitzes, ends in 1057. We are fortunate it extends this far, and the information Skylitzes includes regarding events in Armenia through the decade of the 1040s is unusually detailed. This is in large part down to Skylitzes' focus on the career of Katakalon Kekaumenos.[2] It has been suggested that Skylitzes drew this information from a biography of Katakalon Kekaumenos, although there is no mention of Kekaumenos in the preface of the *Synopsis*, which has led some to suggest either that John the Monk was the writer of the biography or that this was even the pen name of Kekaumenos himself.[3] Skylitzes' work also had a continuation which in all probability was written by the same author as a second edition: it is known to us as *Skylitzes Continuatus*. Arguably the account is a mere copy of the *History* of Michael Attaleiates; as such, it will be referenced here only when it provides additional information to that of Attaleiates, which will be infrequent. The *History* of Attaleiates in itself is our most valuable Byzantine source for the period, even though the work consists of broad summaries until the reign of Romanos IV, 1067–71. His knowledge of military matters and personal understanding of the geopolitical situation on the eastern frontier make him an invaluable source.

Comparatively, our Armenian sources also struggle for continuity from the early eleventh century. Aristakes' narrative on episodes concerning the exiled 'Royal Armenians' is nowhere near as strong as the information he gives on the events in Armenia proper. In support is Matthew of Edessa, who will now become our main narrative source from the Armenian tradition. We have already discussed in the introduction how Matthew's perception of the world was skewed by the two prophesies of Yovhannes Kozern, which predicted the end of the world and identified the major characters of the second coming with the arrival of foreign peoples (Latins and Turks). Yet this does not stop personal polemically charged accusations of failure directed towards both Byzantines and Armenians in their service, and so we must tread carefully, especially when Matthew becomes our sole source for many of the events concerning the Armenians living in the empire in the 1050s and 1060s. Of our other eastern sources Yahya of Antioch ends in 1037, which is a great loss for he has been without doubt our most informative and reliable source on eastern events for the century that his work covers. Our Syriac sources portray a wholly negative picture, highlighting the persecution of the Jacobite Church by the Patriarch Constantine Leichoudes (1058–63); we will witness similar events for the Apostolic Church in the same period, though these are most often secondary in detail and importance. As such, our sources fail to provide a coherent picture of events for much of this period, particularly when attempting to assess the process by which the Armenians became alienated from the Byzantine Empire.

The later annexations and settlements: Vaspurakan, Ani and Kars

It has previously been identified that the changing ethnic-demographic composition of tenth- and eleventh-century Anatolia was a cause of separatism after 1071. After all, the very lands given to the Armenians in Cappadocia and Sebasteia were part of the very same territories that came to later separate themselves from the imperial centre at the time of crisis for Byzantine authority in the east after the civil war of 1071–2 between Romanos IV Diogenes and the Doukas faction in Constantinople.[4] There is no escaping that Byzantium's eastward expansion during the late tenth and early eleventh centuries into western Caucasia and northern Syrian brought with it a plethora of ethnolinguistic units under Byzantine control, not to mention the variety of religious identities that came with it. But the development of Armenian (and other) alienation from Byzantium must be understood within context, rather than simply viewing coexisting ethnic units as natural indisposed towards one another. These conclusions are often drawn from historians writing with the events of the modern world in mind, and this has led to some rather rigid understandings of the ethnic composition and separation across Byzantium's eastern themes in this period.[5]

Certainly, the settlement of the Armenians in the eleventh century did not follow the pattern that had been established in previous centuries. We saw in Chapter 1 that when members of the Armenian nobility migrated into Byzantium they were generally settled nearer Constantinople, or in western themes, and were immediately put to use within the main apparatus of state serving in either the army or administration, sometimes both.[6] It was particularly in the army that we saw Armenians being entrusted with significant commands, fighting wherever they were needed, though they were especially active in the expansion of Byzantium's eastern border throughout the tenth century, at the expense of the disparate Muslim emirates scattered around the Taurus Mountains and northern Syria. Outside of the transferred elite, what can be seen with some certainty is that the average Armenian was settled again where the empire needed them. Settlements in the west, most specifically on the Bulgarian frontiers, were expected to serve as a buffer against an external foe; the success of this policy led to its repetition in the east with Armenian and Syrian settlements being used for the very same purposes to repopulate the newly created themes in south-eastern Anatolia such as Lykandos, Mesopotamia and Cilicia, among many others. Turning to the settlement of the Armenians in the eleventh century, they were also originally settled with a goal in mind: to dilute the power bases of leading aristocratic families that had been able to challenge for the throne. This was a new policy of Basil II who not only lost his throne twice during the 970s and 980s to rebellions but also sought to strengthen the power of the imperial court in the provinces by balancing the regional power bases of Cappadocia, Charsianon and Sebasteia with Armenian settlers loyal to the Macedonian house.[7] It is with this in mind that one should turn to assess the successfulness of the settlement of the Artsruni and judge their immediate experience of living inside the empire in the 1020s and 1030s.

The first settlement of Armenians in the eleventh century occurred around 1020, when the king of the southern Armenian kingdom of Vaspurakan, Senek'erim Artsruni, offered his lands in exchange for estates further west in the region of Cappadocia. Skylitzes lists the territories offered to Senek'erim as 'Sebasteia, Larissa, Abara and many other domains', Aristakes corroborates these lands naming 'Sebasteia and the districts surrounding it', while Matthew of Edessa mentions 'Sebasteia with its innumerable surrounding districts'.[8] It is possible that Senek'erim was granted not only the lands around Sebasteia but also the command of the theme itself, with Skylitzes explicitly claims that Senek'erim was raised to the rank of patrician and made the *strategos* of Cappadocia, yet even he includes in the territory two cities that were in the theme of Sebasteia.[9] We unfortunately have no seal evidence to confirm either position, although we do know that other Artsruni were granted lands and titles by Basil when they first arrived in the empire.[10] Derenik Artsruni, who ruled lands neighbouring Vaspurakan, also handed over his domain of some forty fortresses (if we are to believe Yahya), though we are ignorant of what title and position Derenik and his family were given once they arrived inside Byzantium. Furthermore, both the Armenian edition of Michael the Syrian and Matthew of Edessa mention the Artsruni gaining possession of Caesarea and Xawatanēk, as most likely a further gift of lands as a result of the Artsruni support for Basil II in the revolt in 1022.[11] It is possible that Senek'erim was transferred to the command of Cappadocia in the aftermath of the revolt with the intention that an ally to the crown would prevent further uprisings by the Anatolian aristocracy, a view that is corroborated by the actions taken by Basil against the perpetrators of the rebellion. Taking all of these towns and cities into account, Senek'erim and the Artsruni found themselves placed in command of a sizeable and strategically important area. Our sources are not consistent on the numbers that followed Senek'erim to his new territories in Byzantium; he was allegedly followed by some 14,000 followers from Vaspurakan to Cappadocia, although this specificity is solely reported by the anonymous continuator of Thomas Artsruni's *History of the House of Artsrunik*.[12] Even if we reject this as an exaggerated figure, it is still representative of a sizeable community of Armenians being used as a 'drop-in' social group. There is some corroboration from Matthew who mentions a migration that followed Senek'erim to Cappadocia, but he does not specify a number 'going forth with his whole household and people'.[13] We can glean some commentary on the changing demographics of the eastern themes in the will of Eustathios Boilas, a provincial magnate from Cappadocia. Within it, Boilas lamented that on his journey to his exile in the theme of Iberia he lived 'among alien nations with strange religion and tongue'.[14] Thus the demographic change in Sebasteia and Cappadocia is hard to study further without more data, even though there is little doubt that the placement of the Armenians in Cappadocia and Sebasteia was an intentional policy of Basil II.[15]

Senek'erim would go on to die at some point in the mid-1020s with the usual caveat surrounding the exact date of his death, as our sources are annoyingly hazy on specifics. We do have a surviving funerary inscription in Varag, Vaspurakan, which notes Senek'erim's burial in 1029, though it is likely that this refers to a later symbolic burial of the former king rather than the year in which he died.[16] From our literary sources, Matthew places the date of Senek'erim's death in the same year as that of Giorgi I of Georgia, 1025, but our Georgian sources place Giorgi's death in 1027 and with Matthew's previous poor form on accurate dating, one should trust the Georgian's here as the more reliable record.[17] In any case, the estates of the Artsruni were inherited by Senek'erim's son, David, and it is believed that he also took up the position of *strategos* of Sebasteia or Cappadocia; once again we are lacking firm confirmation as to specifics. Annoyingly, David's own death is only mentioned by Matthew, who places it in 1035/6, and he further informs us that the Artsruni lands passed on to another son of Senek'erim, Atom Artsruni, the oldest surviving brother of David.[18] We will return to Atom and his younger brother Abusahl later in the context of the religious diplomacy of the late 1040s, but what is clear is that the Artsruni were entrusted with a significant administrative command over several successive generations, which does seem a little out of the ordinary for Byzantine administrative practices. So far there is no evidence of any change of the mechanics of assimilation in the migration and settlement of the Artsruni in the early eleventh century. Despite their religious differences, the Artsruni were immediately installed as imperial functionaries in the provinces and for the next fifteen years were to exist peacefully on their estates in the east, revealing that the original bonds made between Basil and Senek'erim had some strength to them, and the Byzantines expected to see shortly the subsequent generation from this Armenian population serving as soldiers and generals across the empire.

This might have been true if it were not for the annexation of Ani during the reign of Constantine IX Monomachos, which brought about another influx of Armenians into the same region that the Artsruni had been living in for more than twenty years. Gagik II of Ani, in return for the forced surrender of his kingdom, was given, according to Matthew of Edessa, 'Kalon-Peghat and Pizu', two towns located near Caesarea, although their exact locations are not known.[19] This seems a rather meagre exchange for Gagik in return for Ani, but our other sources shed further light on additional territories that were offered in compensation. Aristakes informs us that at first Constantine IX offered Gagik 'Melitene and its surrounding districts', but this was refused by the young newly exiled king.[20] When Ani had finally fallen to the Byzantines in 1045, we are told that Constantine instructed Gagik to marry the (unnamed) daughter of David, son of Senek'erim, who had left no heir, and so Gagik gained control over the lands previously held by the Artsruni.[21] Skylitzes offers a different account; he claims that '[w]hen [Gagik] came before the emperor he was honoured with the title of *magister*, receiving lucrative estates in Cappadocia, Charsianon and L[y]kandos from then on he led a peaceful and quiet life'.[22] This new position of Gagik's deserves further examination.

The first sticking point is the claim that Gagik was chosen by Constantine IX to take command of the lands that had been vacant since David Artsruni's death in *c*.1035. The claim by Aristakes that this was because '[David] had left no heir' is misleading. We have already seen that Atom Artsruni assumed control of the lands in Cappadocia and Sebasteia upon his brother's death, and it is unclear why Aristakes does not mention this. Aristakes was well aware of Atom Artsruni, as we will see during the discussions surrounding the Armenian *Katholikos* in 1048. It is possible that the settlement of Gagik in the territories of the Artsruni was to preserve the power balance, as established by Basil II, although it is unlikely that Constantine IX had the same motivations as Basil and we cannot simply expect that the same policy was continued. The second issue is the information provided by Skylitzes that Gagik was given the title of *magistros* and lands slightly to the west of the Artsruni. This is possibly corroborated by Seibt who has identified a seal that may have belonged to Gagik with the title μέγας δοὺξ Χαρσιανοῦ, a theme positioned to the northeast of Cappadocia and west of Sebasteia.[23] Seibt seeks to demonstrate that the lead seal dates from 1071/2, arguing that such a date makes the most sense, as the empire was severely exposed post-Manzikert, and so would explain the exceptional nature of some of Gagik's titles which were intended to ensure his support of the emperor in Constantinople. If this were true, then Gagik would potentially have held concurrent positions in Charsianon, Cappadocia and Sebasteia: an unlikely scenario but not altogether out of the ordinary with many multiple-theme appointments having been made in the preceding 100 years or so. There is little evidence to suggest that the seal represents the political arrangements of 1045 but, in any case, the picture that is painted for us is that Gagik was settled in proximity to the Artsruni and was to take for wife David Artsruni's daughter.

Yet, for some inexplicable reasons Gagik was accorded a position of superiority among the Armenians in the east. This is inexplicable for two reasons. First, we are told by Matthew of Edessa that Atom Artsruni inherited the lands and titles from David upon the latter's death and so governed Cappadocia/Sebasteia as the *strategos* appointed by the emperor in Constantinople. It is indeed possible that Constantine IX decided to remove the title from Atom and give it to Gagik in 1045, but this is not explicitly stated from our seal evidence. Second, the political bonds of friendship and kinship between the Artsruni and the Bagratids were not a forgone conclusion, especially when considering the power structures existing in Armenia before the annexations. While the Artsruni were allegedly inferior to the Bagratid *Shahanshah* in Ani, the ties of loyalty were loose and could in no way be expected to continue after the settlements inside the empire. Unfortunately, we are no closer to understanding how and why Gagik came to be seen as the most prominent of the exiled 'Royal Armenians', but as we will witness later Gagik was seen by the Armenians in Cappadocia and Sebasteia as the leading Armenian magnate during the religious controversies in the late 1050s and 1060s. It is no wonder that Gagik's open insubordination in the 1060s placed a great strain on the empire's ability to defend its eastern frontier against the mounting Turkoman raids, as he held the loyalty of the Armenian princes among the eastern themes and controlled vast swathes of territory that were vital for the defence of the empire.[24] We will return to the influential role of Gagik in the alienation of the Armenians shortly; let us turn to arguably a more prominent example of Armenian interaction with Byzantium in the person of Grigor *Magistros*.

At the same time as the Byzantine annexation of Ani another Armenian prince, Grigor Pahlavuni – later to be known by his Byzantine title *magistros* – handed over his family's estates that included the town of Bjni and the fortresses of Kayean and Kaycon.²⁵ The Pahlavuni family had been staunch supporters of the Bagratid kings and fought valiantly against Byzantine attempts to seize Ani between the years 1043 and 1045. Vahram Pahlavuni, a possible uncle of Grigor, was one of the main architects of the crowning of Gagik II during the interregnum and urged him not to travel to Constantinople in 1045. His resistance to the Byzantines was ultimately in vain and he is reported to have died before the walls of Dvin battling Michael Iasites, the *katepano* of Iberia.²⁶ Grigor, it would seem, was more of a realist in recognizing Byzantine aims in the Caucasus. In return for his lands, we are told by Aristakes, Grigor received the title of *magistros* and 'villages and cities in the Mesopotamian borders'.²⁷ Grigor also received a gold seal and written confirmation of his new lands and the promise of perpetual inheritance for his family, while a seal of Grigor attests his later status as *doux* of both Taron and Vaspurakan, although if we are to take his correspondence into account he may also have been responsible for Mesopotamia.²⁸ It is clear Grigor was entrusted with the defence of a wide frontier command, something that had become more common in the eleventh century, mirroring earlier Byzantine practices of utilizing capable Armenian nobles to rule over a 'hot' frontier.²⁹ We will return later to explore Grigor's career in both terms of his service as a general but also as a literary figure who straddled the Byzantine-Armenian cultural milieu.

The final Armenian kingdom to be annexed by Byzantium was Kars which resulted in the movement of its king Gagik-Abas to estates in the vicinity of Cappadocia in 1064. We are informed by Matthew of Edessa that Gagik-Abas 'abandoned Kars and went over to the Romans. The Emperor Ducas (Constantine X Doukas, 1059-1067) gave [Tzamandos, Larissa, Amaseia, and Comana] to Gagik-Abas, and the Armenian king duly settled there, together with his noblemen, thus abandoning his ancestral home.'³⁰ Interestingly, the lands given to Gagik-Abas were in two distinct regions. Tzamandos and Larissa were technically within the lands held by Gagik of Ani, while Amaseia and Comana (Pontica) were north of Sebasteia, in the area that had previously been given to the Artsruni.³¹ We unfortunately know very little of Gagik-Abas or the settlement of his household in Byzantium. His exchange of lands for estates in the east reveals how the precedent set by Basil II some forty years before was still favoured by the imperial administration, though the usual career path was not offered to him with the commands and titles from which previous migrations had benefitted. It does raise questions as to how the ruling elite in Constantinople viewed the Armenian-dominated territories in Cappadocia and Sebasteia, particularly at a time of rising religious tensions and Gagik of Ani's questionable loyalty to the Byzantine state. It may even suggest that the imperial centre was so detached from the eastern provinces that they were barely aware of the rising resentment of the 'Royal Armenians' towards Byzantium as an entity.

To conclude, there is little reason to think that the Byzantine grants of territory to the 'Royal Armenians' were in themselves problematic. As argued in Chapter 1, the settlement of Armenians in the depopulated frontier zones during the age of reconquest had yielded positive results. What is clear, however, is that the geographical nature of the settlements may well have been a contributory factor.

The distance between the eastern provinces and the centre in this period would aid the disintegration of Byzantine-Armenian relations and exacerbate the fissures in the assimilation process. This, coupled with the political and religious mishandling of the Armenian princes after the settlement of Gagik II of Ani in Cappadocia, exacerbated the Byzantine-Armenian relationship, leading to the later separatism of the 1070s and 1080s.

Religious antagonism

We have previously discussed the nuances of the religious component of Roman identity and the importance that Christianity had in the cultural and ideological world that Byzantium cast over the eastern Mediterranean and beyond. There is no doubt that religion, the adoption and practice of Christian belief, was one of the contributing factors in driving forward the assimilation process, although it was not as strong a factor as some historians have attempted to make it seem. The Christological differences between the Byzantine and Armenian churches have been identified as a direct cause for the alienation of the Armenians from the Byzantine Empire. For example, Gérard Dédéyan focuses almost exclusively on religion to explain Armenian separatism in this period, while Garsoïan views the Miaphysite nature of the Armenian inhabitants in the east as a driving factor behind the Armenian choice of 'a path divergent from that of Byzantium'.[32] This focus on religious antagonism does originate in the primary sources themselves, which often describe the differences between the Byzantines and Armenians through religious identity indicators. Yet, one cannot wholeheartedly summarize the Byzantine-Armenian relationship as one dominated by religious issues. We have seen that other factors contributed to the fluctuating cordiality in the relationship and how in earlier centuries the religious differences had not been as pronounced when assimilation took place. Therefore, this section will attempt to offer a re-evaluation of the increasingly hostile relationship that developed between Constantinople and the Apostolic Church in the mid-eleventh century and argue that the alienation of the Armenians from the Byzantine Empire was not driven predominantly by religious factors.

The information provided for us by our sources forms an extraordinary tangled web of assertions and apocryphal stories that on occasion contradict one another, while others can be refuted through close cross-examination. Such an example can be found when Romanos IV Diogenes was accused by Michael the Syrian of burning down an Armenian Church in Kars and further threatening to force all Armenians living within the empire to convert to Orthodoxy. This event is highly doubtful as we have no confirmation from any other primary source, nor are we aware that Romanos ever ventured near Kars on his campaigns, leading to some certainty that this threat was never made, at least by Romanos IV.[33] The threat of forceful conversion, or rebaptizing, runs consistently through our Armenian sources; we saw previously how Romanos III had pressed Armenian monks of the Black Mountain into his army, while under Constantine X Doukas we are informed that forced baptism was often threatened against the religious communities on the eastern frontier if the Armenian Church would not submit to imperial authority.[34] Such was the extent of the threat of religious persecution that Michael the Syrian, in his account on the failings at Manzikert, claimed:

> The Armenian troops, whom they wanted to force to adopt their heresy, were the first to turn their backs and flee the battle.[35]

Yet this information runs contrary to the accounts of Armenian bravery at the battle found in more contemporary accounts and subsequently the actions of the Armenian-dominated forces that supported Romanos IV in the civil war of 1072. What is clear is that the focus on religious differences between the Byzantines and Armenians has been used to simplify the overall issues that challenged the stability of the Byzantine-Armenian relationship. While it has previously been suggested by some historians that the religious controversy between Constantinople and Armenia had deeper political and cultural roots that were 'cloaked in religious robes', this has been a minority viewpoint.[36] The majority of scholars who have focused on the eleventh century have seized on the religious tensions between the Byzantines and Armenians and have viewed the differences as the underlying cause behind the hostilities between the two groups that flared up in the middle of the century, but a more nuanced approach is required here. While it is undeniable that the Byzantines began to apply substantial pressure on the Armenian Church to bring about a union between the two confessions in the 1050s and 1060s, does this mean that the previous period of religious toleration was at an end? And was it *the* driving force in Armenian alienation, or were there more important factors at play?

It is certain that the Armenians who were settled in Cappadocia and Sebasteia in the eleventh century had access to the institutional structures of the Armenian Apostolic Church. We have already seen that in the tenth century the Apostolic Church had begun to establish new bishoprics throughout the Byzantine east, a development made possible by the waning power of the Muslim emirates who had dominated the region beforehand, alongside the settlement of Armenians in these very regions to provide a buffer zone. It appears that upon arriving on their new estates the 'Royal Armenians' wasted no time in founding and sponsoring new religious houses. The monastery of the Holy Cross was founded by Senek'erim/David Artsruni between the years 1025 and 1030 in the theme of Sebasteia and housed the Cross of Varag that came with the Artsruni migration.[37] Two other convents of St John and St Theodore, respectively, have been identified and their foundations have been dated to the times of the Artsruni settlement. The foundation and construction of a convent to St Gregory the Illuminator, situated some 16 kilometres north-west of Tephrike, has been attributed to a prince called Kiwreł (Cyril) who migrated into the region with the Artsruni, demonstrating that the foundation and patronage of religious houses was not simply the domain of the royal houses that settled in Cappadocia but also the wealthy nobility who followed their monarchs into exile.[38] We are also told by Matthew that Gagik II founded a monastery in the settlement of Pizu, one of the original areas that was granted to the king by Constantine IX.[39] Gagik was to be later buried in the very same monastery after his death at the hands of Byzantine 'agents' in the 1070s.[40] It is clear that the settlement of the 'Royal Armenians' brought about a further expansion of Armenian Church infrastructure in the lands that they were given to govern and one suspects supported a Miaphysite clergy administering the Armenian rites to the local population, thereby continuing Miaphysite practice in these eastern provinces. While we have no data to analyse the rates of conversion from Miaphysite to Chalcedonian religious beliefs, we saw in the ninth and tenth centuries that conversion did occur, with either second- or third-generation migrants coming to adopt Chalcedonian Christianity whether through exposure or the more likely desire to remove barriers to promotion and sponsorship from the imperial court. It is clear that the underlying factor in the production of different results between the tenth and the eleventh centuries was the geographical area of Armenian settlement for the nobility. The 'Royal Armenians' were simply not exposed to the mechanics of assimilation long enough for conversion to take hold. Furthermore, they were placed within the Byzantine-Armenian borderlands that facilitated a continuation of their social and religious norms and thus had access to no driving forces to encourage the Armenian settlers to detach from their hereditary forms of identity.

One can conclude with some certainty that the Armenians, those that were settled in the east in the eleventh century, were able to continue their ancestral customs such as language and faith and consequently this came to severely challenge the mechanics of assimilation that had produced *Romaioi* of Armenian descent in the preceding centuries. We have briefly touched on episodes where accusations of religious tensions/persecutions drove a wedge between the Byzantine and Armenian worlds/peoples, but it is with some certainty that the religious tensions that flared up in the 1050s and 1060s ultimately contributed to driving the forces of alienation to the extreme. As has been outlined before, during the initial stages of Armenian settlement in the eleventh century we do not find examples of imperially sanctioned efforts to challenge the growth of the Armenian Church.[41] The heavy-handed approach of the Byzantines during the reign of Constantine X Doukas against the independence of the Armenian Church was to place a significant strain on the relationship between the Byzantines and the Armenians on the eastern frontier, particularly the 'Royal Armenians'. However, such behaviour is not without precedence.

Some scholars have taken the view that Byzantium's primary goal, through its foreign and settlement policies, was the reduction of the Christian churches independent of Constantinople, a group more commonly brought together under the title Oriental Orthodoxy. Now we have (obviously) been focusing on the experiences of Armenian settlers in the empire, but other ethno-religious groups found themselves going through similar experiences. According to a leading scholar on the Syrian peoples during the ninth and tenth centuries, the Byzantines aimed to subjugated and pursue their ideological aims in the east through three distinct phases:

1. The encouragement of Syrian migrants to settle in the remote borderlands that upon the re-conquests of the ninth/tenth centuries needed repopulating after the expulsion of the Muslim inhabitants.
2. Advocating the relocation of the seat of spiritual power within Byzantine lands, generally in the previously designated territories that the migrants had settled.
3. Then neutralizing the seat of power, generally reducing a patriarch to the rank of an Archbishop and subordinate to Constantinople and integrating the ethnic-religious community fully into the Byzantine church vis-à-vis completing the assimilation process and removing problematic obstacles that obstruct acculturation, in most cases a national/ethnic church.[42]

Cowe believes that this was an intentional policy on the part of the Byzantines to reduce Miaphysite religious groups to subservience to the empire, and he suggests that this was also used to tackle the religious identity of the Armenians.[43] This, Cowe asserts, was a 'means of regularizing and homogenizing [Cappadocia] in order to tie it closely to the centre and reduce the effect of centrifugal forces among the recent immigrants'.[44] This rather sceptical viewpoint is not entirely without merit. The imprisonment of the Syrian Patriarch John VII Sarigta (965–85) between 966 and 969 has strong similarities with the later imprisonment of the *Katholikos* Peter I and his successor Khachik II (1058–65); both were brought about by an invitation to discuss the theological disputes between the Miaphysite and Chalcedonian beliefs followed by swift imprisonment to entice acceptance of religious unity. Interestingly the actions of the imperial centre towards the Syrians followed a very similar pattern to those towards the Armenians, but the theory of planned subordination of an ethno-religious group on the part of the Byzantines by encouraging them to settle within the empire seems ultimately unconvincing, particularly when considering that Basil II had chosen the Artsruni to bring closer central control of Cappadocia through an alliance between the crown and the Artsruni, despite their religious differences.[45]

One can certainly see a similar progression of events in the case of the Armenian settlements in the tenth and eleventh centuries, migrants being used to repopulate areas around either Melitene or Tarsus. Yet it is the 'second phase' that poses certain problems in the comparison with the Armenian migrations, as there were no attempts by the Byzantine to relocate the seat of the *Katholikos* before the eleventh century, and with regards to the migrations towards the middle of the next century, it was not until 1049–50 that the *Katholikos* Peter I was settled in the city of Sebasteia, in the very lands controlled by the Artsruni.[46] The Byzantines certainly prevented the *Katholikos* Peter I from returning to Ani, despite his previous pro-Byzantine tendencies, as they were fearful that he would be used as a figurehead for rebellion against Byzantine control. He was thus kept in Constantinople for several years before being released into the custody of the Artsruni.[47] This aligns with the 'second phase' of Cowe's model in that although there was a difference, the Armenian princely houses held political sway over the lands in which the *Katholikos* was settled, in contrast to the migrant Syrian Jacobites in the preceding century. There are also further questions surrounding Cowe's 'third phase'. We are told by our Armenian sources that the Byzantines desired the wealth of the Apostolic Church, particularly that which had been hoarded by the *Katholikos* Peter I, and this accords with the later claim by Aristakes that the Byzantines wished to impose taxes on the Apostolic Church during the reign of Khachik.[48] Yet we must analyse the events of the 'imprisonment' of Peter and the subsequent events concerning Peter's successors in the seat of St Gregory in an attempt to understand whether Byzantine motives were driven by financial desire or by attempted religious assimilation.

Peter was summoned to Constantinople by Constantine IX Monomachos in 1049. Our Armenian sources inform us that he was kept in great comfort and honoured by the emperor and patriarch, but he was in reality held prisoner in the capital for three years.[49] Eventually, he was released into the custody of Atom Artsruni (an interesting choice as we will see shortly with Gagik's role once settled inside the empire) and came to live near Sebasteia.[50] Here we must return to a previous point. The protection of the *Katholikos*, the spiritual leader of all Miaphysite Armenians, was not granted to Gagik II of Ani but to Atom Artsruni who arguably was of lesser standing than the exiled *Shahanshah*. There are two plausible explanations. The first is that Peter's actions during the Byzantine attempt to seize Ani by force, and his personal responsibility for handing over Ani, may have caused significant friction between the *Katholikos* and Gagik. The second, and less likely one, is that Atom was seen as more representative of Armenian interests in the empire, and that Peter preferred to settle nearer to the Artsruni rather than to the hot-tempered Gagik. Arguably, however, there is a third option and one that is quintessentially Byzantine in character. Providing secular protection to the head of the Apostolic Church held high status, and by granting the responsibility to Atom rather than Gagik would sow discord between the two factions. This does not necessarily mean that the ploy worked, but similar practices of 'divide and conquer' ('control' may be more accurate) are recorded in the granting of titles to Caucasian magnates in the tenth century.

Peter I died in 1058; the new *Katholikos* Khachik II was summoned to Constantinople in late 1059, and here we see the tone of our Armenian sources change.[51] Both Aristakes and Matthew viewed the actions of the new emperor Constantine X Doukas as a deliberate attempt to seize the treasures of the Armenian Church and force the Armenian clergy to accept the Chalcedonian rite.[52] Matthew in fact names the year 1059 as the year when 'the Romans contrived to war against the Armenians in another way; they began to criticize their religious beliefs'.[53] So can we set 1059 as the changing point in religious toleration in the Byzantine Empire? First, we need to acknowledge the issues surrounding the consistency of Matthew's dating, although in the second part of his chronicle he improves dramatically from the first.[54] Second, by taking this date of 1059 at face value would require disregarding previous localized incidents between Byzantine and Armenian clergy, whether through theological debates or small-scale persecutions such as in Sebasteia in AD 987 or the events surrounding Romanos III and his attempt to press-gang Armenian monks into his army during his campaigns in the early 1030s.[55] Despite these examples of localized incidents, one can argue that there was no serious attempt by the Byzantine government to interfere with the Armenian Church on a large-scale basis before this date, and it becomes increasingly apparent that the year 1059 was when direct interference with the Apostolic Church from the imperial centre began. One should question why our primary sources did not see the imprisonment of the *Katholikos* Peter I in 1049 as the beginning of a centralized persecution of the Armenian Church. It would appear that Constantine IX Monomachos had no appetite for attacking the Armenians in matters of faith, nor bringing about a union; clearly his main concern was ensuring that Peter would not cause further trouble with the new Byzantine administration over Ani. The courtesy shown towards Peter during his confinement and the peaceful release of the *Katholikos* into the custody of the Artsruni princes possibly demonstrate that in fact there was no desire yet to challenge the Armenian Church and bring about a union of the Christological disputes that separated Chalcedonian Christianity from the Miaphysite.

Khachik's imprisonment was a significant event in the trajectory of Byzantine-Armenian relations. It signified the beginning of Byzantine attempts to enforce a church union with the Armenians and more importantly resulted in the political alienation of both Gagik II of Ani and the sons of Senek'erim, Atom and Abusahl Artsruni, all of whom travelled to Constantinople to obtain the release of the *Katholikos*. The significance of this event cannot be overstated for the imprisonment and attempted persecution of the Armenian faith is an important trend running through Armenian historiography since the fifth century. The imprisonment of the *Katholikos*, and its wider implications for the representation of Byzantium as an oppressive and persecuting power, produced the narrative structure of self-defence in defiance of political sensitivities. Despite this traditional narrative of Armenian persecution at the hands of a foreign power, it would be prudent to analyse this episode through the lens of our primary sources and see whether the accusations by the Armenian writers have credibility. Was it, indeed, the intent of Constantine X Doukas to destroy the Apostolic Church and subjugate it to Byzantine control, with a hidden agenda of gaining access to the wealth of the Church?

As we have no Byzantine sources reporting the events surrounding Khachik's imprisonment, we must rely on our Armenian sources which claim that the actions taken by Constantine X and his court were solely designed for the seizure of the wealth of the Armenian Church. It is important to remember that the sources were authored by Armenian clerics, and their polemical language must be read in knowledge of the extreme importance the Armenian faith had to their understanding of wider Armenian identity. Matthew mentions that the wealth held by the previous *Katholikos*, Peter I, was an 'immense treasure of gold and silver' which is supported by Aristakes who described Peter I as being man who was 'a great lover of treasure'.[56] This, both sources insinuate, was a major cause for the change in the tone of Byzantine and Armenian ecclesiastical relations, although Matthew was convinced that the underlying motive was 'to compel the Armenians to adhere to the impious faith as set forth at Chalcedon'.[57] In comparison, Aristakes elaborates further that the Byzantines intended to place the Apostolic Church under taxation, which was refused by the *Katholikos* Khachik II, namely as it would surrender the independence of the Armenian Church to the Byzantine state. So why did the Byzantines seek to gain access to the church's wealth? The notion of placing the Armenian Church under taxation is an interesting one and one that speaks of a desire to control an alien population. This desire/fear clearly shows Byzantine awareness of the scope of the expansion of Armenian bishoprics in the east, as well as the subsequent growing wealth of the church and the population that observe Armenian services and traditions. As such, placing the revenues of the lands held by the Apostolic Church under taxation would have yielded substantial receipts for the imperial treasury and slowly bring about more central control on this sizeable religious community that was operating in the eastern themes. In any case, Khachik refused to offer any concessions that would allow the Apostolic Church to be taxed, and he was eventually released, though we do not know precisely how this came about. Like his predecessor Peter, Khachik was allowed to settle in the Armenian lands in Cappadocia, once again securing the seat of the *Katholikos* within the confines of the empire, and he died in 1065.

The death of Khachik provided the Byzantines with a further opportunity to force the Armenian ecclesiastical leadership to the negotiating table with the aim to bring about a union of the two churches. Khachik's successor was chosen with relative speed by a meeting of the Armenian princes and they chose as the new *Katholikos* Vahram Pahlavuni (1066–1105), son of Grigor *Magistros*, an interesting man in his own right and one whom we shall discuss further in the text. Vahram took the name Gregory II and is praised by Matthew of Edessa for his intellect and virtue.[58] Gregory was not, however, summoned to Constantinople. Rather, Constantine X Doukas invited the Artsruni princes to the capital to discuss the possibility of church union and attempted to use political pressure to yield results where previous religious debates had failed.

At some point in 1066 the two princes, Atom and Abusahl Artsruni, were summoned to the capital. We are told by Matthew that they were commanded to 'receive baptism according to the Roman faith', although it is unclear whether this was a threat of forced conversion or simply a summary of the dialogue on matters of faith between the two parties by our source.[59] Whatever the case, they refused to do so, intriguingly stating that they could do nothing without their lord's permission: Gagik II of Ani. It has already been mentioned earlier that there is serious doubt as to whether this relationship existed or whether it was an excuse in order to grant the two brothers more time to wriggle out of the demand from Constantine. It must be remembered that the Artsruni brothers were in fact from a rival royal family to Gagik, who was a Bagratid, and the acknowledgement of the *Shahanshah* in Ani was simply a formality. Nevertheless, such as statement by the Artsruni perhaps reflected Gagik's new role within the Armenian community in Cappadocia; he had after all married the daughter of the deceased David Artsruni, the eldest son of Senek'erim, and received a significant proportion of the Arstruni's estates as a dowry. However we look at this, such an appeal to Gagik speaks volumes on the autonomy that the Armenians felt they had within their lands in

Cappadocia, as it was to their Armenian lord, not the emperor, to whom they felt they owed their allegiance.

We are also told by Matthew that the Artsruni brothers brought with them to Constantinople a *vardapet* called James K'arap'nets'i who was 'erudite in the knowledge of the Holy scriptures' and was able to debate well with the objections the Byzantines had towards the Armenian faith.[60] We are told specifically that 'concerning the two natures in Christ, he inclined a bit to the Roman position', but James had 'raised many objections in reference to various points in the Roman faith'.[61] At the end of the discussions Constantine and the *vardapet* James agreed to produce a document of reunion between the two faiths, something that the Byzantines were obviously very keen to achieve. However, James did not have the authority from his position to produce a document of reconciliation. It is then, we are told, that Gagik of Ani arrived at the capital and tore in two the document that James had authored. Gagik angrily declared: 'This man is only a monk, besides which there are many in Armenia who will neither accept nor conform to such a document as this; moreover, we do not consider him to be one of our accomplished *vardapets*'.[62] Gagik then chastised James in the presence of the emperor and declared that he would write a 'discourse to the Romans concerning the faith of the Armenian nation'.[63] Matthew included a copy of the entire document in his history, although once again we are at the mercy of Matthew's historical record, for no other source provides any details of this highly charged debate.[64] Much as in the work of Stephen of Taron, the inclusion of religious arguments that highlighted the strength and independence of the Armenian Apostolic Church was bread and butter to historians from the medieval Armenian historiographical tradition. Allegedly the reaction from the emperor and his court was positive, and Constantine purportedly 'came to have a very friendly and receptive attitude towards our princes, bestowing many gifts on Gagik, Atom, and Abusahl, as well as on the noblemen of Armenia'.[65] The historicity of this episode is questionable, as are many of the episodes around which Matthew structures larger political/religious discussions. But what it does demonstrate, however, was that serious attempts were made by the Byzantines to bring about a union/subjugation of the Apostolic Church, and the Armenians were forced to defend it from the attacks of the imperial centre. Matthew, writing from the twelfth century obviously saw this as a systematic campaign to destroy the Armenian Church, but wider questions remain as to whether such meetings and debates had much of an effect on Armenian settlers in the east.

Before we can move on, we need to address some inconsistencies that arise in the conclusion to this episode. Matthew does not offer a logical structure for subsequent events. The positivity that is portrayed in the departure of the Armenian princes from the capital does not correlate with the actions of Gagik and his compatriots towards central authority in the years immediately afterwards. It appears, upon closer inspection, that Matthew's commentary on how the attitude of the Byzantines had changed so suddenly is in fact mere flattery towards Gagik, rather than reflecting the truth. It is all the more awkward that in the following passage Matthew tells the infamous, though likely apocryphal, tale of

Gagik and his murder of the metropolitan of Caesarea. From this passage we are told that Gagik was 'quite irritated at the Greeks', presumably from the numerous attempts to bring about the church union, along with his own annoyance at having to defend his faith to the emperor. Additionally, we are told that as Gagik was approaching his home in Cappadocia 'he commanded Armenian troops to violate the distinguished Roman ladies . . . wishing to outrage the Greeks by such behaviour'.[66] Even more intriguing is Matthew's statement that 'Gagik had no intention of ever again returning to Constantinople, rather he was resolved to go to the Persian sultan Alp Arslan and try to regain control of the royal throne of Armenia'.[67] Furthermore, his blatant murder of the metropolitan of Caesarea, seizing his sizeable wealth, and his subsequent refusal to heed the summons from the capital spells out flagrant insubordination to his imperial overlords.[68]

One must attempt to answer why, upon his return from Constantinople, Gagik changed his public behaviour so abruptly. We are informed by Matthew that relations had in fact been normalized with the intervention of Gagik in the theological debates, which in reality were attempts by the imperial court to bring about a union between the two churches. Gagik had originally refuted the document of reconciliation drawn up by the *vardapet* James and yet despite the positive reception from the emperor and the imperial court of Gagik's own discourse, there is no further mention of this aim being fulfilled. It is possible that in contrast to what Matthew reported, relations had not been repaired in the slightest; rather, it was a small reversal for the church in Constantinople forcing it to regroup in order to strike again later at the Armenian Church in wake of the discourse from Gagik. This in turn would make sense of the comment that Gagik was 'already quite irritated at the Greeks', as he was growing frustrated with the persistence of the Imperial Church's attempts to force a union and threats of forced baptism.[69] We are next told that Gagik had a 'deep hatred for the Greek metropolitan [of Caesarea]', not only for having the 'audacity' for naming his dog 'Armen' but also, in the words of Matthew, being 'an evil-minded schismatic and abominable heretic'.[70] Matthew is weak on the details for the religious antagonism between the bishop and Gagik, stating a little further on: '[the metropolitan] brought much affliction upon the Armenians when he heard that the emperor had the intention of forcibly baptizing the princes of Armenia in the Roman faith'.[71] What is clear is that the two men did not get along, and that is putting it mildly.

The apocryphal story of Gagik and the metropolitan of Caesarea deserves to be told in full, not for its historical accuracy, which is highly dubious, but as a literary device from Matthew to symbolize Byzantine-Armenian relations at this time. The story goes that Gagik decided upon his return from Constantinople to stop at the residence of the metropolitan, with an underlying desire to take vengeance on the bishop for his previous slights and actions against the Armenian people. The Metropolitan Mark answered the request for Gagik to lodge with him positively, providing 'a magnificent banquet in [Gagik's] honour'. At the banquet itself Gagik provoked Mark by asking after his dog, which greatly embarrassed the bishop, according to Matthew, as he was aware of the insult he had given by its naming. The excuse from Mark was that the dog 'was solder-like; that is why we call him Armen'. To which Gagik responded; 'We shall now see who is soldier-like, Armen or Roman.' At which point the bishop was bundled into a sack with the dog and Gagik had his attendants beat the dog until he mauled the bishop to death. Afterwards the residence of the Metropolitan was ransacked and Gagik return to his estates, never to heed the summons of the Byzantines again.[72] Whether this episode occurred or not is not particularly important; the inclusion of this tale in Matthew's account is, however, enlightening. For Matthew, this story was for his fellow Armenians of the twelfth century, placing Gagik as a stalwart defender of his and his countrymen's faith against foreign aggressors seeking to subjugate the Armenian Church.

It is clear that religious tensions between the Byzantines and the Armenians had increased in the period after Basil's death, with the previous era of toleration that Basil's reign encompassed having passed. Both the debates of the 1060s and the imprisonment of both the *Katholikoi* Peter and Khachik amplified the gulf between the two parties. Yet, we need to expand the analysis to see whether we can witness the change in attitudes beyond localized incidents. It must be emphasized that imperial and religious policy were not the same thing, and often we find that imperial policy for the eastern provinces was a balance between tolerance and attempts to impose state homogeneity, the most prominent examples of which can be found with Basil's policy towards the frontiers during his reign.[73] Obviously the ethno-religious character of the Byzantine army in the east was very diverse where a significant proportion of the rank and file would have comprised of Miaphysite Christians in Byzantine eyes, necessitating the impartiality of the state in order to maintain order and morale within the army. This would not have been so prevalent with the integration (intermarriage) of the Armenian aristocracy, some of whom came to practise Chalcedonian Christianity, though others held on to their ancestral faith, especially those who had recently arrived in the empire.[74] Michael Taronites, a descendant of the Taronite princes who migrated in the mid-tenth century, married Maria Komnene and in order to marry into the imperial family, it is certain that he observed the Orthodoxy of the Imperial Church.[75] Another example is that of Philaretos Brachamios in the late eleventh century, who was certainly a follower of the Chalcedonian rite, which is understandable, as his family had been present within the empire for several generations before him.[76] Yet, there were non-Chalcedonian members of the aristocracy pursuing successful careers throughout this period, with Ablgharib Artsruni, governor of Tarsus, who was certainly Miaphysite in confession. In fact, there is evidence from a colophon written at the turn of the twelfth century which comments how Ablgharib built 'temples of prayer . . . for there are many who, in the midst of the Greeks, follow the worship of our Armenian race', yet it is also mentioned how 'he remained faithful to the Greeks'.[77] Another example comes with Grigor *Magistros*, who was unashamedly Armenian in faith and made no apparent attempt to convert to improve his career prospects; in fact his impressive career reveals how one's religious faith did not bar someone from high office, especially with one so capable.

While the vast majority of the migrant group of the eleventh century retained their faith in the Armenian Church, there is little difference in how this affected potential assimilation, particularly as we have seen Armenians successfully crossing this hurdle in the ninth and tenth centuries. Armenians were still entering imperial service by the usual means; titles and military commands were granted despite religious beliefs. One has to acknowledge the case of Gagik-Abas II of Kars, the exiled king who was not given a position within the administration of the empire after he settled in the 1060s, though the suggestion that this provides evidence of a change in the policy of containment from the imperial centre to the growing issue of Armenian dominance on the eastern border is hard to prove, especially through the sole prism of religious division.[78]

It is hard to pinpoint accurately when and why the previous status quo of coexistence stopped, and belligerence and intolerance began to rise. We witnessed the peculiarities of the image of Basil II in our Armenian sources, even though he arguably was the chief architect of the Byzantine annexation of the western Armenian kingdoms.[79] In hindsight, it would appear that Basil's tolerance was a high-water mark for the Byzantine-Armenian relationship or so our sources would have us believe. Yet, Basil's successors did not exhibit the same tolerance towards the newly arrived Armenian migrants in the sphere of religion, and as we will see this only helped lay the foundations for the alienation of the Armenians from the Byzantine Empire. That alienation cannot be explained simply through a study of religious animosity; rather, it is through a closer study of the actions of Gagik and the other 'Royal Armenians', and their lack of loyalty to the Byzantine state, that we can understand the full context of Armenian alienation.

The Royal Armenians in the empire

We have already seen in Chapter 1 that upon arrival in Byzantium, Armenian migrants were most often found operating within certain institutions of the state, especially in the army and governance. It has been argued in previous chapters that the adoption of Roman customs was integral for successful assimilation and these customs were defined as 'a subconscious yet simultaneously active belief, support, and loyalty in the universality of Rome, her Emperor, her church, and above all the sanctity of the Empire and its institutions'. Here, our goal is to assess to whether the 'Royal Armenians' of the eleventh century underwent similar experiences and expectations. To be precise, the most important contributory issue for Armenian alienation in the eleventh century was the weakening of the Armenian loyalty to the Byzantine state and emperor. In Chapter 2, we saw how the Artsruni were challenged in their loyalty towards the Byzantine emperor, Basil II, in the revolt of 1022, although participation in Byzantine civil wars did not constitute 'disloyalty' in any real form. Rather, the unintended consequences of the problematic loyalty structures forged between the crown and the Artsruni were to drive their subsequent alienation in the decades that followed. We have also discussed in the previous chapter how the events that brought Gagik II of Ani into the empire fundamentally weakened any possibility of assimilating the exiled king. Our sources hint at two particular factors that drove Gagik's alienation into what would eventually become separatism: first his personal issues with the Byzantines, as a result of political and religious issues that he had to contend with from 1045 to 1071, which added to the second factor, his desire to regain his lost kingdom that had now come under the domination of the Seljuk Turks after the sack of Ani in 1064.[80]

So, when did the Byzantine-Armenian relationship enter the alienation phase? It would be pointless, and most certainly presumptuous, to place a date on when the mechanics of assimilation stopped working if we do not have specific primary evidence to aid us, though the description by Garsoïan as the years after Basil's death as 'the most repressive period' seems a little too generic.[81] At least some sort of relationship between the Armenians and Byzantines seems to have continued up until the Battle of Manzikert in August 1071, and as we will see in Chapter 4, some of these relationships were maintained for several years, if not decades, after. One can say with some certainty that the alienation took root with the arrival of Gagik II of Ani in 1045, although the events concerning the Artsruni in 1040 would suggest that similar sentiments of resentment must have existed among the Armenian elites from the beginning of the decade. This fractious relationship was intensified by the religious conflict, although by conflict we really only mean idle threats and frank discussions around theological differences. We have no evidence of any actual attempts by the imperial centre to impose Chalcedonian practice on the Armenians living in the eastern themes, even if that was their ultimate goal. Despite the later actions of Gagik towards the Byzantines living in the areas of Armenian settlement – one thinks to the tragic figure of the Metropolitan Mark of Caesarea – imperial authority had not completely disappeared through the 1050s and 1060s.

The 'rebellion' of 1040

We have seen so far that the Artsruni were settled during the reign of Basil II and were immediately installed into a high positions within the provincial aristocracy, with Senek'erim being given the title of *strategos* of the theme of Cappadocia, which in turn was inherited by his son David and his nephew also gaining undocumented titles.[82] It has been suggested that the settlement of the Artsruni in Cappadocia may have been a deliberate ploy by Basil to rebalance the power structures in the very regions that had so often challenged the security of his rule.[83] It is entirely probable that the revolt of 1022 may have resulted from some resentment from the Anatolian aristocracy at the settlement of the Artsruni in the area, although our narrative accounts do not offer a reliable chronological record of the events. In any case, the loyalty of the Artsruni was immediately challenged by such a rebellion; we are told that David, son of Senek'erim, 'did not wish to break the pact with Basil' and so brought about the end of the rebellion.[84] The role of the Artsruni in bringing this about seems a little abrupt, with only our Armenian sources even mentioning their involvement; however, they seem to have been rewarded for their efforts with an extension of the lands under their control, and, if subsequent events tell us anything, a renewal of friendship between Basil and the southern Armenian royal family. This begs the question as to whether the loyalty of the Artsruni was simply based on a personal connection with Basil. Such a direct relationship may also offer some assistance in understanding why later emperors were unable to liaise effectively with their Armenian subjects living in the east. We should turn to other examples from the successors of Basil and assess whether the loyalty to the emperor and Byzantine state suffered because the relationship was not maintained at the level that the Armenian princes had experienced when they first arrived.

Basil had ensured that by maintaining the Armenians' prince in the status they had held in their own country they would be able to adjust to their new surroundings with relative ease.[85] Yet, some fifteen years after Basil's death, in 1040, we are informed of a rebellion by the Artsruni princes, Atom and Abusahl. It is worth presenting Matthew's account in full for this pertinent episode:[86]

> In this same year a certain wicked and evil prince from the noblemen of Senek'erim went to the Greek emperor and severely denounced Atom and Abusahl, the sons of Senek'erim, saying: 'They are intent on rebelling against you and thus causing you annoyance and trouble.' The emperor Michael (IV 1034–1041), having heard this, believed these falsely spoken words. He sent his acolyth to Sebastia with fifteen thousand men to bring them to him so that they might not escape, and the acolyth[87] reached the city of Sebastia with his troops. When the sons of Senek'erim heard this, they became stupefied and at the same time frightened. They saw that the prudence of the acolyth was not equal to theirs and thus were afraid to go with him.
>
> Then prince Shapuh[88] said to Atom and Abusahl: 'Do you wish me to scatter the Roman forces throughout the fields?' As he said this, he put seven coats of mail one on top of the other and struck them with his sword, breaking off pieces of the iron mail. The sons of the Armenian king said: 'Let it not be this way, rather we will go with those summoning us.' They gave many gifts to the Roman general and went with him to Constantinople. Upon entering the city, they went weeping to the tomb of the emperor Basil and threw the paper containing the oath given to them on it. Then they said: 'You have brought us to the country of the Romans, and they threaten us with death. O our father, vindicate us before our accusers!' The emperor Michael, hearing such wisdom, marvelled greatly and ordered the denouncer done away with.[89]

These two sections from Matthew are rich in detail on the relationship between the Armenians and the Macedonian house – the latter clearly being viewed as the protectors of the Artsruni settlement by the Armenians themselves. We are first told that 'a wicked and evil prince from the noblemen of Senek'erim' informed Michael IV that Atom and Abusahl were intent on rebelling.[90] We will never know precisely who this unnamed prince was, though we can offer a series of suggestions. First, an Armenian *azat* of the Artsruni who relocated in 1021. Second, one of the extended family of the Artsruni, perhaps in some way related to Derenik, who was given unspecified lands and titles. Third, a member of the Anatolian aristocracy who lived in Cappadocia driven by jealousy and subservience to the Artsruni who held the position of *strategos*. Obviously, we must be cautious when attempting to identify certain characters, and the account of Matthew offers no further clues as to the identity of the accuser. It is entirely possible that the informer identified as a 'prince of Senek'erim' was in actual fact a member of the Anatolian aristocracy attempting to subvert the power base of the Artsruni by accusing them of rebellion, though this is only really supported by the reaction of the Artsruni themselves.

The characters and actions of Atom and Abusahl Artsruni in the two extracts from Matthew offer us some space to evaluate the mechanics of assimilation and its effectiveness on the Artsruni settlement. First, we can see that the two brothers were clearly alarmed at the military force despatched against them and were willing to heed the summons to Constantinople in order to clear their name. The description of the visit to Basil's tomb, while most likely apocryphal, lends weight to the argument that the original alliance between the Artsruni and the Macedonian house was either disintegrating or no longer recognized at the centre. The reasoning behind the accusations, however, is harder to pin down. The claim by Matthew that the accusation came from a nobleman of Senek'erim does not seem rational. Matthew explicitly identifies prince Shapuh as a defender of Armenian interests but does not offer any further description of the accuser. Shapuh's background further calls into question the reliability of the information provided by Matthew. Shapuh had migrated with the Artsruni in *c*.1020 and would have come from the same stock as the unnamed nobleman of Senek'erim. What is more likely is that Matthew mistakenly identified the accuser as a member of Senek'erim's Armenian nobility, rather than a Byzantine noble living in Cappadocia resentful of the patronage the Artsruni had gained at his expense. It is from this perspective that the entire episode gains some reasonable context for the origins of the accusations, although we are left with little else to go on. One must also consider whether Matthew presented this entire episode as a literary device to demonstrate the Armenian infighting that had been prophesized by Yovhannes Kozern. We have already seen, although happening a few years after these events, that the court at Ani was divided against itself in the face of Byzantine opposition after the death of Yovhannes-Smbat and Ashot in 1040/1. Either way, despite the issues surrounding the finer details, Matthew's account of the tensions in 1040 may help explain why Gagik II of Ani was entrusted with the leadership of the Armenian lands in Cappadocia and Sebasteia in 1045.

Grigor Magistros

Before we continue to study arguably the most difficult character of this chapter (and the book at large), Gagik, we should pause to investigate the experience of Grigor *Magistros*, the most prominent Armenian noble of his generation and his role within the Byzantine Empire during the 1040s and 1050s. We have previously seen that he came from the Pahlavuni, a proud Armenian family, and had offered his ancestral lands in 1045, apparently on realizing that the Constantine IX was not going to give up the Byzantine aspirations towards the annexation of Ani. Grigor's career also offers us a chance to view through literary evidence the experience of an Armenian operating in the Byzantine Empire in the mid-eleventh century. First, we need to determine what exactly Grigor's position was when he arrived in the empire. What is clear is that he was directly inserted as a member of the senior officer class and entrusted with the maintenance of imperial authority on the north-eastern frontier, a considerable responsibility. The chronology of his career is problematic. We have seen previously that Grigor was awarded 'villages and cities in the Mesopotamian borders', along with the title of *magistros*.[91] So far, there is no mention of an official position within the hierarchy of the military commands on the north-eastern frontier. Despite claims made by some, there is no explicit evidence to suggest Grigor held the position of *doux* of Mesopotamia and certainly not under the original agreement he made with Constantine IX in 1045.[92] Later, in 1048, Grigor was actively participating in the campaigns of Katakalon Kekaumenos against Turkish incursions. Aristakes informs us of the Byzantine force numbering some 60,000:

> Its heads were Kamenas (Kekaumenos), which translates 'fire', who held sway over Armenia, and Aharon (Aaron), son of Bulghar, who held the Vaspurakan region, and Grigor, the mighty prince of Armenia, who held the dignity of magister.[93]

Here, once again, we lack any statement as to what position Grigor held in this campaign. While our seal evidence tells us that Grigor held the office of *doux* for both Taron and Vaspurakan concurrently, it is impossible that he held the latter position in 1048, for this position was then definitively held by aforementioned Aaron.[94] Nevertheless, Grigor was an active imperial agent defending Byzantium's authority in the Caucasus and shows all the signs of having followed a similar career path to the Armenians of the previous century.

More important, however, is the character and background of Grigor which presents us with other opportunities to examine the Byzantine-Armenian relationship, namely through the shared cultural tradition that transcended the eastern frontier. Grigor had spent a great deal of time among the educated elite of Constantinople, never sharing their religion but holding the same passion for the literature of antiquity, some of which he translated into his native Armenian.[95] Grigor's connection to Byzantium was therefore complicated. He had witnessed blundering Byzantine aggression in the seizure of Ani but also recognized his technical foe as an old friend he had known for his entire life. A recent work on the life and character of Grigor comments thus: 'He could not simply reject Byzantine imperial ideology and culture any more than he could simply adopt it by virtue of its Hellenism.'[96] So how do we categorize Grigor *Magistros*? Arguably Grigor was an Armenian, by origin and religion, but also an active participant in the imperial institutions like so many Armenians before him. One cannot support the claim by another historian that Grigor sought most of all to 'be a member of the Holy

Kingdom of the Romans, because the Byzantines were heirs of the culture which meant most to him'.[97] Grigor engaged with the entity of Byzantium in ways in which the 'Royal Armenians' did not, actively engaging with its cultural inheritance from antiquity, while at the same time holding high offices on the Byzantine frontier. He held on to his religious convictions to his death, though this is not drastically different to examples of first-generation migrants in the ninth and tenth centuries who showed no signs of abandoning their ancestral faith. It may be possible, however, that it was the attachment of said faith, and the subsequent careers of his children within the Apostolic Church, that enshrined the Armenian identity of the Pahlavuni. Despite Grigor's active engagement with some of the most fundamental aspects of the imperial institutions – army, government, positions at court – his children were more heavily engaged in the Armenian, rather than the Byzantine, world after Grigor's death in 1059. Although one must acknowledge that Grigor's legacy led to the Pahlavuni engaging with both the Byzantine and Armenian world in the early twelfth century. While it would be unwise to use the Pahlavuni as an example of the assimilation process breaking down, it certainly highlights the differences between the experiences of those Armenians who migrated in the tenth and the eleventh centuries.

Gagik II of Ani

One must now turn to arguably the most significant Armenian character on the eastern frontier, certainly, in terms of the alienation of the Armenians from the Byzantine Empire. The arrival and placement of Gagik II of Ani on the lands of the Artsruni did not quite have the outcome desired by the outline given in Skylitzes: 'from then on he led a peaceful and quiet life', quite the opposite in fact.[98] Gagik never ingratiated himself with the Byzantine state and barely shared in the experiences that his forefathers had in the ninth and tenth centuries. Despite the placement of Gagik in a region now dominated by both Armenian settlers and nobility, we hear nothing of his contribution to the army or the defence of the Byzantium itself. We have already touched on the doubt surrounding what titles Gagik was given, though we can confirm with some certainty that Gagik married the daughter of David Artsruni and held a prominent position within the leadership of this diasporic community.[99] The marriage, we are told, was 'by the emperor's order, Gagik married the daughter of Dewitt', son of Senek'erim, and ruled that sector, since when Dewitt' died he had left no other heir'.[100] This explanation by Aristakes runs contrary to the information we are given by Matthew, who specifically states that Atom Artsruni, the next eldest son of Senek'erim, held what is described as 'hereditary sovereignty'.[101] We have yet again hit an obstacle. Aristakes is certain that Gagik now held the command of the Armenians in Cappadocia and Sebasteia, while Matthew's information regarding Atom Artsruni suggests that this could not have been the case. We can, however, explore later events that offer us details that our primary sources do not directly record. In 1065, the Artsruni brothers were summoned to the court of Constantine X Doukas to defend the Armenian faith and potentially bring about the much sought-after union of the two forms of Christianity. Matthew paints the scene as one of discomfort for the Artsruni brothers who were unwilling to concede to Constantine's demands concerning the Armenian faith. As an excuse why they could not conform, they said they had to seek the permission of their king:

> We are unable to do anything without Gagik, son of Ashot, for he is a brave man and our king and son-in-law; send for and summon him here, for if we do anything without him, he will burn us to death when we return to our lands.[102]

The context for this unusual claim originates in the tenth century when the Artsruni family directly challenged the authority of the Bagratuni king of Ani and his claim to be king over all of Armenia.[103] While the division in royal authority was certainly real, the king in Ani still held the title of *Shahanshah*, King of Kings, a position that therefore reflected the political landscape of the medieval Armenian kingdoms. This position is further substantiated by the words of Gagik himself, as recorded by Matthew of Edessa: 'I am a king and a son of the kings of Armenia, and all Armenians obey my commands.'[104] Yet, it still does not explain why Atom and Abusahl Artsruni would have seen Gagik as their overlord, as they came from a technically rival house, and Atom had inherited the leadership from David Artsruni in *c*.1035/6. One can suspect that this claim was not in fact true; whether it was an error in Matthew's account or the brothers were making an excuse to get out of a sticky situation. It is entirely possible that Gagik assumed the command as *strategos* of Cappadocia from the Artsruni by the order of Constantine IX; after all, Byzantine offices were not hereditary by right but at the will of the patronage of the emperor. Nevertheless, Matthew's account describes how Gagik travelled to Constantinople to defend the Armenian faith, as he was after all 'brilliant in philosophical debates and invincible in answering questions put to him', alongside Gagik's humble assessment of his own abilities:

> I am well versed in the Old and New Testaments, and all Armenians are witnesses to the truth of my words, for they regard me as equal to the *vardapets*.[105]

Gagik had clearly become the de facto leader of the Armenians in Cappadocia and Sebasteia by 1065, although we are unsure of the technicalities of such authority. While one could argue that even in the 1060s the Armenians were still cooperating with the Byzantine state and emperor by complying with the summons, the arrival of Gagik of Ani had disturbed the previous loyalty structures; that is, the Armenians looked to him, rather than the emperor in Constantinople, as the authoritative political figurehead.

The first steps to separatism

By the mid-1060s, the exiled Armenian royal houses were experiencing the alienating policies of the imperial centre and started to look independently for their own protection. Gagik was said to have corresponded with the Seljuk Sultan requesting the return of the lands around Ani, possibly to rule as a vassal of the Turks. We do not know whether he ever received a response, although his continued residence in Cappadocia is a possible indication that such a request fell on deaf ears.[106] Such an action seems quite remarkable, with magnates attempting to deal separately in terms of foreign policy; indeed, there is a similar incident involving the Armenian princes in negotiating a separate truce with an emir called Ktrich'[107] who apparently had wanted to secretly rebel against the Seljuk Sultan Alp Arslan.[108] This is an unusual episode, as the Armenian princes had treated with a rebellious emir, and more importantly a foreign magnate, as if they were their own state and they had powers, rather than deferring to the emperor and his court in Constantinople for promulgations on foreign diplomacy. Once again this is not definitive proof that the Armenian princes on the eastern frontier were abandoning the empire entirely, but their behaviour was unprecedented and provides the context for how they were to respond to the crumbling authority of Byzantium after the Battle of Manzikert in 1071.

Moving ahead to the reign of Romanos IV Diogenes (1068–71) and his eastern campaign into Armenia in 1071 to counter the Turkish threat, the Armenian princes seem to have still been in communication with the emperor and actively involved in advising Romanos on his plan of action. Matthew of Edessa tells us that when Romanos had reached Sebasteia in the early summer of 1071, he was greeted with great pomp by the brothers Atom and Abusahl Artsruni, though strangely not Gagik.[109] However, we are also informed that the tensions between the Byzantines and the Armenians had risen to a hostile level, as Matthew continues:

> At this time the Romans made slanderous remarks against the inhabitants of Sebastia and against all of the Armenians in general, denouncing them before the emperor saying: 'If at any time the emir Ktrich' strikes at us, the Armenians surely will slaughter us more vehemently than the Turks'.[110]

This narrative is very similar to what can be found in the history of Michael Attaleiates who reports that after the sack of Iconium by the Turkomans in 1069:

> [t]he emperor waited in Kelesine to receive the survivors within the camp, so that they might not be caught wandering about in small groups in the wilderness and be killed by the Armenians.[111]

These two statements from different primary sources indicate that the Byzantine-Armenian relationship was starting to come under serious strain at both a local and wider level. Conversely, Matthew's narrative still indicates an element of cooperation between the Armenian princes and the emperor. Despite being told that Romanos believed the allegations that were levelled against the Armenians in Sebasteia, and the subsequent pillaging of the city by Roman troops along with the snubbing of Atom and Abusahl, the emperor still maintained a relationship, or at least correspondence, with Gagik of Ani. As Matthew recounts:

At that time the illustrious Roman magnates [as well as] the *Shahanshah* Gagik and the emir Ktrich', said to the emperor Diogenes: 'Do not listen to the deceitful words spoken by those belonging to your nations, because all their words are false; for all those Armenians who have survived the combats with the Turks are your auxiliaries'.[112]

Romanos is reported to have yielded to the advice he was given, although he apparently still threatened 'to do away with the Armenian faith on his return [from Persia]', yet further proof of the religiously charged polemic dominating our understanding of Byzantine-Armenian relations.[113] We can still see that the issue of religion is at the forefront of the hostilities between the Byzantines and Armenians within our primary sources. We must consider, however, that Matthew was writing in the early twelfth century, and was a monk in Edessa, so his priority would have naturally been towards matters of faith in terms of hostilities, all of which he may have embellished somewhat. Attaleiates however, our main Byzantine source for the events of the late eleventh century, does indeed corroborate Matthew's views on the religious convictions of the Armenians:

For it seemed that such a large uprising of the foreign nations and the slaughter of those who live under Roman authority could be attributed only to His anger against the heretics, that is the Armenians dwelling in Iberia, Mesopotamia, and as far as Lykandos and Melitene.[114]

It is clear that the animosity between the Byzantines and the Armenians was linked with the religious differences between the two groups, and this in turn was a directly contributing factor to the alienation of the Armenians. Yet, their correspondence with Diogenes, even as late as 1071, indicates that the Armenian separation from the Byzantine state had not entirely come to fruition. What is becoming abundantly clear was that their actions after the strategic defeat at the Battle of Manzikert instigated a new era for the Byzantine-Armenian relationship, rather than the alienation beforehand being terminal.[115]

We have so far been concerned with the interactions of the Armenian elite with that of the Byzantines and how the relationship soured at a time when unity was required to shore up the Seljuk threat. It is important to attempt to further our understanding in how Armenians below the class of the nobility felt about their attachment with Byzantium. Such a task is often near impossible with our sources most often concentrating on the main power brokers and players, but there is one area where we can look more easily at wider Armenian participation and attitudes towards the Byzantines: that being the countless Armenians who served as soldiers in the army. It has often been wrongly assumed, by both primary accounts and secondary works, that the annexation of the Armenian kingdoms in the eleventh century led to the dismantling of the native military forces, such as the dissolution of the Armenian militia of Ani by Constantine IX Monomachos, and that this brought about resentment from the exiled Armenians within the empire.[116] In fact, we are informed by Skylitzes that the troops were absorbed into the regular army, continuing the previous policy of recruiting Armenians into the army, with many serving loyally for decades afterwards.[117] There are certainly examples of issues with the loyalty of some Armenian troops during the campaigns of Romanos IV Diogenes, such as the siege and sack of Hierapolis in Syria during the summer of 1068. The historian Michael Attaleiates informs us that

> the Armenian infantry, who had been ordered to spend the night before the moat as a protective screen, planned to defect and refused to obey their officers.[118]

Yet, such isolated incidents are not entirely reflective of the level of loyalty that the Armenian soldiers displayed towards the Byzantines in general. One can find many examples where Armenian soldiers fought with distinction and were to become prominent supporters of Romanos IV Diogenes during his civil war with the Doukas faction in Constantinople after the defeat and the emperor's release from captivity following the Battle of Manzikert. During the preceding campaigns to Manzikert that were targeting the south-eastern frontier with the Fatimids of Egypt, Romanos used Armenians as settlers in the city Hierapolis after it was captured and the population driven out and further placed an Armenian commander in charge of the garrison, arrangements that sit awkwardly with the previously assumed Armenian disloyalty.[119] In another instance, Romanos had instructed Armenian forces in the vicinity of Seleukeia to attack Turkoman raiders as they passed through the mountains, reinforcing the reliance on the Armenian element within the army for the defence of the empire.[120] Furthermore, during Romanos' final eastern campaign in the environs of Lake Van, the Armenian troops that were at the emperor's disposal were charged with breaching the wall outside of the citadel in Manzikert, which they achieved with great success.[121] The accusations of mass Armenian defections before and during the Battle of Manzikert only appear in Michael the Syrian.[122] Our other sources directly refer to the level of dedication of the Armenian soldiers at Manzikert for the empire.[123] So while tensions between the Armenian princes and the imperial centre were certainly rising, they were not apparently widespread across the entire Armenian population living across the eastern themes of Byzantium, least of all within the institution of the empire that so many Armenians found themselves – the army. We will return to the Armenians and the army in the next chapter, where it will be argued that their dominance facilitated the creation of independent Armenian principalities in the region in the wake of the disintegration of Byzantine influence on the eastern frontier. But there is no doubt that the reliance on Armenian soldiers and generals within the army on the eastern frontier did not bring about the defeat at Manzikert, nor necessarily the desire for separatism, for the chaotic and disparate world of eastern Anatolia in the 1070s and 1080s saw Armenians operating for and against Byzantine imperial authority.

Conclusion

To conclude, it is clear that the assimilation process that had long existed through Roman history was no longer producing the same results for the Armenians who had been settled in the eleventh century. It is all the more remarkable when one contrasts and considers the results of the late ninth and tenth centuries where copious numbers of Armenians slowly but surely adopted Roman customs and came to be seen as fully fledged *Romaioi*. It would be crude and simplistic to point the change in this process to the annexations directly, though they were undoubtedly an indirect cause for the characters and episodes that were to shape the Byzantine-Armenian relationship for the rest of the eleventh century. By the 1060s said relationship was under significant strain, with many of the 'Royal Armenians' no longer feeling attached to the empire in which they lived, for both religious and ideological reasons. One can see from certain actions on the part of the Armenians, headed by Gagik of Ani, that the attempts to enforce religious uniformity by the Byzantine court resulted in resentment. Yet, the religious issues cannot be used as the sole explanation for why the assimilation broke down and found alienation in its stead. Rather it comes back to the broader definition of 'Roman customs' and how the Armenians, from the 1040s onwards, were no longer interacting with the empire as their forefathers had done through such institutions as service in governance or the army which ultimately strained their loyalty to the imperial centre with the position of emperor at its heart. In the end, it was the defeat at Manzikert that produced the conditions for Armenian separatism from Byzantium, but without the alienation experienced by the 'Royal Armenians' in the middle decades of the eleventh century the breakdown of the Byzantine-Armenian relationship would not have reached the levels of separatism that one witnesses in the 1070s and 1080s. This process will be the focal point in the following chapter.

Chapter 4

SEPARATISM, 1071–98

The history of the Byzantine state, and the near-east for that matter, is extraordinarily hard to follow in the decades after the Battle of Manzikert, which took place in August 1071. There are many moving parts and pieces across the geopolitical map, with the disintegration of Byzantine authority, the rapid rise and fall of central Seljuk power, the struggles of local Armenian warlords, and all of this bookended with the arrival of the Frankish crusaders in 1098. For our study this is the period in which the Byzantine-Armenian relationship arrived at its final destination: separatism. The actions and events concerning the Apostolic Church, the 'Royal Armenians' of Cappadocia, the Armenians in the army and Byzantine-Armenian imperial agents will all need to be addressed in turn. As we saw at the end of the last chapter, the alienation of the Armenians in the 1050s and 1060s was a direct result of the erosion of loyalty to the Byzantine state, her emperor and its institutions – the concepts that had otherwise attached previous generations of Armenian migrants to the empire. The main purpose of this final chapter is to understand not only why this came about but also what developed out of this chaotic period of history.

By the mid-1060s it had become clear that the Armenians living on the eastern frontier, particularly in the four neighbouring themes of Cappadocia, Sebasteia, Charsianon and Lykandos, had become alienated from the Byzantine Empire. The events concerning religious debates and ideological differences furthered this disillusionment and were ultimately to sow the seeds of separatism among the Armenian princes. There is little doubt in the integral role played by Gagik II of Ani, who was the most prominent in his disenchantment with the empire and who encapsulated the disintegration of the Byzantine-Armenian relationship in this period. The collapse of Byzantine authority on the north-eastern frontier in the early 1070s has already been expertly researched, and there is little doubt that the 'Royal Armenians' came under significant pressure from the raiding Turkomans who were to begin establishing their own emirates to the north of the Taurus Mountains.[1] Our immediate task, therefore, is to identify the characteristics of the wider Armenian community on the eastern frontier in the summer of 1071, where their loyalties lay, and the strength of Byzantine authority over the region.

Before we can resume our discussion of the Armenians living on the eastern frontier, and their prospects in the immediate aftermath of Romanos IV's defeat near Lake Van, we need to briefly discuss the changes in our primary source evidence from which our partial understanding of this period comes from. In regards to the Byzantine perspective, we must now rely heavily on the *History* of Michael Attaleiates up to 1079, the first year of Nikephoros III Botaneiates' reign. Skylitzes' first edition of the *Synopsis* finishes in 1057, although his second edition (Skylitzes Continuatus) brings the narrative up to 1079. This second edition, known as the *Epitome*, contains very little new material in it; in fact it follows Attaleiates' *History* very closely, while also utilizing Psellos' *Chronographia* for additional information.[2] As such, the *Epitome* will only be referenced when Skylitzes offers us information that we do not otherwise gain from Attaleiates. As Attaleiates' account finishes in 1079 we are reliant on two further works, that of Nikephoros Bryennios and Anna Komnene. Bryennios' history of the events in Anatolia offers a different perspective than that of Attaleiates, particularly when concerning the 'achievements' of Botaneiates whom Attaleiates does not hesitate to flatter. Yet Bryennios' account only adds a couple of years to the end of Attaleiates' *History* finishing in 1081. It is the *Alexiad* of Anna that we must use to cover the events through to 1100. There are issues with the reliability of Anna's factual details, due in large part to her distance from the events, writing well into the twelfth century and her aim to distance Alexios from the responsibility for the collapse of imperial authority in the east. As such, our Byzantine sources offer us only limited window of information for the events unfolding in the east during this period and struggle to present the full story of the collapse of imperial authority across the eastern provinces in the 1070s and 1080s.

Turning to our Armenian narrative sources we are now left solely with Matthew of Edessa, which without doubt raises some serious concerns over accuracy of events and dating. Aristakes' account tragically ends with Manzikert: a great textual loss, for his account of the eleventh century has largely been the litmus test for Matthew's errors. We are entirely reliant on Matthew for his account of the fracturing of the leadership of the Apostolic Church and have already discussed how Matthew, in some similarity to previous Armenian authors, interpreted the internal strife and discord within the church as part of the divine plan for the Armenian people. Despite the polemical language Matthew uses in condemning the sins and divisions of the Armenians as a whole, his belief in their eventual redemption through God's mercy was unwavering. It is in this period that we find Matthew describing events with more vigour and verve, with a greater grasp on the recent history for the Armenian inhabitants in the region, largely as his sources for information would have been more readily available, existing in the oral tradition of his own lifetime in the first half of the twelfth century. The arrival of the Latins alongside the attempted preservation of Armenian rule in Cilicia and along the upper Euphrates become key elements within Matthew's narrative and as such will be major focal points in this chapter. Additionally, we are assisted by the chronology produced by Samuel of Ani, although he offers only a vague narrative of the events in this period.

Michael the Syrian's chronicle offers limited information on this obscure period, and it is to our Latin and Muslim sources that we must turn to fill in the gaps. While the Latin narrative accounts of the First Crusade are only relevant for the period 1096–8, our Muslim sources help us reconstruct the chronology of the 1080s and 1090s, particularly concerning the Turkic settlements of eastern Anatolia in the heartlands of where the 'Royal Armenians' had been settled earlier in the century. The Seljuk historiographical tradition is largely focused on the origins and history of the Turkic peoples, providing only limited and inaccurate details of the penetration of the Byzantine frontier in the eleventh century.[3] The most informative universal chronicles from the broader Muslim historiographical tradition come from Ibn al-Athīr and Sibṭ b. al-Jawzī, both writing in the thirteenth century.[4] Both of these chronicles are inconsistent in their information on the eastern frontier in the late eleventh century, although they do on occasion offer valuable additions, particularly when used in combination with our other sources. In summary, our primary sources describe a disparate and confusing world for the Armenians on Byzantium's eastern frontier in the aftermath of Manzikert, and it is a constant struggle to construct a flowing narrative account of this era. Yet we are able, through this patchwork of sources from varying historiographical traditions, to trace the disintegration of Byzantine influence over the Armenians in the east and the manifold ways in which separatism manifested itself in the lordships from Cilicia to northern Syria.

Romanos IV, Manzikert and the Islamic world

The Battle of Manzikert in August 1071, for all the doubts over the strategic and military losses in the battle itself, was without question the most significant event for the geopolitical status quo on the eastern frontier since the campaigns of John I Tzimiskes. The repercussions of the battle affected not only the Byzantine world but, in the longer term, Christendom at large, specifically the west, and consequentially the Islamic world too. The very importance of Manzikert is reflected in both our Byzantine and Muslim sources, although both historiographical groups undoubtedly paint the battle as a watershed with the benefit of hindsight. It is not the purpose of this book to offer a new narrative on the battle itself; there are many other works out there that look at the military tactics, political weaknesses and capability of the two commanders Romanos IV and Alp-Arslan.[5] Therefore, a very brief sweep will be offered before moving on to the immediate effects the loss of the battle had on Byzantine politics and the Byzantine-Armenian relationship at large.

Romanos IV acceded to the throne in 1068, having been selected by the Empress Eudokia on advice to choose a popular figure from the army and who came from distinguished Roman lineage.[6] Romanos' reign was largely dominated by a series of campaigns to the eastern frontier in 1068, 1069 and 1071 – the first two being focused on the Syrian battleground with the Fatimids of Egypt. We have already noted these previously when discussing Romanos' use of Armenian soldiers and settlers to stabilize the gains he made in this sector, and it is interesting to note that northern Syria, anchored by the city of Antioch, was seen as the utmost priority, not the Armenian highlands where Romanos' legacy would be immortalized in defeat two years later. The geopolitical situation in 1071 called for a campaign in the direction of Armenia, with bands of Turcomans raiding at will through the Caucasus, reaching as far west as Iconium. Furthermore, Seljuk garrisons now held important frontier fortresses which were key to Byzantine defensive strategy. Therefore, the recovery of places such as Khliat and Manzikert became the primary aims of the 1071 campaigning season, with Romanos personally leading the expedition having spent the previous twelve months stuck in the capital.

Once Romanos arrived in Armenia, he divided his forces to take the two intended targets of Khliat and Manzikert, not aware that the Seljuk Sultan was less than 100 miles away with his own force of some 30,000 horsemen. Modern estimates put Romanos' troops after his division of the army at around 20,000, and Attaleiates gives the impression that the troops remaining with Romanos were inferior in quality and experience than those that marched ahead to Khliat. Not only did the army fail to regroup into one cohesive unit once the Turks were detected but Romanos also had to contend with surmounting disloyalty from his generals – the main antagonist being Andronikos Doukas. In the eyes of some courtiers Romanos had usurped the throne when Constantine X Doukas had died in 1067, leaving a powerful but resentful Doukas faction in the court headed by Constantine's brother, John, who held the powerful position of Caesar within the Byzantine court. John's son, Andronikos, was bizarrely entrusted with commanding the reserve during the battle, and so when Romanos desperately needed relieving after being surrounded by Seljuk cavalry Andronikos withdrew from the field with his force intact, leaving Romanos to be captured and his part of the army destroyed.

We are informed by our sources that Romanos was freed by his captor Alp-Arslan, the victorious Sultan of the Seljuk Empire, who had treated the defeated emperor with all the respect that his rank warranted, gaining praise from Attaleiates: 'Even if the Turks do not have a law of loving one's enemy, he unconsciously carried out this divine law through his naturally virtuous disposition.'[7] In the wake of the defeat and capture of Romanos IV at Manzikert the prominent Doukas faction in Constantinople saw their chance to regain the throne from a man they had always seen as a usurper.[8] Romanos received news of his deposition when he arrived in the Armeniakon theme, which complicated the delicate diplomatic position in the east quite considerably.[9] Romanos had been forced to agree to certain conditions to obtain his release for the details of which we have several competing accounts. Ibn al-Athīr speaks of 1,500,000 dinars for ransom, an expectation of a levy on Byzantine forces at the Sultan's request and the release of prisoners held by the empire.[10] Zahir al-Din Nishapuri, a Persian writer of the twelfth century, largely reports the same details with some additional information:

> [Romanos agreed to] commit a thousand dinars to the private treasury each day, that he would send this tax on two occasions in the course of each year, that, in time of need when the call for help came, he would send as aid ten thousand

experienced horsemen, and that he would release every Muslim prisoner in the Byzantine Empire.[11]

The treaty was ignored by the regime in Constantinople; indeed, Skylitzes claimed that the failure of the Doukas regime brought about a change from Turkish raiding to that of conquering; either way, their main concern was to bring the deposed emperor to heel and prevent him from mustering substantial support from his allies in the east.[12] Here, the Doukas faction ultimately failed. Romanos fell back to Cappadocia and summoned troops loyal to his cause for the coming fight with the imperial forces sent from Constantinople under the command of Andronikos Doukas.[13] Many of these were Armenians in the military hierarchy who owed their positions to the patronage of Romanos, and this too is confirmed by our Muslim sources.[14] Indeed, according to the account by the historian Sibṭ ibn al-Jawzī, a Turkish historian of the late twelfth/early thirteenth century, after Romanos had paid part of the tribute to Alp-Arslan he came into conflict with the regime of Michael VII Doukas and was eventually imprisoned and blinded by 'Sinakharib, the king of the Armenians'.[15] Furthermore, the Armenian king was purported to have brought over many of the forces that had supported Romanos and began terrorizing various nearby localities such as Iconium and Melitene, even going so far as to promise to support the Sultan. Now let us deconstruct the various claims that are made here and compare them with what we know from elsewhere. First, that 'Sinakharib' (Senek'erim) died in c.1027 means this cannot be the Artsruni king or even his son David (who was mistakenly identified as Senek'erim by Aristakes), who died in c.1035. It is possible that the Armenian king identified in the sources was in fact Gagik II of Ani and we have seen in the previous chapter that it was likely that Gagik had contacted Alp-Arslan regarding the control over Ani (we will explore the career of Gagik post-1071 later). Second, the Armenian opposition towards Romanos IV is not corroborated by our wider non-Muslim sources. Rather, an extensive study on the roles and careers of various Byzantine-Armenians highlights the natural affinity many had with Romanos IV, especially with their most recent experiences in the campaigns of Romanos from 1067 to 1071.

One of the most important Byzantine-Armenian commanders in the east in the aftermath of Manzikert was Chatatourios, described by Attaleiates as 'a noble man who had in the past given much proof of his valour', holding the title of *doux* of Antioch and responsible for the troublesome south-eastern frontier while Romanos led his army east into Armenia in 1071.[16] It is probable that Matthew of Edessa is describing the very same person when he states: '[a] certain brave Armenian soldier called the *vestis*, who was the d[o]ux of Antioch'.[17] It must be noted that Matthew could be confused, as the date he gives for this event is 1065-6, when Nikephoros Botaneiates was holding the position, but it is more likely a dating error than misidentification. Despite the loss and deposition of Romanos IV Diogenes, Chatatourios came to support his patron, highlighting the strength of personal loyalties during bouts of civil war.[18] The imperial court attempted to contact Chatatourios and ordered him to attack Romanos; this was to be a serious misjudgement on their part, for Chatatourios had no desire to see the emperor to whom he owed his position deposed, and so he combined his forces with those of Romanos and fought against the imperial army commanded by Andronikos Doukas in Cilicia in 1072.[19] Attaleiates reports that Chatatourios was captured in battle and hints at his death:

> He was brought before the general naked and wretched both on account of his present condition and the harm that he was about to suffer.[20]

Although Psellos reported that after Chatatourios' capture:

> clothes and equipment were provided for him, and, though he was kept prisoner, no constraint was put upon him, as befitted a brave leader.[21]

We are not told with any certainty by Attaleiates or Psellos what became of Chatatourios or who was sent to replace him in his position as *doux* of Antioch and must turn elsewhere for information.

Yet before we can do so there is a more important figure to assess, who like Chatatourios was employed in the army and actively participated in the campaigns of Romanos IV: Philaretos Brachamios. During 1071 Philaretos was not operating in the highest echelons of the military hierarchy out on the eastern frontier, although he was entrusted with moderate responsibilities by Romanos. His absence at Manzikert is not hard to explain and later claims that he wished to take advantage of an imperial defeat do not stand up to scrutiny. Romanos had twice previously campaigned against the Emirate of Aleppo (in 1068 and 1069, respectively), campaigns in which Philaretos most certainly took part, and it is in this sphere of conflict that Philaretos can be thought to have remained while Romanos passed north on his way to Manzikert in the summer of 1071. It is in the aftermath of Manzikert that Philaretos' loyalties began to take shape, for there is no evidence that he attempted to assist Chatatourios in his support for Romanos. This is certainly unusual, as the hierarchical military command must have placed Chatatourios above Philaretos, the latter holding no formal Byzantine title at this point.[22] It is entirely plausible that he had been entrusted with maintaining the frontier to protect Chatatourios' rear as he advanced into Cilicia. Some scholars, such as Treadgold, have argued that Philaretos held command over most, if not all, of the eastern tagmata from 1072 onwards, with the title of *domestikos* which he received in 1078 reflecting the troops under his command, though this is more of an assumption than actual reliance on primary evidence.[23] In the aftermath of the defeat of Romanos IV's forces in Cilicia in 1072 it would appear that Philaretos was able to assume command over a substantial body of troops in a region that had suddenly become a political vacuum. While it is impossible to know the numbers now under Philaretos' command, Matthew of Edessa claims that they were around 20,000. So without doubt Philaretos was able to dominate the immediate geographical area of northern Syria and Cilicia after the collapse of imperial authority in *c.*1072.[24] Despite Romanos' surrender and death through blinding in 1072, his lieutenants in the east began to pursue policies of separatism from the central authority, not necessarily out of loyalty to the memory of a beloved emperor, nor through loyalty to their Armenian brethren, but more likely by virtue of the opportunities that arose in the wake of the disintegration of imperial authority in the east. There are some serious questions surrounding the extent of the loyalty of various Byzantine-Armenian characters in the region, the most important of whom was Philaretos. Some historians have argued that his rebellion in the 1070s represented a refusal to accept the political revolution in Constantinople in the autumn of 1071, while others believe that in fact, he was nothing but an opportunistic warlord who saw his chance to break away from an imperial servitude that he resented. We will return to focus on the career of Philaretos later, but it is with some certainty that we can view the geopolitical situation on the south-western frontier as fluid at best.

The last vestiges of Byzantine authority on the eastern frontier in the 1070s were undoubtedly centred on the city of Antioch and focused in the authority commanded by either the *Doux* or *Katepano* who represented the emperor's interests. It appears that the holder of this position changed with increasing regularity from Romanos IV's fall from power through to the capture of Antioch by Philaretos Brachamios in 1078, reflecting the fragile political situation at the Byzantine court. One can see through the constant changes and political tussling over the position of *doux* that Antioch was seen as the fundamental strategic centre of Byzantine interests in the region, and therefore one must spend time analysing how Antioch was governed and by whom. While the Doukas family still held sway in Constantinople in the 1060s we are informed that a certain eunuch by the name of Nikephoros was appointed *doux* of Antioch by Constantine X Doukas, most likely holding the position between c.1063 and 1067.[25] Nikephoros' fall from power in Antioch was sudden, according to our primary sources, with an imperial decree reaching the city that caused him to be imprisoned for murder on the orders of the Empress Eudokia acting in sole authority.[26] Attaleiates does not inform us of his successor, though we can gain the information from an earlier episode in his history. Nikephoros Botaneiates (the future emperor Nikephoros III, 1078–81) was mentioned as a possible suitor to marry the Empress Eudokia upon the death of Constantine X Doukas in 1067:

> But there was a debate over who the right man was for the times and for this dignity, since Botaneiates was away governing Antioch.[27]

It is not unreasonable to assume that it was Botaneiates who was sent to Antioch to dispose of Nikephoros the eunuch and who assumed the role of *doux* of Antioch. The details of Botaneiates' tenure are uncertain and the appointments between Botaneiates (1068) and 1069 are ambiguous.[28]

The chronology of appointments from the death of Chatatourios in 1072 is hard to piece together. Nikephoros Bryennios informs us that Isaac Komnenos was sent to replace the *magistros* Katakalon, who had been serving as *doux* of Antioch since the death of his father, Joseph Tarchaniotes.[29] Joseph seems to have held the position after the death of Chatatourios in 1072, though the date of his own death is not accurately known. Isaac governed in Antioch from 1074 to 1078, so one can presume that Joseph's son, Katakalon, ruled for a year or less.[30] It would appear that the next appointee was Vasak Pahlavuni, the son of Grigor *Magistros* and brother to *Katholikos* Gregory II. Vasak was an intriguing choice and one which may offer some insight into the decision-making of the imperial court. The date of Vasak's term of office is a matter of debate, but what we can infer from his appointment was the awareness of the main threat to Byzantine authority: Philaretos.[31] Vasak came from the Pahlavuni princely house, and it is surprising that such an appointment was made to represent the emperor's interests in the region. It was hoped by the imperial court that Vasak, possibly working with Ablgharib Artsruni, would be able to limit the power of Philaretos and his growing lordship, forming an alliance of resistance alongside his brother the *Katholikos*. Bryennios documents the rising fear of the imperial court of the growing power of Philaretos, with Bryennios specifically describing Philaretos' actions as a revolt indicating that from the perspective of the imperial court his actions were harming imperial authority around Antioch.[32] In any case, the ploy did not yield the results that Constantinople hoped for; Vasak was killed by 'the perfidious Romans' (according to Matthew), while the Doukas faction was to be overthrown a few months later by Nikephoros III Botaneiates.[33] If we are to believe Matthew, Philaretos was to justify his capture of Antioch by seeking to avenge the murder of Vasak, but we will never truly know whether this was an attempt by Philaretos to present himself as the defender of Armenian interests in the region.[34] It is with little doubt that we can view Philaretos' actions as a way of entrenching his position as the dominant warlord among the fractured Armenian polities. Clearly the position and control of Antioch underpinned central authority in the east, and the continuous appointments to the post of *doux* illustrate the perceived value of the city for the Byzantines. The loss of Antioch to Philaretos was a damaging blow to Byzantine claims of authority in the area and, in reality, brought the end of Byzantine control in the region. It is no wonder that control of the city was to become such a contentious issue between Bohemond and Alexios in 1098, as both surely knew that it could be used to create an independent lordship around the Euphrates frontier. We will resume our analysis of the various Armenian lords and princes in the aftermath of Manzikert shortly, but we must briefly return to examine the Turkoman incursions into Anatolia and provide the context for the external pressures that the 'Royal Armenians' were to face in the years immediately after Manzikert.

Many previous works have struggled to paint a coherent and reliable narrative of the decade from Manzikert to the accession of Alexios I Komnenos largely as a result of the inward focus of Byzantine sources on the events that plagued the empire internally. We have already addressed the changing perspective of Michael Attaleiates' *History*, wherein Attaleiates treats the westward encroachment of the Turks as a matter of only secondary concern.[35] From the Muslim perspective we are no better off for clarity. We have already seen that despite later Muslim accounts commenting upon the significance of Manzikert, and the actions of Alp-

Arslan, there is little evidence to suggest that a general order was given for Turkic settlement in north-eastern Anatolia. We can glimpse the later Seljuk perspective from the twelfth-century source of Zahir al-Din Nishapuri for the first Turkoman principalities founded in the immediate aftermath of the battle. According to Nishapuri, Romanos immediately abandoned any effort to keep his part, instead of the treaty allegedly taking 'the road to rebellion and sedition'.[36] It was noted in particular that Romanos did not want to fulfil the financial obligations of the tribute and this was the chief cause of Alp-Arslan's command:

> The amirs are to penetrate deeply into the dominions of Byzantium and as far as every territory which they seize and obtain is concerned, let each one, along with his relations and children have it, and let no one besides him have access to it or control over it.[37]

This later attempt to legitimize the creation of semi-independent lordships across Anatolia must be understood within the geographical context of these Turkic settlements and the twelfth century. Unlike their kin who settled in western Anatolia, or even in Syria, those who settled on the old Byzantine north-eastern frontier never truly abandoned their nomadic ways, nor saw themselves as direct subjects of ruling Seljuk Sultans either in Iraq or from Iconium in Rum.[38] Yet the emirates, as listed by Nishapuri, that were founded in the aftermath of Manzikert did not all come into existence immediately in 1071. Rather, the process by which the north-eastern borderlands, and western Anatolia for that matter, fell into Turkic hands was a more convoluted and drawn-out process. Detailed information of Turkic settlement in north-eastern Anatolia only becomes available a decade later in the mid-1080s. It is entirely possible that the Armenian holdings to the north of the Taurus Mountains offered significant resistance to the various raiding Turkic bands; as we will see later, our sources only document the dispersion of Armenians towards Cilicia with the death of Gagik II. But without solid primary evidence we are very much at a loss for a full explanation of the replacement of the Armenian bloc in Sebasteia and Cappadocia with that of disparate Turkic emirates in the 1070s and 1080s.

The separatism of the Armenian lords

We have already seen that within seven years of Manzikert Byzantine authority on the south-eastern frontier had all but disappeared; in its stead came a series of Armenian lordships that represented the fractured loyalties and political structures in the region. This section will look at the Armenians in two groups. The first will be the 'Royal Armenians', living on their estates which stretched over the four themes of Cappadocia, Charsianon, Sebasteia and Lykandos, whose fate seems to have been tied closely to Gagik of Ani, and sadly much of the information regarding the migration southwards after Gagik's death is lost. The second group were those Armenians operating as imperial agents, serving the Byzantine state as governors or generals along the south-eastern sector of the frontier. These particular Armenians were not in any way a single identifiable group; they all had varying degrees of Byzantine authority in their official positions and some were firmly established in the empire, others recent arrivals. Arguably they could be divided into two subgroups for examination: the Armenians in Cilicia, in contrast to those on the Euphrates frontier. Yet, I believe that they should be treated together to provide the full breadth of the Byzantine-Armenian relationship at the end of the eleventh century.

The 'Royal Armenians'

We last left the 'Royal Armenians' dwelling on their estates among the eastern themes. They were shown to have played only a minor role in the campaigns of Romanos IV and were possibly subject to the emperor's ire on account of rumours circulating of Armenian attacks on Byzantines in the region. The lack of contribution to the campaigns of 1071 resulted in large part from the alienation of the 'Royal Armenians' from the empire, as was most obviously demonstrated by the behaviour of Gagik II of Ani. Gagik allegedly had not only murdered the metropolitan of Caesarea in cold blood but also contacted Alp-Arslan regarding the rule of Ani and Greater Armenia in general, a clear indicator that all was not well.[39] Unfortunately, our information on the actions and conditions of the Armenian estates is severely limited. What we do know with some certainty was that the Danishmend emirate was established in *c.*1084, under an emir called Tanushman taking control of 'Sebasteia, Caesareia, and other regions'.[40] Clearly by 1084 the Armenian estates were no longer intact; so what happened to the 'Royal Armenians'?

In part, they became more active on the local political scene, and our primary evidence starts to document a web of marriage alliances between the various Armenian lords in the region. The daughter of Gagik II married a certain Ablgharib Artsruni, while it is plausible that the daughter of Gagik-Abas was to marry a relatively unknown Armenian soldier called Gabriel.[41] Ablgharib seems to have been a member of the Artsruni house, though we cannot say for certain as to how he was related to the senior line of Senek'erim and his descendants. Ablgharib was a rising star in the region, having recently been given the governorship of Tarsus and Mamistra by Michael VII in 1072, although the claim that this was to counter the rising power of Philaretos is debatable.[42] The use of marriage alliances had certainly strengthened Gagik's position in the east; and we have already seen how Gagik had been able to slot seamlessly into the Armenian community in 1045 by marrying David Artsruni's daughter.[43] It is not far-fetched, therefore, to see these attempts by Gagik as a tried and tested method to bring about some unity among the desperate Armenian lords in the region during the early 1070s.[44]

Yet, the marriage alliances may have indeed been Gagik's downfall. According to the thirteenth-century account of Vardan the situation was far more complicated:

Now the lord of Ani, Gagik, who went to Constantinople, was greatly importuned by Zoe, Theodore's sister, to become a Roman, marry her, and rule over the Greeks.[45] But he did not agree. He made his younger son son-in-law to [Ablgharib], son of Xacik, one of the princes of Vaspurakan, who controlled Missis, Adana, Paparon, and Lampron.[46] But [Ablgharib] hated [Gagik's son] and put him in prison. When his father heard of this, he went to extricate him; but on his return to his lodging the Romans strangled him. So the foul [Ablgharib] killed his son-in-law with poison.[47]

Vardan's history, we must remember, was a compilation from the thirteenth century, and we have other sources that document this event. Gagik, we are told by Matthew, was seized by Byzantine forces at the fortress of Kizistra in the Taurus Mountains, under the command of three brothers, 'sons of Mandale'.[48] Despite a show of force by the Armenian forces of Gagik, and the presence of the Artsruni brothers Atom and Abusahl along with Gagik-Abas II of Kars, they were unable to obtain the king's release.[49] This is the last direct reference to the Artsruni brothers. Their fate after the death of Gagik would have been a similar experience to the migration of many Armenians into the Taurus Mountains, as Turkish emirates gradually seized control of the regions around Sebasteia and Caesarea.[50] We are told briefly by Samuel of Ani that upon Gagik's death, '[t]he other Armenian princes, terrified, fled and dispersed'.[51] These Armenians fled south to Cilicia in particular and cautiously observed the more powerful Armenian lords jostle for position. Gagik was strangled, and his body hung from the ramparts of Kizistra, an event that would become very important in legitimizing later Rubenid rule of Cilicia. Opinion on the role of Philaretos in the death of Gagik of Ani is split in both our primary and secondary sources. Our evidence comes from Matthew of Edessa, who is polemical in his description of Philaretos and clearly blames him for the death of the Armenian king:

> Then the wicked Philaretos sent to them and said 'Why are you afraid of doing anything violent to a King? You will gain nothing by letting him go or by keeping him'.[52]

The information on the exact date of the death of Gagik is scant, causing historians to have widely differing years when it occurred. Matthew of Edessa has it in the year 1079–80, while Vardan does not explicitly date the event.[53] Gagik's death heralded the end of the ruling Bagratid house, and the traditional secular forms of Armenian authority were broken. It is difficult to establish which faction brought around Gagik's death, and Armenian infighting certainly played its part. Ultimately, however, Gagik died at the hand of Byzantine agents, though it was undoubtedly favourable to the Armenian warlords living to the south of the Taurus Mountains. Furthermore, Gagik's murder may have also brought about the collapse of the estates of the 'Royal Armenians' to the north. It is suspected that many of the minor nobles who had settled with the Artsruni, Bagratids or Gagik of Kars began to migrate south into defensive areas in the Taurus Mountains, although our source evidence is limited at best.[54] We are told by Vardan that Ruben, the founder of the Rubenid dynasty that came to create Armenian Cilicia, had allegedly been one of the nobles of King Gagik, though this is one of the rare occurrences of detail relating to the family's history before the settlement in the Taurus Mountains. This is corroborated by Samuel of Ani who mentions 'Prince Rhouben, a relative of Gagic and master of the fort of Cositar, having learned of the death of the king, went to Cilicia and took up residence in the city of Colmesol'.[55] The death of Gagik was a significant event for the Armenians of the east, yet it appears that despite the outpouring of grief in our sources, many of the other Armenian lords went about their business in building separate lordships in the region.

In the previous chapter it was shown that the Armenian princes living in Cappadocia and Sebasteia were not directly involved in the Manzikert campaign, although Armenian troops played a significant role in the battle. It was demonstrated that Gagik apparently refused to answer the summons of the emperor since his involvement in the death of the metropolitan of Caesarea, although Matthew's account seems confused, as Gagik appears to have been at a gathering of the Armenian princes with Romanos at Sebasteia.[56] What effect this lack of contribution from the Armenians had on the success of the Manzikert campaign is not of concern here, though it is clear that loyalty towards the Byzantine state and emperor was no longer evident from the Armenian princes who dominated the political landscape around Sebasteia and Cappadocia. Nevertheless, the Armenian princes were able to maintain some integrity of their lands, fending off Turkic occupation, despite the sack of Sebasteia and Caesarea in 1059 and 1067, respectively.[57] Up to the death of Gagik at the end of the 1070s the Armenians maintained a distant relationship with Constantinople, and the relations between Gagik and imperial agents in the east were complicated, to say the least. It would not be far-fetched to link Gagik's distrust of imperial agents in the east with the events he experienced in Constantinople in 1065.[58] Gagik's murder at the hands of the Byzantines offers at least some reflection on the nature of relations between the two. It is beyond doubt that the imperial centre had little control over the situation in the east and had other issues to deal with closer to home, such as the Pechenegs in the Balkans and rebellious Frankish warlords in Anatolia. The suspicion surrounding Ablgharib of Tarsus and Philaretos over their role in Gagik's murder further illustrates the isolation of Gagik and the Armenians to the north of the Taurus Mountains from their neighbours to the south, and it is not unreasonable therefore to assume that Gagik viewed himself as independent from Byzantium in every way.[59] Some secondary sources maintain that Gagik was put to death on Byzantine orders, even citing Matthew as evidence, although no such reference occurs in Matthew's account; he only stipulates that he died at the hands of the Romans who controlled the fortress of Kizistra.[60] Nevertheless, Gagik's death was certainly a point of divergence for the Armenians living in eastern Cappadocia; whatever the exact nature was of Gagik's political influence in exile, his murder heralded the end of Bagratuni Armenia.[61]

That is not to say that the Armenians themselves ended as an observable entity. Our leading narrative source Matthew was well aware of the events in his lifetime such as the rising power of the Rubenid dynasty in Cilicia, which in Matthew's adulthood maintained quasi-independence from the resurgent Byzantium under the Komnenian dynasty. While Gagik's death was an important setback to Armenian unity in the north, the king was not the sole embodiment of Armenian separatism, as the actions of the Rubenids and Philaretos and his lieutenants were to show in the coming decades.

The 'imperial agents': Philaretos Brachamios and others

The death of Gagik did not directly spell a period of dramatic change for the Byzantine-Armenians living on the south-eastern frontier. In fact, the seeds of separatism had already produced a variety of quasi-independent Armenian lordships in Cilicia and around the upper Euphrates, most holding little attachment to the exiled king. The most prominent of these lordships was ruled by Philaretos Brachamios, a former commander in the Byzantine army who took full advantage of the political vacuum that developed after 1072 to forge his own domain. The details we can gain from our primary sources on the foundations of Philaretos' lordship is both vague and sparse, such as the narrative from Attaleiates:

> Assembling a multitude of Armenians and men of different origins, [Philaretos] created for himself a battle-worthy force and had resisted the previous emperor's (Michael VII) attempts to subdue him, arranging matters for himself as he saw fit.[62]

There is little doubt over how Philaretos was perceived by the regime of Michael VII Doukas; he had been a loyal lieutenant of Romanos IV and now was a rebel.[63] The sentiment was most likely mutual, as Philaretos never seems to have recognized the authority of Michael VII, nor his court and its appointments. Yet, there are still questions surrounding the level of support that Philaretos offered Romanos in his conflict with the Doukas faction; what our evidence seems to suggest is that he withdrew to the environs of Marash where he began to consolidate his own power base.[64] Through the early 1070s there is little evidence to suggest that Philaretos sought any legitimacy from the new regime in Constantinople. Instead he seems to have focused on consolidating and then expanding his authority over the Byzantine-Armenian lords who held control over several important urban centres, such as Melitene, Lykandos and Tarsus, yet Philaretos was not the only potentate in the region accumulating power.[65] We have seen earlier that Ablgharib Artsruni had been appointed the governor of Tarsus and Mamistra in 1072 by the regime of Michael VII, although he, too, was to pay little attention to the tribulations of the imperial court. In fact, Ablgharib began to sponsor other Armenian lords in Cilicia, such as Oshin, a member of the Hetumid family. The origin and identity of Oshin are difficult to establish but worth exploration. It is distinctly possible that the figures identified by the names of Oshin/Ursinus/Aspietes, three names given by our primary sources, are actually all the same individual. Indeed, they were all described as Armenian in some form, were active warlords who survived in the

Taurus Mountains and participated in the affairs of the region for some time.⁶⁶ Nevertheless, the individual called Oshin seems to have emigrated into Cilicia in 1072, abandoning his ancestral lands in eastern Armenian 'Mairiats-Dchourk, near Gantzac', as noted by Samuel of Ani, which means that he came from outside of the Byzantine-Armenian circle that dominated the geopolitical landscape in this time frame.⁶⁷ Upon arriving in Cilicia Oshin either established the fortress of Lampron or was given it by Ablgharib to rule over; we cannot say for certain which is true; either is possible. Samuel of Ani's account has Oshin taking the land from the Saracens, thus associating him with the heroic deeds of the legendary Armenian figure David of Sassoun.⁶⁸ Yet, as noted by Der Nersessian, the Armenian sources with closer proximity to Oshin and the Hetumids describe him as a faithful servant of Ablgharib who was given Lampron to guard on behalf of Ablgharib.⁶⁹ Either way, Oshin was to embody one of the many minor Armenian lords active in the region whose descendants were to become major players in the foundation of Armenian Cilicia in the twelfth century. Yet, neither Oshin nor Ablgharib was able to challenge Philaretos' primacy among the Armenians throughout the mid-1070s, despite some claims of a possible conflict between Ablgharib and Philaretos in 1078. While the two warlords certainly represented two different camps within the wider Armenian community, the claims by certain commentators that Ablgharib represented the 'Doukas faction' while Philaretos represented the 'Diogenes faction' are far-fetched.⁷⁰ The two may have been rivals at one time, but the claim that they were somehow representative of two competing Byzantine interests is not borne out by our evidence.⁷¹ Indeed, while it is true that Ablgharib held a series of Byzantine titles and controlled several former 'imperial cities' in the 1070s, there is little evidence that Ablgharib, or for that matter Philaretos, was acting on behalf of the emperor or with Byzantine resources.

Yet we must try to construct an accurate timeline of the various Byzantine titles Philaretos was given and evaluate what this tells us about the Byzantine-Armenian relationship as a whole.⁷² The account of Attaleiates only refers to Philaretos as a soldier at this point, calling him στρατιωτικὴν in his narrative, with Skylitzes Continuatus offering στρατηγός αὐτοκράτωρ.⁷³ Yet the lead seal evidence that most likely dates to before Michael VII came to the throne in 1071 has Philaretos holding at certain points the positions of *taxiarches* and then *protospatharios* and *topoteretes* of the *tagmata* from Cappadocia. Cheynet has suggested that at this point in his career he may have met Romanos IV before he became emperor.⁷⁴ From 1068 his career of office holding increased exponentially as he acquired the dignities of *magistros*, *doux*, *kouropalates* and *domestikos ton scholon* (of the east).⁷⁵ One cannot be entirely reliant on the accuracy of the seal dating; indeed, many of the more senior titles are only reported in our literary sources at a much later date. It is clear that Philaretos owed his original position of power to the patronage of Romanos IV, serving directly under the emperor in 1069, and it is possible that in 1070 he received the rank of *kouropalates* and the title of *doux* (one must ignore the claim by Anna Komnene that Philaretos received the office of *domestikos* from Romanos which was a much later promotion).⁷⁶ In Attaleiates' account, Philaretos is only associated with the title of *kouropalates* after he declared his submission and loyalty to the Emperor Nikephoros III Botaneiates in 1078 and the office of *doux* was most likely a reflection of Philaretos' control of Antioch. The image of Philaretos as a loyal and respectful lieutenant of the new emperor is nothing more than fanciful.[77] Philaretos was to receive the highest of dignities as his career peaked, holding the ranks of *protokoropalates*, *sebastos*, then *protosebastos*, which were followed by his promotion in offices through to the *domestikos* of the east.[78] These titles do indeed highlight an element of Byzantine interaction with the Armenian lordships on the eastern frontier, but they do not in any way change the character of Philaretos' loyalties and actions.[79] Rather, the titles granted to Philaretos reveal only that the imperial court wanted to appear active in the region. It does not in any way reflect Byzantine control over these individuals or the region itself, especially after Antioch fell to Philaretos in 1078. Byzantine influence had become a mere shadow of its former self.

So how was Philaretos able to expand his control over the region of Cilicia and northern Syria at the expense of Byzantine governors still present in certain cities during the 1070s? Attaleiates states that Philaretos was able to bring 'imperial cities under his power', although sadly does not specify which cities and when this occurred, and it is unlikely that he was able to immediately seize the aforementioned important cities on the south-eastern frontier.[80] Whatever Philaretos' official title was before Manzikert, there is no doubt that his power and influence came through his military command, whether merited or not.[81] Indeed, his preference for having the icon of Saint Theodore, the patron saint of the eastern armies, reinforces the relationship Philaretos had with the military.[82] Yet the authority he wielded in the early 1070s is hard to reconstruct, certainly in comparison with the other Byzantine-Armenian imperial agents in the area such as Ablgharib Artsruni in Tarsus. Matthew of Edessa noted Philaretos' first base of operations was a town called Msher (Marash), which is to the south-east of Melitene; this could also be the area in which he was stationed by Romanos IV for the purpose of defeating Turkic raids.[83] So it would seem that at first Philaretos was willing to use his imperial authority to rally the support of his immediate neighbours to his cause, though it is highly doubtful that he was acting to protect the integrity of the empire in the region, as suggested by Michael the Syrian.

Indeed, the case of Edessa, and how it came under the sway of Philaretos, helps us better understand the motives behind the expansion of the lordship. Let us look at Matthew's account in full:

> In this period (1077/78) Basil,[84] the son of Abukab[85] [who was] formerly the tent keeper of David [III of Tao] the *Kouropalates,* at the behest of Philaretos collected a cavalry force and went against the city of Edessa. For six months he harassed the city with many assaults. In this same year Basil repaired the ramparts of the fortress-town of Romanopolis which the Roman emperor Romanus had built. After this he once again harassed the city of Edessa. Then the townspeople became stirred up against their dux, who was called Leon and who was the brother of Dawatanos, and so this Leon fled and took refuge in the upper citadel. In the meantime the dux's proximus took refuge in the Church

of the Holy Theotokos, entering the sanctuary and tightly holding on to the edges of the altar. However, the townspeople entered the church and savagely killed the *proximus* right in front of the altar of God. So on that very day Edessa was delivered into the hands of Basil, the son of Abukab; he was a benevolent and pious man, compassionate towards orphans and widows, and a benefactor and conciliator of people. Basil's father Abukab had formerly resided in Edessa and during his time had built up and organized the city and its surrounding territory.[86]

Matthew clearly suggests that Basil was sent on the orders of Philaretos to bring the city under his control, and with a small force Basil was able to gain the support of the townspeople to overthrow the *doux* Leon, an official who had some relationship with Byzantium. There is little evidence of the origins of this Basil. He is said to have been the son of the former tent keeper of David III of Tao, putting him at best in late middle age, which may also suggest he was of Iberian stock and therefore Chalcedonian in practice, although the absence of polemic insults from Matthew is intriguing.[87] The actions of Basil, on behalf of Philaretos, highlight how far the level of imperial authority had diminished in the region – so much so that Philaretos had no need to fear reprisals from Constantinople for annexing territory that was held by an imperially appointed official. Basil gains high praise from Matthew as 'a benevolent and pious man' and it is in all probability that Matthew had oral testimony to rely on for Basil's reputation. The relationship between Basil and Philaretos is hard to judge, but we can gain further insight from the information given surrounding his death and succession in 1083/4. Basil's successor was a man named Sarkis, apparently elected by the assembled population in the cathedral of the city, holding the title of *doux*; it is more likely that this had become the customary title of the ruler of the city, rather than representing a direct appointment from Constantinople at this juncture.[88] After six months the aristocracy launched a coup led by a man named by Matthew as Ishkhan.[89] The aristocratic party offered control of the city to Philaretos, who readily accepted, and had all those involved in the struggle blinded, with Matthew recounting the gruesome demise of the leaders and imprisonment of many of the leading men of the city in Philaretos' capital of Marash.[90] The one thing that the aristocratic rebellion can tell us is that Sarkis did not see Edessa as any sort of 'fief' from Philaretos, and so questions arise over the nature of the previous relationship between Philaretos and Basil. While we do not have firm evidence to give us any accurate detail, it would appear more than likely that Philaretos did not have the military capabilities to rule over his lordship by another force, especially on the eastern fringes of his lands on the Euphrates. The fact that Ishkhan handed the command of the city over to Philaretos in 1083/4 tells us with some certainty that Philaretos did not control the city directly or indirectly through a vassal. In any case, Philaretos' rule over Edessa did not last for long, as his lordship was being squeezed by the various Turkic factions both from Syria and Anatolia – something that we will return to shortly.

In general terms we can see that by ignoring Byzantine authority during the reign of Michael VII Doukas and gaining the support of the local Armenian and Syrian aristocracy, whether through alliance or force, Philaretos' lordship arose within a geopolitical vacuum and came to occupy much of the old south-western frontier.[91] Philaretos' success was not down to greatness, nor exceptional military ability: his underlying strength was his ability to harness the support of the most populous identifiable group in the region, the Armenians. We have already seen that Armenians had been used to repopulate cities that were retaken by the Byzantines during the age of reconquest. This policy was still in force during the campaigns of Romanos IV. For example, in 1068 during Romanos' first campaign to the east the emperor besieged and captured the town of Hierapolis in Syria, an important strategic foothold located to the north-east of Aleppo. We are informed that the town was placed under the governorship of an Armenian called Pharasmanios Apokapes and designated to be a new Armenian settlement.[92] Philaretos was to exploit these very Armenians who had only recently been settled in the region by using both Byzantine and Armenian concepts to enhance his legitimacy in the region. From the Byzantine perspective, Philaretos allied himself with various remnants of imperial officers and agents, eventually holding prominent Byzantine titles that only really served to legitimize his rule, while from the Armenian perspective, Philaretos' main aim was to present himself as the guardian of Armenian interests, specifically the secular protector of the Armenian *Katholikos*. These two constructs were masterfully adapted to the needs of Philaretos, and by 1080 he was at the peak of his powers. The lordship he had created now stretched across a sizeable area in northern Syria and Cilicia, occupying major strongholds and holding its own against neighbouring foreign entities.

Arguably, Philaretos' lordship could only last as long as the various powers around him were distracted elsewhere, and by the early 1080s the Muslim powers converged on his principality. The main Muslim threat to Philaretos' domain was the lordship of Sulayman b. Qutlumush, based between Nicaea and Iconium. Sulayman was a Turkic warlord who had successfully and pragmatically involved himself in Byzantine internal affairs throughout the 1070s. While at first operating as an ally providing auxiliary forces to Nikephoros III, by 1081 the new emperor Alexios I Komnenos was forced to agree to a treaty with Sulayman, the first of its kind enshrining Byzantine recognition of a Turkic entity existing within the confines of the empire.[93] After the treaty, we hear no more from any source on Sulayman's activities until November 1084 when he departed from his base in Bithynia for his campaign into Cilicia towards Antioch, this, incidentally, being the first mention of Sulayman in most Muslim chronicles.[94] It is with great difficulty that one can reconstruct the genuine motivation for Sulayman's intervention in Cilicia and northern Syria, as the perception of our Muslim accounts that depict Sulayman as exerting his authority as a loyal subject of Malik-Shah most likely represents later political thought.[95] Sulayman appears to have already started campaigning in Cilicia in 1082/3, capturing Tarsus (possibly from Oshin of Lampron) and other towns:

Sulayman b. Qutlumush conquered Nīqīyā, which is a town on the coast and resembles Antākiya, as well as places in its vicinity, such as Tarsus, Adhana, Massīsa (Mamistra), and 'Aynzarba (Anazarbos).[96]

The capture of these settlements is also recorded in the chronicles of al-'Azīmī and Michael the Syrian, the former dating the events to 1083/4 and the latter attributing the conquests to Malik-Shah's Syrian campaign.[97] Yet, the claim by some modern scholars that Sulayman was recovering former imperial territories on behalf of Byzantium appears a little far-fetched. As we have seen, neither Ablgharib nor Oshin held any distinct loyalty to Byzantium in the 1070s, let alone nearly a decade later. Turning to the capture of Antioch itself, both our Byzantine and Muslim sources indicate an element of factionalism within the ruling elites in Philaretos' lordship. The Muslim accounts talk of Philaretos imprisoning his son in Antioch, and so when Philaretos ventured to Edessa to take control of the city in late 1084, the unnamed son contacted Sulayman inviting him to take the city. The Byzantine account of Anna documents the dismay at Philaretos' apparent conversion to Islam in order to hold his lands as a fief of Malik-Shah. Like the Muslim sources, Anna's account has Philaretos' son as the main agent who brings about the intervention of Sulayman, and despite local resistance in Antioch itself, Philaretos' rule over Antioch was brought to an end.[98]

Philaretos' relationship with his Muslim neighbours was as complex as his relationship with Byzantium. One example of this relationship was his interaction with the governor of Mosul, Sharaf al-Dawla Muslim ibn Quraysh, who held power in neighbouring Aleppo. According to our Muslim sources, Philaretos had been paying tribute to Sharaf al-Dawla, although we do not know when this practice began.[99] Ibn al-Athīr's account only relays this information when Sharad al-Dawla demanded the same tribute from the new ruler of Antioch, Sulayman. What the nature of this tribute signifies is that by the end of Philaretos' career he owed his position more to the neighbouring Muslim powers than he did to Byzantium. In any case, Philaretos' control was faltering, and with the fall of Antioch in 1084, Philaretos attempted to preserve what was left of his lordship by paying direct homage to the Seljuk Sultan Malik-Shah. This did not end well for Philaretos, for apparently the Sultan dismissed Philaretos from his court when he learned of the capture of Antioch and Edessa.[100] Edessa does not seem to have fallen to external force but rather to another coup by the factions inside the city. We are told that when Philaretos journeyed to Malik-Shah's court to pay homage, he left 'an illustrious Roman official', an unnamed eunuch bearing the title of *parakoimomenos*. Although Matthew of Edessa's account is full of praise for the eunuch's character, his opinion was not shared universally, and one of Philaretos' officers named Parsama murdered the eunuch while at prayers and assumed control of the city.[101] It is this event that, Matthew suggests, brought about the final destruction of Philaretos, who is said to have converted to Islam in an attempt to hold on to a mere fraction of his lordship. This desperate gamble may ultimately have failed, as Michael the Syrian recounts: 'He went to Maras[h], where he died. It is said that before dying he was again a Christian.'[102] As for Edessa, Malik-Shah was to send the emir Buzan to conquer the city which he accomplished after a three-month siege.[103]

The exploits of Philaretos Brachamios clearly accelerated the disintegration of Byzantine authority in the 1070s. Although some commentators see 1078 as the year that he returned to the imperial fold, Philaretos' actions up until the mid-1080s offer little evidence that he was operating as a Byzantine agent on the old south-eastern frontier. Indeed, Philaretos was nothing more than a separatist warlord who engaged with both the Byzantine and Muslim political structures to prolong his lordship. In the end he failed, and his territory was carved up by the expanding Turkic warlords in northern Syria and Anatolia, respectively. Yet before any conclusions can be reached on the state of the Byzantine-Armenian relationship it is necessary to assess how several other Armenian lords in the area maintained their autonomy up until the arrival of the First Crusade. The focus will fall on three particular areas: Melitene, Kesoun and Edessa with their respective lords Gabriel, Kogh Vasil and T'oros, all of whom interacted closely with the participants of the First Crusade and had a prior relationship with the Byzantine Empire.

The Armenian Church

A significant factor in the developments in Asia Minor in this period was the situation of the Armenian Church. We have seen consistently through our primary evidence that the Armenian ecclesiastical writers placed great emphasis on the religious aspect of their identity, seeing it as the guiding principle of being an Armenian, particularly when surrounded by either Chalcedonian or Muslim powers that potentially threatened the existence of the Apostolic Church. It is thus surprising that in this period of fractured political unity among the Armenians the great 'vehicle' of identity did not play a more prominent part in holding the Armenian communities together. In fact, to view adherence to the Apostolic Church as 'a vehicle of ethnic cohesion', or certainly the overemphasis placed by certain commentators on these aspects, has clouded our understanding.[104] In this section then, a new perspective will be offered. It will be argued that it is no coincidence that at the very same time as the fracturing of political unity occurred for the Armenian lords in the region, they suffered a division in ecclesiastical leadership, several co-*Katholikoi* existing at the same time. This was partially brought about not only by the need for legitimacy of many of the lords – particularly Philaretos – but also by the personal choices of the *Katholikos* Gregory II.[105]

In the mid-eleventh century we saw that religious tensions and threats of forced conversion fuelled the alienation of the Armenians from the Byzantine Empire, and this was evident in two particular areas. First, the geographical proximity of the lands granted to the exiled princes in Cappadocia and Sebasteia allowed the continuation of Armenian religious practices and the expansion of the Armenian Church through the formation of new bishoprics in various urban centres and the foundation of new religious houses by the exiled 'Royal Armenians' on their estates. Second, the intent of the imperial centre to bring about religious assimilation and union in the 1050s and 1060s created considerable animosity between the two groups, although the extent to which this was a dominant factor is highly questionable.[106] We have already seen that it has often been claimed that the main division between the Byzantines and the Armenians, that is, 'the vehicle of separatism', was religious conflict, but again one cannot condone the application of this simplistic characterization of the Byzantine-Armenian relationship in the period 1071–98. Indeed, the complexities can be seen in the case of Philaretos Brachamios, where we will survey and analyse the interactions between Armenians of different confessions: between those who followed the Apostolic Church and those who had converted to the Chalcedonian Church of Constantinople. This, too, will reveal that the differences were not as drastic as they have been made out to be; this involves challenging the religiously charged polemical language of our primary sources, most of which were authored by churchmen who saw the actions through a strongly religious lens.

The leadership of the Armenian Apostolic Church, headed by the *Katholikos*, underwent significant strain in this period as competing political powers attempted to control the church by having the *Katholikos* reside within their lands. The death of Gagik II of Ani ended the Bagratid line of kings and left the Armenians in need of a new figurehead. It would be natural to assume that the fiercely independent Church of the Armenians would be able to provide such a figure; the political actions of the competing powers on the eastern frontier, however, prevented this from becoming reality. While by the turn of the twelfth century the *Katholicate* started to resemble a hereditary monarchy, the fragmentation of ecclesiastical authority in the preceding decades effectively made unity under the heir of St Gregory nigh impossible.

The *Katholikos* Gregory II, whose pontificate officially stretched from 1066 to 1105, was a member of the Pahlavuni family and son of Grigor *Magistros*.[107] It was to be Gregory who threw the leadership of the Armenian Church into confusion at the time it was most needed, for he decided in 1070 to take up the monastic calling for a solitary life dedicated to prayer. Gregory, with his secretary George, planned to journey to Rome and then through the Egyptian desert. He informed a meeting of the secular Armenian powers of his decision, and despite their protestations Gregory was resolved to leave the patriarchal see.[108] Interestingly, the election of the *Katholikos* was decided by the secular, not ecclesiastical, powers. This was also true of the election of Gregory himself in 1066, when he was encouraged to stand by Gagik of Ani.[109] But Matthew informs us that Gregory said directly to Gagik:

> Appoint anyone you wish as catholicos, but do not hinder me from the road of righteousness.[110]

Gagik and the princes then decided to go behind Gregory's back and asked George, the secretary of the *Katholikos*, to take the patriarchal see, to which George readily agreed. This was to begin a fractious relationship between Gregory and George, which Matthew describes as a deep hostility, which was to resurface roughly three years later.[111] The influence of the secular powers over the leadership of the church was related to the importance of religious affiliation to Armenian identity. Yet, as we will see, the death of Gagik and the shattering of the political leadership of the Armenian community in the east was to provide a change in protocol for the selection of the *Katholikos*.

Gregory seems to have never departed on his trip to Rome, and despite his express desire for the pursuit of an ascetic life in 1072/3, we are told by Matthew that he successfully deposed George, who 'deeply hurt, went to the city of Tarsus, where he died'.[112] Gregory went to live in a place called Mutarasun, near Kesoun to the south-west of Melitene.[113] In this instance, it would appear that the secular Armenian powers were not called upon to adjudicate in the dispute between the two *Katholikoi*. Matthew saw them both as *Katholikos*, which would indicate that the appointment of George as his replacement forced Gregory to stay and dispute this decision. We sadly have no further information on how Gregory was able to regain the position he had renounced, but one can speculate that his noble heritage and precedence helped in his recovery of his seat. What is strangest of all is that Gregory in this instance rejected the possibility of two sharing the patriarchal see, and yet his actions only a short while later seem to reveal a change of heart.

As Philaretos started to expand and consolidate the lands around his base at Marash, his quest for legitimacy became more prominent in his dealings with the Armenian Church. Despite Gagik II still ruling to the north of the Taurus Mountains, Philaretos demanded that Gregory reside somewhere in his lands, though Matthew does not specify exactly where. Gregory refused the summons but replied to Philaretos:

> I authorize you to put his lordship Sargis, the nephew of his lordship Peter [1019–58], on the patriarchal see.[114]

This was a very unusual instruction in the light of the opposition that Gregory had previously voiced to the appointment of George in 1070, and that he was now willing to offer an alternative candidate to meet the demands of Philaretos. It appears that Gregory did not view this as his resignation from the patriarchal see, something that Yarnley accepts at face value, as his actions over the coming years were still those of the leader of the Armenian Church.[115] Furthermore, we see that Gregory saw it as his right to suggest a fellow co-*Katholikos* and not to seek approval from Gagik or any secular lords that had put his predecessor and himself on the patriarchal throne. In the case of Sargis, Philaretos, we are told, summoned 'an assembly of bishops, abbots, and monks' to come together in order to confirm Sargis' appointment.[116] Here we have a divergence from the protocol observed in the confirmations of Khachik and Gregory, in the election of a new *Katholikos*. It is unlikely that Philaretos felt strongly about this, as is suggested, not only by his strong-armed actions towards the church but also the confessional differences he had with the Apostolic Church, as we are informed that Philaretos 'professed the Roman faith', that is, a Chalcedonian.[117] In any case Philaretos had been able to achieve control over an Armenian religious leader, something he presumed would bring about the loyalty of his numerous Armenian subjects. Yet Sargis' pontificate was not to last long, for he died possibly only a year after his elevation to the seat of St Gregory. Matthew tells us that Philaretos nominated as his successor a man called Theodore Alakhosik.[118] Theodore dwelt in the town of Honi where Sargis had previously resided, but as a result of the fluidity of the political landscape, Honi was captured by a Turkic emir, whose name is only given in Armenian – Polchtachi according to Matthew and 'Bouldadji according to Yarnley.[119] Philaretos wrote to Theodore asking him to settle in Marash, the de facto capital of Philaretos' domain, but Theodore was unable to leave because of his new Turkish masters. Philaretos was unperturbed and resolved to create yet another *Katholikos* whom he could control. At first he turned to the archbishop of the monastery of the Holy Icon of the Virgin Mary, a man named John, who refused the offer, so instead a man by the name of Paul, the superior of the monastery of the Holy Cross of Varag, was consecrated by an assembly of bishops and abbots.[120] Matthew viewed these events as solely motivated by the 'iniquitous and malicious behaviour' of Philaretos, which despite the emotive language used is largely accurate, based upon the precedent set by Philaretos in the consecration of Sargis two years before. This event has two particular points of interest. First, Gregory II was not consulted for his approval, though this could be explained by Gregory's residence in Egypt at the time. Second, it shows that Philaretos took the religious recognition of his rule seriously, for he was positioning himself as the defender and leader of the Armenians in the east, and in order to maintain the loyalty of his subjects he needed control of a *Katholikos* to legitimate his rule.

We are also informed that Gregory II went to Armenia and consecrated his nephew Parsegh as bishop of Ani, an important position in the old royal capital.[121] Here we encounter a disjointed and confusing narrative provided by Matthew, who suggests that Parsegh was to claim the patriarchal see in Armenia in 1081/2 with the support of the Armenian king of Lori, Gurgen-Kvirike II (1048–89). Gregory, on the other hand, finally departed on his planned journey, visiting Rome and eventually Egypt where he was to establish his patriarchal residence. After some time, sadly not specified by Matthew, he consecrated his nephew, also called Gregory (Gregory III, 1113–66), as *Katholikos* and returned to Armenia. Matthew seems here to have been confused with what exactly Gregory II had bestowed upon his nephew. It would seem that he actually nominated Gregory III as a successor to the patriarchal see, rather than creating yet another *Katholikos* that could potentially undermine his authority or split the leadership of the Armenian Church even further.

It is clear that the leadership of the Armenian Church had fragmented on an unprecedented scale, with even Matthew lamenting on the dissension within his own Church:

> the holy see was not governed according to the will of God or individual merit or even free election, but according to the principles of violence, power politics, and manipulation of high offices.[122]

Matthew clearly saw the actions of Philaretos as exceptionally damaging in the division of the *Katholicate*, but the seeds of this development were first sown with the transferral of the *Katholikos* Peter I to the lands of the Artsruni princes in Sebasteia in 1049. The Armenian patriarchal see remained in geographical proximity to the exiled king Gagik II of Ani for protection from the Byzantines who had attempted to subordinate the Armenian Church to Constantinople. Peter's immediate successors in turn were selected and remained attached to the Armenian population that was now dominant in Cappadocia and Sebasteia. The relationship between the exiled princely houses of Armenia and the *Katholikos* grew closer, and as mentioned before, the secular powers held sway over the election process to the seat of St Gregory. Matthew's last reference to the secular influence over the position of *Katholikos* comes in 1070 with the attempted resignation of Gregory II, and it was the body of secular princes who created the first division in the highest office of the church. Despite Matthew garbling his narrative, it is clear that Gregory never accepted the decision on his replacement, and here one can witness a resurgence of the church handling the appointment of *Katholikos* directly, or more accurately, Gregory intentionally consecrating successors personally. Consequently, the rising power of Philaretos and his desire to exercise control over the *Katholikos* seriously harmed the leadership of the Armenian Church, with Gregory allowing others to share in the office of *Katholikos*. This was further compounded by the fluctuating borders of Philaretos' domain that in turn created yet more *Katholikoi*. Matthew's account can, however, be misleading. Parsegh of Ani and Gregory III of Egypt, respectively, should be seen as designated successors, rather than co-*Katholikoi* to Gregory II.[123] Matthew claims that Gregory's see was divided into four: Vahram (Gregory III) in Egypt, Theodore in Honi, Parsegh in Ani and Paul in Marash, yet all of these were acknowledged/appointed by Gregory, therefore the fault for any division lay with Gregory.[124]

The division of ecclesiastical leadership as seen here is remarkably similar to the fractured geopolitical scenario that many Armenians were living through on the south-eastern frontier in the 1070s and 1080s. While the church did not provide the vehicle of separatism for the Armenians, it certainly played an important role in the varying claims for legitimacy from the Armenian lordships in the region. We will see that in the aftermath of Philaretos' fall many of his lieutenants who held on to local power bases continued to tussle over the role of the church's guardian. But one must not forget that although the Armenian Church was an integral part of medieval Armenian identity, not all the major players were Miaphysite in belief. For example, the lord Oshin of Lampron has been identified as Orthodox in faith by secondary sources, although this in reality highlights how the mistaken merging of him with other warlords in the region has led to the wrong conclusion. Oshin came from the heart of eastern Armenia, and there is no primary evidence to suggest that he was anything but Miaphysite. The religious beliefs held by Philaretos' former lieutenants, as we will see shortly, have been a major point of discussion. Even when considering the religious confession of Armenians like Oshin, Gabriel or Ablgharib there seems to be no direct link between religious antagonism and the destruction of the Byzantine-Armenian relationship. It is clear, after all, that the religious preferences of the Byzantine-Armenian lords did not shape their ultimate goal – survival.

From Philaretos to the First Crusade (1086–98)

The collapse of Philaretos Brachamios' lordship in c.1086 heralded a new period for the Armenians living in Cilicia and northern Syria. Unlike Gagik's death in the decade before, Philaretos' fall from power shattered the remnants of any unity within the Armenian communities. The period from 1086 to 1098 was a turbulent time; having lost secure leadership in both the secular and ecclesiastical spheres the Armenian lords had to tread a careful line. The reason why no new Armenian lord had taken the places of Philaretos is quite simple: the surrounding Turkic powers, under the suzerainty of Malik-Shah, were now more able to interfere with regional politics than they had been during the previous decade. And yet, after Malik-Shah's death in 1092 Turkic unity was as fragile as that of the Armenians, something that in many ways allowed the various Armenian lordships to last until to the advent of the First Crusade.[125] In this respect, Philaretos' career was to cast a long shadow, as many of his former lieutenants scratched out an existence either as independent or Seljuk-approved rulers in forts and cities across the region. It is in this section that we will try and trace the various individuals and assess their relationship with the Byzantine Empire. Many of these Armenian lords had served under Philaretos in some capacity. Gabriel of Melitene had been installed as governor of the city by Philaretos and was able to continue to rule the area independently from 1085/6 up to the establishment of the Latin states in Antioch and Edessa.[126] Kogh Vasil (Basil the Crafty) held Kesoun, although there are questions as to whether he seized the city before or after Philaretos' death.[127] He, too, was able to hold on to his lordship until his death in 1112.[128] The situation in Edessa was a little more complicated. By the mid-1090s an Armenian by the name of T'oros had established himself as the leading magnate in the city. There were some, however, who had not served under Philaretos, such as warlords Oshin and Rupen. These various Armenian lords allow us to assess the extent of Byzantine influence in the region and how they engaged with their former imperial overlords. Let us take a look at each of these men in turn.

We know very little about Gabriel of Melitene's origins, despite his prominent role in the foundation of the royal family of Jerusalem when he arranged for his daughter Morphia to marry Baldwin of Bourcq, who not only succeeded his uncle as the second Count of Edessa but later became king of Jerusalem in 1118.[129] But it is his career before the First Crusade that we are most interested in. We are informed by Michael the Syrian that Gabriel had been placed in command of Melitene by Philaretos and continued his rule over the city after the death of his former master.[130] Our sources tell us that Gabriel sought to protect his domain by sending his wife to the Caliph in Baghdad to gain an edict ensuring his position in the new geopolitical climate. Michael the Syrian neatly summarizes the collapse of Byzantine authority in the region:

> When Philardus died, Gabriel reigned [in Melitene]; and when he saw that the Turks had defeated the Greeks he sent his wife to Baghdad, and she brought him from the caliph of Taiyaye, an edict which granted him the principality of Melitene.[131]

While we do not have confirmation whether this was successful, the fact that he held his position in 1097 indicates some sort of agreement had been made. The mission led by Gabriel's wife is extremely important for measuring the extent of Byzantine authority in the region and Gabriel's own political loyalties. We know from seal evidence that Gabriel held the title of δούξ σεβαστός, while also being recognized as *protokouropalates* which certainly shows that the distribution of Byzantine court titles was still continuing in the east but cannot be used to assert loyalty to Byzantium on Gabriel's part.[132] Rather, what we witness here is similar to the final years of Philaretos' rule, Gabriel seeking legitimacy from the two major powers in the region, the Seljuk court in Baghdad and the Byzantine court in Constantinople. The acceptance of Byzantine titles in fact tells us far more about what the court of Alexios was trying to achieve than informing us regarding Gabriel's political loyalties. As we will see with other Armenian magnates in the region, the distribution of titles was seen as part and parcel of Byzantine political posturing, but it does not illustrate the continuity of Byzantine influence in the region beyond that of a mere façade.

Yet, from our sources we gain a picture of Gabriel being the most 'Byzantine' of the Armenian lords in the region, not only for his previous career in the Byzantine army and as holder of Byzantine titles but also for his religious confession. Michael the Syrian saw Gabriel as a Greek, however, most likely stemming from his religious profession. But one should be careful not to overemphasize this considering the context of the author.[133] Our other sources shed some light on this. Albert of Aachen saw Gabriel as primarily Armenian, while William of Tyre described him as 'Armenian by birth, language, and habit, but Greek in faith'.[134] When one considers Gabriel's daughter, Morphia, she, too, was identified as an Armenian but also practised the Chalcedonian rite, thereby suggesting that her father had either partly assimilated or was a second-/third-generation migrant whose parents or grandparents had adopted the Chalcedonian rite.[135] What we have here is a clear lack of uniformity from our primary sources in identifying certain characteristics of Gabriel. What our sources do agree on is that Gabriel belonged to the Byzantine-Armenian society that had existed before its collapse in the 1070s. Yet none describe Gabriel as operating as a Byzantine agent in the region by the time of the arrival of the First Crusade. In reality, Gabriel was just one of many quasi-independent Armenian lords in the region, carefully playing the major powers off against each other, in order to preserve his control of his lordship that consisted of Melitene and its immediate environs. What his career before the arrival of the First Crusade shows us is that he was no longer attached the Byzantine Empire, acting as independently as possible in the volatile geopolitical climate of the late 1090s.

We left Edessa in the hands of the Turkish warlord Buzan who ruled over the city until his death in 1094/5, falling in battle against Sultan Tutush of Damascus.[136]

We are told by Matthew that '[w]hen the sultan arrived in Edessa, he appointed the Roman official T'oros, the son of Het'um, as the city's commander', while Ibn al-Athīr records that '[a] Greek, called the *curopalates*, was there, who 'farmed' the town for Buzan'.[137] In any event, T'oros' takeover and rule of Edessa were an oddity in a Turkish-dominated political scene. Indeed, most of our information on T'oros of Edessa comes from the account of Matthew who must have been able to tap into the oral testimony of his fellow citizens who witnessed the events at first-hand. While it would appear at first glance that T'oros' name should be a useful indicator as to his identity, T'oros is simply the Armenian of Theodoros, by which name he is referred to in Michael the Syrian's account.[138] From what we know of his background, T'oros had previously ruled over Melitene, before moving on to Edessa, and was married to another daughter of Gabriel of Melitene, who, as discussed earlier, was most likely of the Chalcedonian confession.[139] Yet, T'oros' religious affiliation is not mentioned by Matthew, and this silence offers reasonable doubt that T'oros was Chalcedonian. One can observe the polemical language utilized by Matthew to describe Armenians who followed the Chalcedonian confession, namely Philaretos, and his silence on the matter carries some weight. Fulcher of Chartres regarded T'oros as a Greek, but Latin perceptions of identity in the east were understandably unreliable, as they had only recently encountered the inhabitants of the region. The reference to being Greek may nevertheless be an indication of his Chalcedonian beliefs.[140]

Yet with regard to his political affiliations we have both written and physical evidence that sheds light on his loyalties towards the Byzantine Empire.[141] The first mention of T'oros in Matthew's account refers to him as a Roman official.[142] Furthermore, Matthew consistently refers to T'oros as the *Kouropalates* of Edessa, indicating that he had some official recognition from the Byzantine court for his position in the east.[143] The Greek inscription on the Harran Gate at least offers some support to how T'oros wanted his rule to be seen: that being on behalf of the Byzantine emperor. Unfortunately, the inscription in its present form is badly damaged, but thanks to the work of a nineteenth-century German scholar, von Gaertringen, we have an almost complete transcription.[144] The date of the inscription 6602 A.M., which equates to 1093/4, offers perhaps an indication that T'oros was linking his rule directly to that of Alexios, the named Roman emperor in the inscription. Yet, to use the inscription to argue that Byzantine authority was still a reality in the region by the late 1090s is far-fetched. T'oros was just the product of the tumultuous internal politics of Edessa, which, as assessed earlier, had a frequent turnover of leader in the preceding decade. His claim to being appointed by the emperor in Constantinople, at this time Alexios I Komnenos, was merely an attempt to seek legitimization by the nearest Christian power. One must not forget that T'oros also sought legitimacy from the far greater threat to his rule in Edessa, the various Turkic powers in the vicinity. We can see that on his last-known seal the titles of *Kouropalates* and *amēr* appear in tandem, signifying the delicate balancing act that T'oros was performing to hold on to the city.[145] Any pro-Byzantine feelings T'oros may have held did not help him when a better option presented itself to the people of Edessa; T'oros was murdered by the populace of the city shortly after adopting Baldwin of Boulogne as his heir.¹⁴⁶ Despite some comments by secondary works, the overthrow of T'oros does not seem to have represented an Armenian-led anti-Byzantine coup, nor does the claim that 'all our sources' depict that T'oros was hated hold up to scrutiny.¹⁴⁷ At least the account from Matthew's perspective considers T'oros a capable governor, and his death as a result of intrigue and acceptance of Frankish rule does not sit well with Matthew.¹⁴⁸ In any case, to view T'oros as an active Byzantine agent holding Edessa on behalf of the empire is far-fetched. In fact, our primary evidence explicitly tells us that T'oros was acting in accordance with the other minor Armenian lords in the region, holding legitimacy from the major powers in the region but ultimately separate from them.

Turning now to the opposite end of the spectrum, the career of the Armenian lord Kogh Vasil (or Basil the Robber) came to represent the most 'Armenian' of all the independent lordships that were formed after the collapse of Philaretos' domain. One can see that Kogh Vasil was far more independent from Byzantium than Gabriel of Melitene and T'oros, eventually even holding the prestigious responsibility of the secular guardian of the Armenian *Katholikos*. Indeed, our main source of information on Kogh Vasil comes from Matthew of Edessa. Matthew resided in Kesoun, the capital of Kogh Vasil's domain, shortly after the death of the Armenian lord and speaks highly of him, often commenting on the reputation Kogh Vasil had established in his domain. Unlike Gabriel, there is no dispute over Kogh Vasil's Armenian identity.¹⁴⁹ In religious terms one can see how he came to be the main protector of not only the *Katholikos* Gregory II but also Gregory's successors.¹⁵⁰ Kogh Vasil's adherence to the Apostolic Church has been noted by some secondary commentators as the underlying strength of his rule and support from the surrounding Armenian populace.¹⁵¹

It is beyond doubt that Kogh Vasil was one of the individuals who can firmly be placed in the separatist camp for not accepting the authority of Byzantines, Franks or Turks. He did indeed hold a Byzantine title, as seal evidence suggests, that of σεβαστός, but this does little more than highlight the Byzantines' attempts to still appear relevant to the local lordships in the region.¹⁵² Matthew sadly does not inform us of Kogh Vasil's origins, but his death in 1112 places him in a similar generation to that of Gabriel and T'oros, thereby suggesting his early career was under Philaretos which is confirmed by Michael the Syrian:

> At that time there were Armenians who had occupied certain places since the time of Philardus. One of them was Kogh-Basil, who occupied Kaisum and Ra'ban.¹⁵³

Clearly Kogh Vasil had little desire to interact with his former masters, but with our main information coming from his interactions with the Franks of the northern Latin states in Syria and their hostilities with the surrounding Turks, we can gain no true understanding of how Kogh Vasil felt towards Byzantium. From his actions, Kogh Vasil demonstrated no real desire to return under the imperial yoke, and like other surrounding Armenian lords he sought to retain dominion over his lordship centred on Kesoun. Indeed, the mourning of his death by his former subjects, as described by Matthew, reveals the fundamentally Armenian character of his rule despite his previous relationship with Byzantium:

> Around this prince were united remnants of the Armenian army, members of the Bagratid and Pahlavid families, sons of the kings of Armenia, and finally all those of Pahlavid lineage, together with the military aristocracy of Armenia all these remained with Vasil and were highly respected and honoured by him. Moreover, the Armenian patriarchal see was transferred to Vasil's territory for this Armenian prince had gained control of many areas through his bravery and strength. Thus all the monks, bishops, abbots, and vardapets gathered around him and were very well treated by him.[154]

In summary, the major Armenian lords in the region all had similar characteristics, not explicitly expressed through religious or political affiliation but rather their will to retain dominion over their lands that they had obtained by either gaining them from Philaretos before his downfall or by performing a political balancing act between the powerful Muslim forces in the region.

It was into this world that the First Crusade entered when it descended on to the Cilician plain and into northern Syria, finding a people ready and waiting for the dramatic changes of the coming years. As Ralph of Caen summed up the situation:

> at this time the Turks ruled, the Greeks obeyed, and the Armenians protected their liberty in the difficult conditions provided by their mountains.[155]

As the participants of the First Crusade arrived on the eastern marches of Anatolia in September 1097, the army split in two. The larger force crossed the Taurus Mountains along the eastern route to the north of Marash, where previously the Byzantine-Armenian separatist Philaretos Brachamios had held sway,[156] while a smaller splinter force, led by Tancred and Baldwin of Boulogne, took the more immediate route on the western side of the mountain range through the pass known as the Cilician Gates, entering the plains of Cilicia around 14 September 1097.[157] On the road to Antioch both sections of the crusading army were met and assisted by Armenians across the various towns and cities of the Cilician plain and the southerly foothills of the Taurus Mountains.[158] In February 1098, Baldwin arrived in Edessa and shortly afterwards the people of the city murdered T'oros and invited Baldwin to be their ruler instead.[159] According to some sources it was an Armenian who betrayed Antioch to the crusaders in June the same year.[160] Thus to some extent the crusaders inherited from the Armenians the Byzantine cities of which they had been the guardians since the collapse of imperial rule some fifteen years before.

Conclusion

There is little doubt that in order to comprehend how and why the Armenians were scattered throughout Cilicia and northern Syria at the time of the arrival of the

First Crusade, one must understand the complex relationship between Byzantium and the Armenians in the final three decades of the eleventh century. The most prominent careers of Armenian lords have been analysed, many of whom had held commands within the Byzantine army at around the time of Manzikert in August 1071. We have seen that despite attempts by the Byzantines to hold on to their influence in the region they were largely ignored by a succession of Armenian lords who now operated at a more local or regional level, protecting their lordships and engaging in local diplomacy with other Armenians. The 'Royal Armenians' did not last particularly long, as the increasingly damaging Turkoman raids took their toll on their estates in Cappadocia and Sebasteia. We lack any substantial detail concerning the speed and destruction that was wrought on the communities north of the Taurus Mountains, but Gagik's death, and the attachment placed by the later Rubenids on their historical connection to the exiled king, demonstrates that Gagik was never truly part of Byzantium and always seen as the embodiment of the now-defunct Armenian kingdom.

Over the course of the 1070s we witnessed the collapse of Byzantine authority on the eastern frontier and this can be accredited to two key factors. The first was the lack of attention paid to the eastern frontier by the centre which removed any possibility of shoring up the crumbling imperial authority in the region. The second revolved around the key figures in both political and military capacities pursuing an independent policy from Byzantium, a mixture of sheer survival and pursuit of a separatist agenda. The death of Gagik Bagratuni was certainly a catalyst for change in the Armenian loyalty towards the Byzantines, but the rise of the Rubenids did not provide a replacement for this lost allegiance. The fragmented political landscape nearly twenty years later reveals that the Armenian people were leaderless, divided among each other with remnants of imperial officials and opportunist warlords creating a series of petty lordships throughout the region.

While many of the Armenians operating through the period 1071–98 could be seen as Byzantine-Armenians, many of them did not hold their attachment to the Byzantine Empire with much consideration as Byzantine authority broke down in the region. In the words of one recent commentator: 'These were former Roman officials of Armenian origin creating a post-imperial future for the region.'[161] Yet, this has not stopped far-fetched attempts to see the interactions of these Armenian lords with that of the First Crusade as genuine efforts to reconnect with Byzantium.[162] Indeed, while some of the Armenian lords did accept titles and were seen as Byzantine agents by contemporary commentators (usually Byzantine), the Armenians were now separated from the empire, operating in a very different world. This was a world where the scattered lords had to settle or graft out some sort of independence from the dominant Turkic powers that surrounded their strongholds. It was to the bewilderment of the participants of the First Crusade that they found a people so willing to assist and supply their enterprise. Yet it is not hard to see in hindsight that in comparison to the lacklustre efforts of the Byzantines in the 1070s and 1080s, the participants of the First Crusade were actively expanding the borders of Christendom back to near the status of pre-1071. Without doubt, the greatest contribution of the First Crusade to the Armenians of Cilicia and northern Syria was an opportunity to rebuild a new Armenian state. Yet, this time they were to be truly sundered from the imperium that was Byzantium, the empire their illustrious ancestors had indelibly marked.

CLOSING REMARKS

This book opened with the start of the Armenian relationship with the Roman Empire, and it is remarkable that these two powers, peoples, cultures and later faiths held such a symbiotic bond for over a millennium. The year 1098 does not end the interaction between the Romans and Armenians; nearly a century later the newly crowned Leo I of Cilician Armenia (1198/9–1219) received his diadem from Constantinople, though he had been courting with other powers to recognize his new position as king. But Rome was never to hold the draw and attention of the Armenian world, and arguably it never regained its status after the collapse of the late eleventh century, despite what the Komnenian authors tell us about the twelfth century. But a degree of fluidity is needed around the bookend of dates in a study such as this. What was crucial, however, was the identification and analysis of the Byzantine-Armenian relationship over this time frame, assessing why centuries of successful assimilation gave way to alienation and subsequent separatism. It was argued that previous studies of Armenians in the Byzantine Empire have been hindered by a variety of preconceived notions on the subject of identity on both sides, thereby obstructing a clear analysis on how the Armenians themselves assimilated and what processes were undertaken in order to become fully fledged *Romaioi*. It was therefore imperative for a new understanding of the mechanics of assimilation, what sort of lives, careers and behaviours these newly arrived migrants were expected to adopt. Fundamentally, it was argued that the change in the Byzantine-Armenian relationship from the ninth and tenth centuries through to the end of the eleventh can be characterized in four distinct, but ultimately linked, phases: assimilation, annexation, alienation and separatism. Before the study could begin the investigation properly it was necessary to produce a definitive understanding of what was meant by assimilation, and this was done through the development of a model:

1. The area of territorial settlement
2. The acceptance and adoption of 'Roman customs'
3. The religious conversion/conformity of the migrants

It has now come to the point where some conclusions are needed on why the Byzantine-Armenian relationship underwent the four phases, as identified earlier, and why these changes occurred.

The main argument of Chapter 1 was to showcase the assimilation phase of the Byzantine-Armenian relationship. The chapter demonstrated how Armenians, before the eleventh century, engaged with the mechanics of assimilation as defined by the 'assimilation model'. It was noted that our primary evidence restricts the study of assimilation to members of the nobility, as it was this particular social group that garnered the most interest from our narrative sources. Initially, the discussion focused on certain passages from the literary circle originating from the court of Constantine VII Porphyrogennetos. In looking at the territorial placement of Armenian migrants it was shown that the geographical area in which they were settled was to have an impact on the speed and effectiveness of their assimilation. Thus, those placed nearer Constantinople were able to adapt efficiently to their new surroundings, while those settled in the east held on to their Armenian identity for longer though not forever. In bringing together a wide variety of sources one could trace the Armenians' origins of many of the great aristocratic Byzantine families and the worlds they operated in. For many of the Armenians this was predominantly service in the army or imperial governance.[1] In showing the relative ease, and huge success, these institutions had in assimilating Armenians, it was also argued that the religious divide between the Byzantines and Armenians was not represented fairly in our sources. It can clearly be observed that the ninth and tenth centuries were periods of religious toleration and peace between the two Christian denominations, with only occasional flashpoints of antagonism, most at a local level.[2] Furthermore, we do not have substantial evidence to suggest that difference in the religious practices in any way barred Armenian assimilation. It is certainly true that as assimilation progressed, many of the assimilated Armenians had adopted the Chalcedonian rite, but it is impossible to analyse the level or rate of this 'conversion' without adequate primary evidence. In summary, our sources suggest that a large number of Armenians were able to assimilate into the Byzantine Empire and produced many of the dominant personalities on the Byzantine political scene through the late ninth, tenth and eleventh centuries.

The focus then moved away from the direct evaluation of the mechanics of assimilation and argued that in order to fully understand the transition of the Byzantine-Armenian relationship from assimilation to alienation, it was imperative to fully comprehend the events and long-term effects of the annexations of the western Armenian kingdoms during the reign of Basil II. The chapter had two main aims. The first was to outline the context of the annexations with a discussion of Byzantine foreign policy in the tenth century, which directly led on to the explanation of why Basil was forced to directly intervene in the area during the first half of his reign. This was then followed by analysing the causes behind the annexation of Vaspurakan, and the Treaty of Trebizond, which brought about the settlement of the Artsruni in Cappadocia and the agreement to bequeath the kingdom of Ani to the Byzantium, respectively. The second aim was to outline the unforeseen consequences of these annexations and how these laid the foundation of later alienation. One must expand on these a little.[3]

The contextualization of Byzantine foreign policy during the tenth century is necessary in order to produce a coherent understanding of Basil's direct intervention in Caucasia during his reign – one which seemed to go against previous policies of frontier cooperation between the empire and the local magnates that his predecessors had maintained. It was seen that rather than repeating the older view that Basil was motivated by expansion, he was in fact concerned and primarily motivated by the internal factionalism that had risen during the early years of his reign and very nearly brought about the end of the ruling dynasty of the Macedonians. Basil's minority had been dominated by Nikephoros II Phokas and John I Tzimiskes, while his grandfather Constantine VII Porphyrogennetos had spent the greater part of his reign sharing power with Romanos I Lekapenos. Furthermore, Basil's early reign had been convulsed by two major civil wars, the risings of Bardas Skleros and later Bardas Phokas, both of which were serious threats to the ruling house. The assistance provided by David III of Tao in the revolt of Bardas Phokas had shown Basil the rising independent powers that were operating on the frontier and ones that could unduly influence the internal politics of the empire. It was this action by David that forced the pragmatic Basil to insist on inheriting David's lands upon the latter's death, providing the later issues that once again forced Basil to interfere with the polities of western Caucasia.

The second task of the chapter was to argue how the annexations towards the end of Basil's reign were to ultimately sow the seeds of alienation of the Armenians in the mid-eleventh century as a result of two unforeseen consequences. First, it was seen that Basil was forced to return east in 1021 with the rising belligerence of the Georgian kingdoms that now dominated much of Byzantium's north-eastern border. Seeking to enforce imperial rights on occupied lands in the region of Tao/Tayk, Basil marched into the region in force. Despite claims that it was Basil's intention all along to subjugate the western Caucasian polities to Constantinople, our sources are in near-complete agreement that the principal aim of his north-eastern campaign was the neutralization of Georgia. It was during Basil's stay at his winter quarters in Trebizond that a deal was struck between Basil and Yovhannes-Smbat on the status of the kingdom of Ani. Yovhannes-Smbat sought Byzantine recognition of his title as *Shahanshah* and in return he would bequeath his kingdom to the empire upon his death. While certain voices saw this as a result of external pressure our sources actually tell us how it was internal factionalism within the kingdom of Ani itself that brought about Yovhannes-Smbat's offer. Yet neither Basil nor Yovhannes-Smbat could ever have foreseen the problems that undermined the Byzantine claim to Ani in the early 1040s. The enforcement of the treaty and the feelings of betrayal held by its exiled king, Gagik II, were to fester on the sprawling Armenian estates in Cappadocia and Sebasteia. The second unforeseen consequence was to be the result of the settlement of the Artsruni in Cappadocia, which was originally intended to dilute the power base of the military officer class that had so often threatened Basil's reign. This almost immediately backfired when the Armenian settlers got caught up with the Rebellion of 1022. While the Armenian narrative accounts depict the Artsruni as agents of the emperor who internally brought down the revolt, from other historiographical traditions this does not seem to be so clear. In any case, the aftermath of the revolt meant that the Artsruni held a stronger loyalty to Basil II himself rather than to the

Byzantine state. This bond actually weakened the mechanics of assimilation and meant that even fifteen years after the emperor's death, the Artsruni held more to the memory of Basil than loyalty to the position of emperor and the empire itself. In summary, the annexations of the Armenian kingdoms created the conditions for the later alienation, but it is important to re-emphasize that the alienation of the Armenians was the product of the mid-eleventh century that had its origins in the 1020s.

Following on from the annexations of the Armenian kingdoms in the early to mid-eleventh century, we arrived at the third phase of the Byzantine-Armenian relationship: alienation. Three factors were identified as driving the feelings of alienation: the settlement of the Armenians on lands nearer their ancestral homeland, the religious animosity that occasionally flared up into heated theological debates and the failure to adopt 'Roman customs' by the newly settled Armenians. Let us take a look at each of these in turn.

It was argued that the settlement of the exiled Armenian princely houses in Cappadocia and Sebasteia created issues that could not have been foreseen by Basil who was responsible for the original settlement of the Artsruni. The subsequent settlements of members of the elite from Ani and Kars, in precisely the same region, created a large demographic of Armenians who did not respond to the mechanisms of assimilation in the same manner as their compatriots had in the preceding decades: previously the Armenians had been scattered throughout the empire, often used to repopulate buffer zones on frontiers such as the Balkans. The estates that were given to the Armenians were too close to the Armenian homeland, meaning that many did not have to adapt to their new surroundings, whether that was religiously or linguistically. Nor were the Armenians motivated to pursue careers within the imperial institutions, preferring to remain with their compatriots on their estates, continuing very much the same existence they had lived back in Armenia.

The most common theme of animosity between Byzantines and Armenians has been through the religious differences between their official churches. While this did indeed have some effect on the growing resentment of the Armenians living within the empire, it was neither the sole nor the most prominent factor that drove alienation. It has been assessed in depth how the Byzantines attempted to bring about uniformity among its eastern subjects through religious conformity, with some particularly difficult episodes revolving around imprisonment of the Armenian *Katholikos* and attempts at religious debate to bring about a statement of union. But all of this animosity would have been of only minor concern without the main bonding agent of alienation: the weakness of the adoption of 'Roman customs'.

We saw with the conclusion of Chapter 2 that the two unforeseen consequences of the annexations revolved around the failure of the Armenian migrants to adopt the loyalty structures enshrined in the definition of 'Roman customs'. The 'Rebellion of 1040' opened the fissures in the Byzantine-Artsruni relationship, exposing the inherent weakness in the personal loyalty between Basil and the exiled dynasty. This was further exacerbated with the coercive annexation of Ani and the settlement of Gagik in the very same region as the Artsruni. Viewed by Armenian historians, both medieval and modern, the forced exile of the Armenian king has been characterized as either 'treacherous coercion'[4] or 'deceived by enemies both at home and abroad'.[5] Gagik never pretended to be a Byzantine, nor does he ever seem to have held any feelings of loyalty to the Byzantine state. The failure of the imperial centre to engage with the Armenians and encourage them to pursue careers within the great institutions of state, namely the army, further propelled the force of alienation. This is why during the episodes of religious discussion between the Armenians and the Byzantines that the imperial centre had an inherent flaw in trying to control their Armenian subjects in Cappadocia and Sebasteia: they were first and foremost loyal to Gagik, rather than to the emperor. Gagik's staunch defence of the Armenian faith was in many ways an act of defiance against those who had taken his kingdom away from him, and one can see that after the discussions in Constantinople in 1065 Gagik pursued a policy of separatism within his territories in Cappadocia and Sebasteia.[6] While indeed the 'Royal Armenians' had mostly disappeared within a decade of the collapse of the Byzantine eastern frontier after Manzikert, their actions showcase the weakening position of Byzantium with its subjects, and the attachment to the royal exiles was held dearly by the next generation of Armenian rulers in Cilicia and northern Syria.

In the final chapter the focus was to explain how the alienation phase, as observed previously, developed into the separatism that came to define the Byzantine-Armenian relationship in the post-Manzikert world. First, the analysis concentrated on the fallout from the Battle of Manzikert in 1071 from both a Byzantine and Islamic perspective. From the two historiographical traditions we gain a very murky picture of events in eastern Anatolia, namely as a result of the sources being written from both geographical and temporal distances. The first section attempted to trace the residues of Byzantine influence in the region, while also explaining why the Turkic penetrations across Anatolia did not have initial success across the Taurus Mountains and onto the Cilician plain.

The answer to this limited success was twofold. The Islamic world entered another phase of internal weakness with the death of Alp-Arslan in 1072 that allowed Armenian warlords to expand and consolidate the various Armenian lordships in the region. Surprisingly, this force of unity did not come from the 'Royal Armenians', with Gagik II failing in his attempts to become the rallying point for Armenian separatism. Instead we witness his murder at the hands of semi-independent imperial agents in the region. Ironically, it was to be the death of Gagik that paved the way for the supremacy of Philaretos Brachamios, although even Philaretos was not able to unite all of the surrounding Armenian lordships to his side. Eventually, the pressure from the surrounding Turkic warlords led to the complete collapse of Philaretos' lordship but not before several Armenian warlords were able to entrench themselves in various cities and forts in the surrounding area.

There remain some questions over the strength of the religious bond that many Armenians shared and why this too failed to produce some element of cohesion among the various Armenians lords. The simple answer to this is twofold. First, many of the Armenian warlords in the region did not follow the Apostolic confession. Whether this was because of elements of assimilation taking hold or that some were Armenian Chalcedonians, the result is the same; religion could not unite all of the lords in the region. The second was the Apostolic Church itself was incredibly divided. This can largely be validated by the fracturing of the ecclesiastical leadership under *Katholikos* Gregory II, who in many ways was its main architect. At the same time as the leadership enshrined in the royal lineage of the Bagratuni was destroyed, the ecclesiastical leadership of the Apostolic Church was fractured, in many ways mimicking the political geography. While our source, Matthew of Edessa, firmly places the blame for this disunity on the 'perfidious Romans' or the 'anti-Christ' Philaretos, the actions of Gregory II seem to have been the catalyst.

The fall of Philaretos' lordship did not spell the end of Armenian rule in the region, for some of the surviving lieutenants of Philaretos such as Gabriel of Melitene, T'oros of Edessa and Kogh Vasil were all able to hold on to their localized power bases. Some certainly held their position with the permission of the Seljuk court, but after Malik-Shah's death in 1092 there was not central authority in which these Armenian lords could engage with. Nevertheless, despite small residues of Byzantine authority existing in the region through the form of imperial titles and seals, none of these warlords attempted to reintegrate into the Byzantine Empire when the First Crusade liberated many of the Armenian settlements from Turkic garrisons. On this point, most of all, can one finally understand in context as to why the Armenians were so willing to assist the Franks of the First Crusade during their passage through Armenian lands.

APPENDIX I

THE HARRAN GATE

The Greek transcription on the Harran Gate:[1]

1. Ἀλέξ[ιος ἐ]σώθη ἡ Ῥωμαϊκὴ ἐξουσ[ία
2. διὰ τὴ]ν μακαριοτάτην περίπτω[σιν
3. πρωτοσεβάστῳ το[ῦ] Σεβαστοῦ κ(αὶ) Α[ὐ]τοκ[ράτορος] τοῦ . . .
4. [. . .]ην Χρι(σ)τιανους μέχρι τῆς δευρὶ [ἐ]κ τῆς τῶν Τούρκων ἐπικρατείας βασυλ(έως) [Ῥω]μαί[ων . . .
5. Ἀλεξί]ου τοῦ φιλοχριστο[υ] Αὐτ[οκράτορο]ς Ῥ[ωμαί]ων Κ[ο]μνηνοῦ ἐν ἔτει ϛχβ', [ἰν] δ. β'

Dating:

ϛχβ', [ἰν] δ. β'. The Greek numerals state 6602 A.M. To get Anno Domini date one minus 5509 which equals 1093. The indiction, which is the second, corrects the cyclical anomalies of the months to 1094.[2]

NOTES

Byzantium and Armenia

1   Cornelius Tacitus, *Annals*, trans. M. Grant (London: Penguin Classics, 2003), XIII, 34–41.
2   Tacitus, *Annals*, XV, 29.
3   Anthony Kaldellis, *Streams of Gold, Rivers of Blood: The Rise and Fall of Byzantium, 955 A.D. to the First Crusade* (Oxford: Oxford University Press, 2017), 2.
4   Such an argument is put forward by Jean-Claude Cheynet, 'Les Arméniens de l'Empire en Orient de Constantin X à Alexis Comnène (1059–1081)', in *L'Arménie et Byzance: Histoire et culture*, ed. N. Garsoïan, Byzantina Sorbonesia 12 (Paris: Publications de la Sorbonne, 1996), 67. We will explore this idea a little further in the section on Modern Historiography.
5   Ashot was indeed recognized by the Abbasids as king, with the court in Baghdad sending a crown, largely in recognition of the new geopolitical situation in the Caucasus.
6   Tim Greenwood, *The Universal History of Stepannos Taronets'i*, vii; Tara Andrews, *Matt'ēos Uṙhayec'i and His Chronicle* (Leiden and Boston, MA: Brill, 2017), 44–5.
7   Anthony Kaldellis, *Romanland: Ethnicity and Empire in Byzantium* (Cambridge, MA: Harvard University Press, 2019), 156. See 157 where Kaldellis ably deconstructs previous scholarship who have propagated multigenerational Armenian identity in individuals and families who lived in the Byzantine Empire.
8   This is not in any way to dilute or dismiss the travesty of these events that affected groups, such as the Armenians, in a tragic way during the twentieth century. But through re-evaluating the definitions of medieval identity, for both the Byzantines and Armenians, we can gain a richer understanding of how the medieval ancestors of a whole series of modern ethno-national peoples understood and identified themselves within their own context.
9   A recent study on the correspondence of imperial agents, specifically from the eastern frontier, still judges that the Byzantines saw the Armenians as a fundamentally foreign element: AnnaLinden Weller, *Imagining pre-Modern Imperialism: The Letters of Byzantine Imperial Agents Outside the Metropole* (Unpublished Thesis, Rutgers, 2014), 4.
10   Peter Charanis, 'Armenians and Greeks in the Byzantine Empire', in *Social, Economic and Political Life in the Byzantine Empire*, ed. P. Charanis (London: Variorum Reprints, 1973), No. VIII, 25–32, at 32.
11   Peter Charanis, 'The Formation of the Greek People', in *The 'Past' in Medieval and Modern Greek Culture*, ed. S. Vryonis (Malibu, CA: Undena Publications, 1978), 88, 90.
12   Charanis, 'Armenians and Greeks', 32.
13   Nina Garsoïan, 'The Problem of Armenian Integration into the Byzantine Empire', in *Studies on the Internal Diaspora of the Byzantine Empire*, ed. H. Ahrweiler and A.

14 Alexander Kazhdan, 'The Armenians in the Byzantine Ruling Class Predominantly in the Ninth Through Twelfth Centuries', in *Medieval Armenian Culture*, ed. Thomas Samuelian and Michael Stone (Chico, CA: Scholars Press, 1983), 438–45; Alexander Kazhdan and Giles Constable, *People and Power in Byzantium: An Introduction to Modern Byzantine Studies* (Washington D.C.: Dumbarton Oaks, 1982), 153–4.
15 Isabelle Brouselle, 'L'intégration des Arméniens dans l'aristocratie byzantine au IXe siècle', in *L'Arménie et Byzance: Histoire et culture*, ed. N. Garsoïan, Byzantina Sorbonesia 12 (Paris: Publications de la Sorbonne, 1996), 43–4.
16 Cheynet, 'Les Arméniens', 67; Brouselle, 'L'intégration des Arméniens', 44.
17 For further investigation of the understudied contributions of justice and finance to the assimilation process see Angeliki Laiou, 'Institutional Mechanisms of Integration', in *Byzantium and the Other: Relations and Exchanges – Angeliki E. Laiou*, ed. C. Morrisson and R. Dorin, vol. III (Farnham: Ashgate Publishing, 2012), 161.
18 S. Peter Cowe, 'Armenian Immigration to the Sebastia Region, Tenth-Eleventh Centuries', in *Armenian Sebastia/Sivas and Lesser Armenia*, ed. R. Hovannisian, UCLA Armenian History and Culture Series: Historic Armenian Cities and Provinces, 5 (Costa Mesa, CA: Mazda Publishers, 2004), 111–36.
19 Gilbert Dagron, 'Minorités ethniques et religieuses dans l'orient byzantin à la fin du Xe et au XIe siècle: l'immigration syrienne', TM 6 (1976): 177–216.
20 Tacitus, *Annals*, XI, 24.
21 One prominent example of the promotion of Romanization by a governor can be found in Tacitus, *Agricola*, 21.
22 Aelius Aristides, *Roman Oration*, trans. in J. Oliver, 'The Ruling Power: A Study of the Roman Empire in the Second Century after Christ through the Roman Oration of Aelius Aristides', *Transactions of the American Philological Association* 43 (1953): LIX.
23 ILM 116, printed in J. Gascou, *Inscriptions an-tiques du Maroc 2, Inscriptions Latines*, 284–7, no. 448.
24 A. Gibb, 'I. Quintus Lollius Urbicus. Builder of the Wall between the Forth and Clyde', *The Scottish Antiquary, or, Northern Notes and Queries* 14, no. 55 (January 1900): 140–6.
25 Cassius Dio, *Roman History*, LXXVIII, IX.
26 For use of Punic in the fifth century see Augustine, *Epistola* 17. The Isaurians were to last well into the sixth century, with a great rebellion against the Romans lasting from 492 to 497. Some later emperors were said to have Isaurian ancestry, although this was not held against their Roman credentials.
27 There is some debate as to whether this occurred in Constantine's reign or that of his son and heir Constantius II (337–61). Eusebius, *Vita Constantini*, XLIV.
28 For examples in Africa see F. M. Clover, 'Emperor Worship in Vandal Africa', *Romanitas-Christianitas*, ed. G. Wirth (Berlin and Boston: De Gruyter, 1982), 661–74.
29 *Oxford Dictionary of Byzantium*, II, 989–90.
30 Jack Tannous, 'Romanness in the Syriac East', in *Transformations of Romanness: Early Medieval Regions and Identities*, ed. W. Pohl, C. Gantner, C. Grifoni, and M. Pollheimer-Mohaupt (Berlin and Boston, MA: De Gruyter, 2018), 457.
31 Tannous, 'Romanness in the Syriac East', 458–9.
32 κ(υρι)ε βοητι της πολ/ λεος κε ρυξον τον αβα/ ριν/ κε πυλαξον την ρω/ μανιαν/ κε τον γρ/ αψαν/ τα/ ἀμη/ ν Rudolf Noll, 'Ein Ziegel als sprechendes Zeugnis einer historischen

Katastrophe (Zum Untergang Sirmiums 582 n. Chr.)', *Anzeiger der philosophisch-historischen Klasse der Österreichischen Akademie der Wissenschaften* 126 (1989): 139–54.

33 By 'contemporary' I am referring to the world view of the compiler/author, not necessarily the views of the original sources that they used which in some cases were hundreds of years apart.

34 For an extreme view of lack of originality in Byzantine literature see Cyril Mango, *Byzantine Literature as a Distorting Mirror. Inaugural Lecture, University of Oxford, May 1974* (Oxford: Clarendon Press, 1975) and Paul Speck, 'Byzantium: Cultural Suicide?', in *Byzantium in the Ninth Century: Dead or Alive?*, ed. Leslie Brubaker (Aldershot: Ashgate, 1998), 73–84. For an alternative, see Roger Scott, 'The Classical Tradition in Byzantine Historiography', in *Byzantium and the Classical Tradition*, ed. M. Mullett and R. Scott (Birmingham: Centre for Byzantine Studies, University of Birmingham, 1981), 61–74, and the essays in: Anthony Littlewood (ed.), *Originality in Byzantine Literature Art and Music: 13th Annual Byzantine Studies Conference Papers* (Oxford: Oxbow Books, 1995).

35 Constantine Porphyrogennetos, *De Administrando Imperio* [henceforth *DAI*], ed. G. Moravcsik, trans. R. J. H. Jenkins (Budapest: Pazmany Peter Tudomanyegyetemi Gorog Filologiaai Intezet), CFHB 1, 13, 70–1: τοῦ μηδέποτε βασιλέα Ῥωμαίων συμπενθεριάσαι μετὰ ἔθνους παρηλλαγμένοις καὶ ξένοις ἔθεσι χρωμένου τῆς Ῥωμαϊκῆς καταστάσεως.

36 *DAI*, 13, 72–3: Ὁ κύρις Ῥωμανός, ὁ βασιλεύς, ἰδιώτης καὶ ἀγράμματος ἄνθρωπος ἦν, καὶ οὔτε τῶν ἄνωθεν ἐν βασιλείοις τεθραμμένων, οὔτε τῶν παρηκολουθηκότων ἐξ ἀρχῆς τοῖς Ῥωμαϊκοῖς ἐθισμοῖς. I have placed 'national' in italics as there is no justification for this from the original Greek as included by Jenkins' translation.

37 John Skylitzes, *Synopsis Historiarum*, ed. J. Thurn, CFHB 5 (Berlin and New York: Walter de Gruyter, 1973), 231; English translation: *A Synopsis of Byzantine History 811-1057*, trans. J. Wortley (Cambridge: Cambridge University Press, 2010), 223; *The Complete Works of Liudprand of Cremona*, trans. Paolo Squatriti (Washington D.C.: The Catholic University of America Press, 2007), 179, 183–4; *DAI*, 26, 112–13.

38 Anna Komnene, *Alexias*, ed. D. Reinsch and A. Kambylis, 2 vols, CFHB 40 (Berlin and New York: Walter de Gruyter, 2001), I, 10, 35; English Translation: *The Alexiad*, trans. E. Sewter and P. Frankopan (London: Penguin Publishing, 2009), 30.

39 Skylitzes, *Synopsis Historiarum*, ed. 336, trans. 319; Yahya of Antioch, *Cronache dell'Egitto fatimide e dell'impero bizantino (937-1033)*, trans. B. Pirone (Milan: Jaca Book, 1998), 196. In general, see Jonathan Shepard, 'Marriages towards the millennium', in *Byzantium in the Year 1000*, ed. Paul Magdalino (Leiden and Boston, MA: Leiden, 2003), 1–33.

40 Niketas Choniates, *Nicetae Choniatae Historia*, ed. J.-L. van Dieten, CFHB 3 (Berlin and New York: Walter de Gruyter, 1973), 37; English translation: *O City of Byzantium, Annals of Niketas Choniates*, trans. H. Magoulias (Detroit, MI: Wayne State University Press, 1984), 22: ἀμέλει καὶ ὡς ὁμοροῦσιν αὐτοῖς προστιθέμενοι Ῥωμαίους ὡς ἐχθροὺς ὑπεβλέποντο· οὕτω χρόνῳ κρατυνθὲν ἔθος γένους καὶ θρησκείας ἐστὶν ἰσχυρότερον.

41 Matthew of Edessa, *Armenia and the Crusades*, trans. E. Dostourian (Lanham, MD: University Press of America, 1993), II, 60, 137. This could indeed be referring to religious traditions that together combined into Matthew's understanding of what made someone Roman.

42 Garsoïan, 'Armenian Integration', 53–124, at 66, n. 59.

43 *DAI*, 13, 74–5: οὕτω καὶ ἕκαστον ἔθνος οὐκ ἐξ ἀλλοφύλων καὶ ἀλλογλώσσων, ἀλλ' ἐκ τῶν ὁμογενῶν τε καὶ ὁμοφώνων τὰ συνοικέσια τῶν γάμων ποιεῖσθαι καθέστηκεν δίκαιοω.

44 Theophanes the Confessor, *Chronographia*, ed. C. de Boor, 2 vols (Hildesheim and New York: G. Olms, 1980), I, 455; English translation: *The Chronicle of Theophanes Confessor*, trans. C. Mango and R. Scott (Oxford: Clarendon Press, 1997), 628: τῶν Γραικῶν γράμματα καὶ τὴν γλῶσσαν, καὶ παιδεῦσαι αὐτὴν τὰ ἤθη τῆς Ῥωμαίων βασιλείας. This particular passage has also been noted by Florin Curta in: *The Edinburgh History of the Greeks, c.500 to 1050, The Early Middle Ages* (Edinburgh: Edinburgh University Press, 2011), 292.

45 Leo the Deacon, *Leonis Diaconi Caloënsis Historiae Libri Decem*, ed. C. Hasii, CSHB (Bonn: Weberi, 1828), IX.vi, 149, viii, 152; English translation: *The History of Leo the Deacon: Byzantine Military Expansion on the Tenth Century*, trans. A.-M. Talbot and D. Sullivan (Washington D.C.: Dumbarton Oaks Research Library and Collection, 2005), 192–3, 196; Skylitzes, *Synopsis Historiarum*, ed. 250, 304, 308, trans. 240, 289, 292; John Kinnamos, *Epitome*, ed. A. Meineke, CSHB (Bonn: Weber, 1836), 34–5, 71–2, 77; English translation: *The Deeds of John and Manuel Comnenus, by John Kinnamos*, trans. C. Brand (New York: Columbia University Press, 1976), 35–6, 61–2, 65; Choniates, *Nicetae Choniatae Historia*, ed. 52, 64, trans. 31, 37: τροφῆς δὲ καὶ παιδείας μεταλαχὼν ʿΡωμαϊκῆς

46 Choniates, *Nicetae Choniatae Historia*, ed. 171, trans. 97: τὰ δ' ἄλλα σύμφυλοι ὄντες καὶ <φίλοι> πάνυ Ῥωμαίων

47 Skylitzes, *Synopsis Historiarum*, ed. 151, trans. 146: ὅθεν καὶ Ῥωμαικοῖς ἔθεσι καὶ στολαῖς καὶ τῇ ἄλλῃ πάσῃ πολιτικῇ κατασατάσει ἄγονται ἄχρι τῆς σήμερον. This passage is in fact an interpolation MSS ACEB; for further information see Thurn's preface in the edition, xxix.

48 There are some obviously important debates around the continuity of said tradition after 1204 and the trauma that the fall of Constantinople had on this ideological world view. However, there is evidence that this concept was still held dear during the late Byzantine period. For example, in c.1396 the Patriarch Anthony IV rebuked the grand duke of Moscow for belittling the position of emperor, stating that he was '[the] single emperor whose laws, ordinances and decrees hold throughout the world, who alone, with none other, is revered by all Christians'. *Acta et Diplomata Graeca Medii Aevi Sacra et Profana*, 6 vols, ed. F. Miklosich and J. Muller (Aalen: Scientia Verlag, 1968), ii, 190–2, Ernest Barker, *Social and Political Thought in Byzantium from Justinian I to the Last Palaeologus* (Oxford: Oxford University Press, 1957), 553–4.

49 Greenwood, *The Universal History*, vii; Andrews, *Matt'ēos Uṙhayec'i*, 44–5.

50 It is important to acknowledge that not all Armenians identified with the Miaphysite Apostolic Church. The group known as 'Armenian Chalcedonians' – Armenians who were Chalcedonian but whose liturgical language was Armenian – is not included in this section. They will be addressed in the section 'Religious Conversion and Conformity' of Chapter 2.

51 Greenwood, *The Universal History*, vii.
52 Greenwood, *The Universal History*, viii.
53 Greenwood, *The Universal History*, 70.
54 Andrews, *Matt'ēos Uṙhayec'i*, 74–5.
55 MacEvitt, 'The Chronicle of Matthew of Edessa: Apocalypse, the First Crusade and the Armenian Diaspora', *DOP* 61 (2007): 157–81, at 170–4; Andrews, *Matt'ēos Uṙhayec'i*, 75.
56 The character of Philaretos Brachamios will be one of the more prolific figures to come under criticism in Chapter 4.

Chapter 1

1. Manea Erna Shirinian, 'Armenian Elites in Constantinople: Emperor Basil and Patriarch Photius', in *Armenian Constantinople*, ed. R. Hovannisian and S. Payaslian, UCLA Armenian History and Culture Series: Historic Armenian Cities and Provinces (Costa Mesa, CA: Mazda Publishers, 2010), 9, 53–72, at 53. Both the *Vita Basilii* and Joseph Genesios' *On Imperial Reigns* were written in in the mid-ninth century, some 140 years after the events reported here.
2. Shirinian, 'Armenian Elites in Constantinople', 55–9; Kaldellis, *Romanland: Ethnicity and Empire in Byzantium*, 155–95.
3. Charanis, 'Armenians and Greeks', 27.
4. Theophanes Continuatus, *Chronographiae quae Theophanis continuati nomine fertur liber quo Vita Basilii Imperatoris amplectitur*, ed. I Ševčenko, CFHB 42 (Berlin and Boston: Walter de Gruyter, 2011), [henceforth *Vita Basilii*], 10–11: τὸ δὲ γένος εἶκεν ἐξ Ἀρμενίων ἔθνους.
5. Charanis, 'Ethnic Changes in Seventh-Century Byzantium', *DOP* 13 (1959): 23–44, at 34, n. 64. Only in a later work does Charanis cite Michael the Syrian for the existence of an Armenian Church in the capital at the time of Alexios I Komnenos: Peter Charanis, *The Armenians in the Byzantine Empire* (Lisbon: Fundação Calouste Gulbenkian, 1963), 55.
6. Leo the Deacon, *Leonis Diaconi Caloënsis Historiae Libri Decem*, IV.vii, ed. 64, trans. 113; Skylitzes, *Synopsis Historiarum*, ed. 275, trans. 264.
7. Michael the Syrian, *Chronique*, trans. J. Chabot, 4 vols (Paris: Ernest Leroux, 1906), iii, XV.vii, 185.
8. *DAI*, 50, 239; Charanis, *Armenians in the Byzantine Empire*, 29; further details of the careers of Manuel's sons are discussed later. Tekis, or Tephike, was a region in the Upper Euphrates settled extensively by Armenians.
9. Skylitzes, *Synopsis Historiarum*, ed. 279, trans. 268; Stephen of Taron, Patmutʻiwn tiezerakan, ed. S. Malxaseanc (St Petersburg: publisher unknown, 1885), III, VIII, 183, English translation: History of Stepʻanos Tarōnecʻi, trans. T. Greenwood, Oxford Studies in Byzantium (Oxford: Oxford University Press, 2017), 235. The principality of Taron was the westernmost area of the Kingdom of Armenia during the medieval period.
10. Sebeos, *The Armenian History Attributed to Sebeos*, trans. R. Thomson (Liverpool: Liverpool University Press, 1999), I, 15, 31; Garsoïan, 'Armenian Integration', 57; Charanis, 'Ethnic Changes', 30.
11. Theophanes the Confessor, *Chronographia*, ed. 429, trans. 593; Michael the Syrian, *Chronique*, ii, IX.xxiv, 518.
12. It should be noted that there is a discrepancy in the details of which groups of people were involved in this transfer. The Syriac edition only mentions Syrians as part of the transfer, while the Armenian edition mentions Armenians and Syrians. Michael the Syrian, *Chronique*, iii, VII.i, 2; *The Chronicle of Michael the Great*, trans. V. Langlois (Venice: San Lazzaro degli Armeni, 1868), 260, 262; Theophanes the Confessor, *Chronographia*, ed. 452, trans. 623; Charanis, *Armenians in the Byzantine Empire*, 15–16.
13. *Vita Basilii*, 3, 17. The episode is also captured by the later compiler of history Skylitzes found: Skylitzes, *Synopsis Historiarum*, ed. 116, trans. 117. This will be explored further later.

14 Theophanes Continuatus, *Chronographiae quae Theophanis Continuati nomine fertur Libri I-IV*, ed. M. Featherstone and J. Signes-Codoñer, CFHB 53/1 (Berlin and Boston: Walter de Gruyter, 2015) [henceforth *Theophanes Continuatus*], 137–59; Nina Garsoïan, *The Paulician Heresy: A Study of the Origin and Development of Paulicianism in Armenia and the Eastern Provinces of the Byzantine Empire* (The Hague: Mouton, 1967), 129.
15 Anna Komnene, *Alexias*, XIV.8, ed. 455, trans. 425.
16 Stephen of Taron, *Patmut'iwn tiezerakan*, III, XX, ed. 201, trans. 251.
17 Speros Vryonis Jr, 'The Vita Basilii of Constantine Porphyrogenitus and the Absorption of Armenians in Byzantine Society', in Ευφρόσυνον· Αφιέρωμα στον Μανώλη Χατζηδάκη, 2 vols (Athens: Ekdosē tou Tameiou Archaiologikōn Porōn kai Apallotriōseōn, 1992), ii.676–93, at 679.
18 Charanis, 'Armenians and Greeks', 28–9.
19 The Paulicians are noted in the primary accounts of the Second Crusade when they come across the heretical Armenian sect.
20 Skylitzes, *Synopsis Historiarum*, ed. 136, trans. 134.
21 This occurred *c*.871/2, although the location of Lokana is unknown. Dédéyan states that he received titles, functions and state revenues in exchange, though without primary source evidence: Gérard Dédéyan, 'Mleh le grand, stratège de Lykandos', *REArm* 15 (1981): 73–102, at 74, n. 8.
22 Skylitzes, *Synopsis Historiarum*, ed. 176, trans. 170. His career is explored further later in the chapter.
23 A title he would gain later in his career. Ashot 'the long armed' was related to the Bagratuni dynasty that ruled from Ani: Constantine Porphyrogennetos, *De Thematibus*, ed. A. Pertusi (Vatican City: Biblioteca Apostolica Vaticana, 1952), 75; Mark Whittow, *The Making of Orthodox Byzantium, 600-1025* (Basingstoke: Palgrave Macmillan, 1996), 315; Dédéyan, 'Mleh le grand, stratège de Lykandos', 75.
24 Also called Malīh in Arabic sources: Dédéyan, 'Mleh le grand, stratège de Lykandos', 72.
25 Melias' career in Lykandos will be explored in detail later in the chapter.
26 Leo the Deacon, *Leonis Diaconi Caloënsis Historiae Libri Decem*, X.vii, ed. 169, trans. 212. n.64. ὅτε κατὰ τὴν Λάπαραν τὸ πεδίον (μεθόριον δὲ τοῦτο τῆς χώρας τῶν Ἀρμενίων).
27 Leo the Deacon, *Leonis Diaconi Caloënsis Historiae Libri Decem*, II.viii, ed. 28, trans. 80; Constantine Porphyrogennetos, *De Thematibus*, 75–6, 143–6.
28 For examples of this before the eleventh century see 107–17.
29 A key argument that will be resumed in Chapter 4.
30 *Vita Basilii*, 3, 16–17, sometime between 780 and 797.
31 *Vita Basilii*, 3, 16–17.
32 *Vita Basilii*, 3, 17.
33 Skylitzes, *Synopsis Historiarum*, ed. 116, trans. 117. The account by Skylitzes is obviously a copy of the information he found in the *Vita*. It is still prudent to draw comparisons between the two.
34 The Greek in the *Vita* is at points repeated verbatim in Skylitzes. I would argue that Ševčenko's translation is finer. Maiktes never enters the accusative (nor Leo leave the accusative) in the passage. L.9-12 all keep Maiktes as the subject.
35 Joseph Genesios, *Iosephi Genesii Regum Libri Quattuor*, ed. A. Lesmüller-Werner and I. Thurn (Berlin and New York: Walter de Gruyter, 1978), IV.3, 58, english

translation Genesios on the Reign of the Emperors, trans. A. Kaldellis (Canberra: Australian Association for Byzantine Studies, 1998), 74.
36 *Vita Basilii*, 12, 49.
37 Genesios, *Iosephi Genesii Regum Libri Quattuor*, ed. IV.3, 58, trans. 74.
38 *Vita Basilii*, 12, 49. ἅτε καὶ αὐτὸς ἐξ Ἀρμενίων ἕλκων τὸ γένος
39 Genesios, *Iosephi Genesii Regum Libri Quattuor*, ed. IV.26, 78, trans. 97. ἀγχιστείας
40 For further debate on the author known as Genesios and his lineage to Constantine the Armenian see Kaldellis, *Genesios*, Translator's note, 2.
41 Cheynet has previously observed that assimilation may have taken around three generations to complete; see Cheynet, 'Les Arméniens', 67.
42 Karekin Sarkissian, *The Council of Chalcedon and the Armenian Church*, The Karekin I Theological and Armenological Studies Series (New York: The Armenian Church Prelacy, 1975), 2.
43 Mt. 22.21; Donald Nicol, 'Byzantine Political Thought', in *The Cambridge History of Medieval Political Thought c.350-c.1450*, ed. J. Burns (Cambridge: Cambridge University Press, 1988), 51–79, at 52–3.
44 This point is excellently summarized by Haldon, who sees it as a contributory factor in the survival of the empire in the seventh and eighth centuries: John Haldon. *A Critical Commentary on the Taktika of Leo VI*, Dumbarton Oaks studies 44 (Washington D.C.: Dumbarton Oaks Research Library and Collection, 2014), 6.
45 Dédéyan makes this assumption by the interpretation of the word Θεράπων meaning servant.
46 Constantine Porphyrogennetos, *De Thematibus*, 75.
47 *DAI*, 50, 240–1; Dédéyan, 'Mleh le grand, stratège de Lykandos', 79.
48 *DAI*, 50, 238–9: ὁ δὲ Μελίας εἰς τὴν Μελιτηνὴν ἔτι πρόσφυγος.
49 *DAI* uses the word κλεισουριάρχην. κλεισούρα translates as 'narrow pass' and by expansion came to describe the military district defending the narrow passes in the Tarsus Mountains. John Haldon and Hugh Kennedy, 'The Arab-Byzantine Frontier in the Eighth and Ninth Centuries: Military and Society in the Borderlands', *ZRVI* 19 (1980): 79–116, 99–102.
50 *DAI*, 50, 240–1, explicitly notes Melias' career and loyalty: διά τε τὴν συνοῦσαν αὐτῷ πρὸς τὸν βασιλέα τῶν Ῥωμαίων πίστιν
51 Stephen of Taron, *Patmut'iwn tiezerakan*, III, XIV, ed. 190–1, trans. 242–3. <u>My emphasis.</u>
52 Stephen of Taron, *Patmut'iwn tiezerakan*, III, XIV, ed. 191, trans. 242.
53 Yahya of Antioch, 'Histoire', ed. and trans. I. Kratchkovsky and A. Vasiliev, *Patrologia Orientalis* 23 (1932): 424; for opinion on which brother it was see C. Holmes, *Basil II and the Governance of Empire 976–1025* (Oxford: Oxford University Press, 2005), 98, n. 69. It would appear that the title *Magistros* is the indicator for the person being Grigor not Bagrat.
54 Skylitzes, *Synopsis Historiarum*, ed. 339, trans. 321; Stephen of Taron, *Patmut'iwn tiezerakan*, III, XXXIII, ed. 261, trans. 297.
55 For full history of the family see Nicholas Adontz, 'Les Taronites en Arménie et à Byzance', *Byzantion* 9 (1934): 715–38.
56 Skylitzes, *Synopsis Historiarum*, ed. 341, trans. 323.
57 Skylitzes, *Synopsis Historiarum*, ed. 341, trans. 323; Stephen of Taron, *Patmut'iwn tiezerakan*, III, XXXIII, ed. 261, trans. 297.
58 Skylitzes, *Synopsis Historiarum*, ed. 342, trans. 324–5.

59 A member of the Taronites family was to marry into the Komnenos family; see Garsoïan, 'Armenian Integration', 95, n. 160.
60 Cheynet, 'Les Arméniens', 67.
61 W. Seibt, *Die Skleroi* (Vienna: Verlag der Österreichischen Akademie der Wissenschaften, 1976); J.-C. Cheynet, 'Les Phocas', in *Le Traité sur la guerrilla (De velitatione) de l'empereur Nicéphore Phocas*, ed. and trans. G. Dagron and H Mihăescu (Paris: Editions du Centre national de la recherche scientifique, 1986), 289–315. The careers of Bardas Skleros and Bardas Phokas will only be summarized briefly in this chapter. For an in-depth analysis of their revolts against Basil II see Chapter 2.
62 Although somewhat dated see Stephen Runciman, *The Emperor Romanus Lecapenus and His Reign* (Cambridge: Cambridge University Press, 1963); Luisa Andriollo, 'Les Kourkouas (IXe-XIe siècle)', *Studies in Byzantine Sigillography* 11 (2012): 57–87.
63 J.-C. Cheynet, *Pouvoir et Contestations à Byzance (963-1210)*, Byzantina Sorbonensia 9 (Paris: Publications de le Sorbonne, 1996), 213–27.
64 Seibt, *Die Skleroi*, 20, see Table 1, seal 2 and 3.
65 Seibt, *Die Skleroi*, 23; for the two sons Niketas and Antonios see 24–7.
66 A man called Pantherios has been identified as a Skleroi; see J.-C. Cheynet, 'Notes arabo-byzantines', in *Mélanges Svoronos* (Rethymnon: Panepistēmio Krētēs, 1986), 145–52, at 145–7.
67 *George the Monk Continuatus*, 917, found in: Theophanes Continuatus, *Theophanes Continuatus, Ioannes Cameniata, Symeon Magister, Georgius Monachus*, ed. I. Bekker, CSHB (Bonn: Weber, 1838).
68 Seibt, *Die Skleroi*, 27–8: Pantherios was most likely appointed by Romanos I's sons Stephen and Constantine, yet the family does not seem to suffer with the regime change in 944.
69 Seibt, *Die Skleroi*, 30.
70 Skylitzes, *Synopsis Historiarum*, ed. 287–91, trans. 274–8. For commentary on the pro-Skleros source used by Skylitzes see Holmes, *Basil II*, 272–4.
71 Matthew of Edessa, *Armenia and the Crusades*, I, 16, 26; Tzimiskes seems to have been a nickname of Armenian origin – Chmushkik (Չմշկիկ) possibly referring to his short stature.
72 The revolts of Basil's reign are considered in full in the following chapter.
73 Attaleitates dismissed the claim that the Phokas family were descended from the Roman Fabii see Cheynet, 'Les Phocas', 289.
74 Cheynet, 'Les Phocas', 292.
75 Seals attest to protospatharios and droungarios of Aigaion Pelagos, among others; see Cheynet, 'Les Phocas', 292, n. 8–12.
76 *Oikeioi* equates to companions. An unusual seal notes that a Phokas held the position *épi tou manglabiou*, a member of the Manglabites corps of imperial bodyguards: Cheynet, *Sceaux de La Collection Zacos (Bibliothèque Nationale de France), se rapportant aux provinces orientales de L'empire byzantin* (Paris: Bibliothèque nationale, 2001), II, no. 276.
77 A post in the imperial stables and accompanying the emperor on horseback: Cheynet, 'Les Phocas', 293.
78 *George Monachus Continuatus*, 882–9.
79 For minor military commands see Skylitzes, *Synopsis Historiarum*, ed. 229, trans. 221. For promotion: Skylitzes, *Synopsis Historiarum*, ed. 238, trans. 230; Cheynet,

'Les Phocas', 197. For a scathing note on Bardas' subsequent career: Skylitzes, *Synopsis Historiarum*, ed. 240–1, trans. 232.
80 Alexander Vasiliev and Marius Canard, *Byzance et les Arabes*, 3 vols (Brussels: Institut de philologie et d'histoire orientales, 1935–68), ii.i, 350–1.
81 *Three Byzantine Military Treatises*, ed. and trans. G. Dennis, CFHB 25 (Washington D.C.: Dumbarton Oaks, 1985), 139.
82 *Three Byzantine Military Treatises*, 152–3; *Le Traité sur la guerrilla*, 151.
83 Charanis, *Armenians in the Byzantine Empire*, 34.
84 Platana is some nine miles west of Trebizond while Giaprino is further west near Giresan. Constantine VII Porphyrogennetos, *The Book of Ceremonies (De Ceremoniis)*, trans. A. Moffatt and M. Tall, 2 vols (Canberra: Australian Association for Byzantine Studies, 2012), ii, 44, 652, 656.
85 The primary sources start to distinguish from the older and larger 'Roman' themes with the new smaller and more militarily active 'Armenian' themes: Haldon, *Taktika of Leo VI*, 111.
86 Constantine VII Porphyrogennetos, *De Ceremoniis*, II, 45, 667.
87 *Sylloge tacticorum*, 35.4-5; John Haldon, 'Chapters II, 44 and 45 of the Book of Ceremonies: Theory and Practice in Tenth-Century Military Administration', *TM* 13 (2000): 201–352, at 305–6.
88 Leo the Deacon, *Leonis Diaconi Caloënsis Historiae Libri Decem*, IV.vii, ed. 64, trans. 113; Skylitzes, *Synopsis Historiarum*, ed. 275, trans. 264; Garsoïan, 'Armenian Integration', 59.
89 Nikephoros Phokas, 'Nikephoros Phokas Rules on the Land Claims and Homicide in the Armenian Themes', in *The Land Legislation of the Macedonian Emperors*, trans. E. McGeer, Medieval Sources in Translation 38 (Winnipeg: Hignell Printing, 2000), 86–9.
90 Symeon the Logothete, *Symeonis Magistri et Logothetae Chronicon*, ed. Staffan Wahlgren, CFHB 44 (Berlin and New York: Walter de Gruyter, 2006), 262–3; *George Monachus Continuatus*, II, 841.
91 Runciman, *Romanus Lecapenus*, 63.
92 *DAI*, 13, 72–3.
93 Theophanes Continuatus, *Theophanes Continuatus*, VI, 377.
94 Symeon the Logothete, *Symeonis Magistri*, 269. Skylitzes gives him the name Romanos: Skylitzes, *Synopsis Historiarum*, ed. 140, trans. 138.
95 Andriollo, 'Les Kourkouas', 63.
96 *DAI*, 45, 212–13.
97 Theophanes Continuatus, *Theophanes Continuatus* (Bonn), 428; Skylitzes, *Synopsis Historiarum*, ed. 230, trans. 222.
98 See earlier in the text for the Phokas family, who replaced the Kourkouai in 945.
99 Skylitzes, *Synopsis Historiarum*, ed. 256, trans. 247.
100 John Nesbitt, Nicolas Oikonomides and Eric McGeer, *Catalogue of Byzantine Seals at Dumbarton Oaks and in the Fogg Museum of Art* (Washington D.C.: Dumbarton Oaks, 1991–2005), iv., no. 55.13; Andriollo, 'Les Kourkouas', 68.
101 Leo the Deacon, *Leonis Diaconi Caloënsis Historiae Libri Decem*, VII.ix, ed. 126, trans. 173–4.
102 Leo the Deacon, *Leonis Diaconi Caloënsis Historiae Libri Decem*, IX.v, ed. 148, trans. 192.
103 *DAI*, XLIII, 194–9.
104 *DAI*, XLIII, 196–7; Skylitzes, *Synopsis Historiarum*, ed. 236, trans. 228. Cheynet identifies Nicholas and Leo as the sons of Tornik, despite the *DAI* and other sources using the singular παιδίον.

105 It is possible that Krinitis is the same man mentioned later in the *DAI* serving as the military governor in Peloponnesus: *DAI*, L, 234–5.
106 For further discussion on bilingualism, particularly in the eastern provinces see Gilbert Dagron, 'Formes et fonctions du pluralisme linguistique à Byzance (IXe -XIIe siècle)', *TM* 12 (1994): 219–40, at 238–9; Garsoïan, 'Armenian Integration', 102.
107 Skylitzes, *Synopsis Historiarum*, ed. 320, 322, trans. 303, 306.
108 This is, however, unlikely. The name Melias was relatively common as noted: Dédéyan, 'Mleh le grand, stratège de Lykandos', 78, n. 27.
109 Lyn Rodney, 'The Pigeon House Church at Cavuşin', *Jahrbuch der Österreichischen Byzantinistik* 33 (1983): 301–39, for argument on the link of shared royal imagery between Cappadocia and Tao see Antony Eastmond, *Royal Imagery in Medieval Georgia* (University Park, PA: The Pennsylvania State University Press, 1998), 29–34.
110 Yahya, *PO23*, 353–4; Matthew of Edessa, *Armenia and the Crusades*, I, 16, 26.
111 Garsoïan, 'Armenian Integration', 67; Hratch Bartikian, 'The Religious Diplomacy of Byzantium in Armenia during the Tenth and Eleventh Centuries', in *Armenian Studies: In Memoriam Haïg Berbérian*, ed. D. Kouymjian (Lisbon: Calouste Gulbenkian Foundation, 1986), 55–62, at 55.
112 Sarkissian, *The Council of Chalcedon*, 185.
113 Sarkissian, *The Council of Chalcedon*, 4. There was a violent rebellion against the Sassanids in the same year, which may account for the lack of representatives.
114 For historiographical outline of the date of the schism of the Armenian Church see Sarkissian, *The Council of Chalcedon*, 6–12; Nina Garsoïan, 'Quelques précisions préliminaires sur le schisme entre les églises byzantine et arménienne au sujet du concile de Chalcédoine', in *L'Arménie et Byzance: Histoire et culture*, ed. N. Garsoïan, Byzantina Sorbonensia 12 (Paris: Publications de la Sorbonne, 1996), 99–112, at 100.
115 Sarkissian, *The Council of Chalcedon*, 20.
116 For western settlements: Theophanes the Confessor, *Chronographia*, ed. I, 429, trans. 593; eastern settlements: Leo the Deacon, *Leonis Diaconi Caloënsis Historiae Libri Decem*, II.viii, ed. 28, trans. 80; Constantine Porphyrogennetos, *De Thematibus*, 75–6, 143–6.
117 Garsoïan, 'Armenian Integration', 68.
118 H. Bartikyan, 'Concerning the Byzantine Aristocratic Family of the Gavras', *Patma-Banasirakan Handes* 3 (1987): 190.
119 Constantine Trypanis, *Medieval and Modern Greek Poetry* (Oxford: Clarendon Press, 1951), 43. One will see similar comments coming from Attaleiates later in the eleventh century, someone who held negative attitudes towards the Armenians.
120 Stephen of Taron, *Patmut'iwn tiezerakan*, III, XL, ed. 268, trans. 302.
121 For various examples of cordial relations between the two confessions see Timothy Greenwood, 'Armenian Neighbours (600-1045)', in *The Cambridge History of the Byzantine Empire c. 500-1492*, ed. J. Shepard (Cambridge: Cambridge University Press, 2008), 333–64, at 357–9.
122 There is a division among scholars as to whether Yovhannes was pro-Chalcedonian or not. For discussion on the historiographical debates see the introduction: *Yovhannes Drasxanakertc'i, History of Armenia*, trans. K. Maksoudian (Atlanta, GA: Scholars Press, 1987), 4.
123 Yovhannes Drasxanakertc'i, *History of Armenia*, trans. K. Maksoudian (Atlanta, GA: Scholars Press, 1987), LIV, 189–97.
124 Yovhannes Drasxanakertc'i, LIV, 189; Nicholas I Patriarch of Constantinople, *Miscellaneous Writings*, ed. and trans. L. Westerink, CFHB 20 (Washington D.C.: Dumbarton Oaks Center for Byzantine Studies, 1981), 198, 32–5.

125 Matthew of Edessa, *Armenia and the Crusades*, I, 19, 29–32.
126 Nicholas I Patriarch of Constantinople, *Letters*, ed. and trans. R. J. H. Jenkins and L. Westerink, CFHB 6 (Washington D.C.: Dumbarton Oaks Center for Byzantine Studies, 1973), 139, 446–51.
127 Michael the Syrian, *Chronique*, iii, XV.vii, 185.
128 Kazhdan, 'The Armenians in the Byzantine Ruling Class', 438–51, at 444; Brouselle, 'L'intégration des Arméniens', 50.
129 Matthew of Edessa, *Armenia and the Crusades*, I, 16, 26–7.
130 Stephen of Taron, *Patmutʻiwn tiezerakan*, III, XXXI, ed. 258, trans. 295; Lang, *Armenia*, 193.
131 Stephen of Taron, *Patmutʻiwn tiezerakan*, III, XXXII, ed. 259, trans. 296.
132 Michael the Syrian, *Chronique*, iii, XIII.iv, 130.
133 Michael the Syrian, *Chronique*, iii, XIII.iv, 131.
134 Cowe, 'Armenian Immigration to the Sebastia Region', 112–15.
135 Stephen of Taron, *Patmutʻiwn tiezerakan*, III, VIII, ed. 181, trans. 233.
136 Stephen of Taron, *Patmutʻiwn tiezerakan*, III, VIII, ed. 182, trans. 234.
137 Stephen of Taron, *Patmutʻiwn tiezerakan*, III, XX, ed. 202, trans. 252; Bartikyan, 'The Religious Diplomacy of Byzantium', 58; Garsoïan, 'Armenian Integration', 73, 83.
138 Garsoïan, 'Armenian Integration', 93.
139 V. Arutjunova-Fidajan, 'The Ethno-Confessional Self-Awareness of Armenian Chalcedonians', *REArm* 21 (1988–9): 347.
140 Bartikyan, 'Concerning the Byzantine Aristocratic Family of the Gavras', 190.
141 Arutjunova-Fidajan, 'The Ethno-Confessional Self-Awareness of Armenian Chalcedonians', 346.
142 Arutjunova-Fidajan, 'The Ethno-Confessional Self-Awareness of Armenian Chalcedonians', 346.
143 Laiou, 'Institutional Mechanisms of Integrations', 164.
144 *Peira*, 14.16 and 54.6 in: *Jus graecoromanum*, IV, ed. I. and P. Zepos, 8 vols (Athens, 1931), 47, 224; Laiou, 'Institutional Mechanisms of Integrations', 164.
145 Cheynet, 'Les Arméniens', 67; Brouselle, 'L'intégration des Arméniens', 50.

Chapter 2

1 Skylitzes, *Synopsis Historiarum*, ed. 4, trans. 2; Warren Treadgold, *The Middle Byzantine Historians* (Basingstoke: Palgrave MacMillan, 2013), 247, for expanded discussion on Theodore of Side and Sebasteia see 247–58; Holmes, *Basil II*, 96–7.
2 Treadgold suggests that John the Monk may have been the author of Kekaumenos' biography: *Middle Byzantine Historians*, 263–5; see also Shepard, 'Scylitzes on Armenia in the 1040s, and the Role of Catacalon Cecaumenos', *REArm* XI (1975-1976): 269–311.
3 Gregory of Narek, *The Festal Works of St. Gregory of Narek: Annotated Translation of the Odes, Litanies, and Encomia*, trans. A. Terian (Collegeville, MN: Liturgical Press, 2016); Jean-Pierre Mahé, 'Basile II et byzance vus par Grigor Narekacʻi', *TM* 11 (1991): 555–73, at 559.
4 Aristakes Lastivertcʻi, *Matenagrutʻyan banasirakan kʻnnutʻyun*, trans. G. Manukyan (Yerevan: Erevani Hamalsarani Hrataraktʻutʻyun, 1977), I, 19.
5 Matthew of Edessa, *Armenia and the Crusades*, I, 53, 49.

6 Matthew of Edessa, *Armenia and the Crusades*, I, 50, 46; Aristakes, II, 27.
7 Stephen of Taron, *Patmut'iwn tiezerakan*, III, XLIII, ed. 276, trans. 308.
8 Aristakes, VI, 59; Matthew of Edessa, *Armenia and the Crusades*, II, 57, 133; C. Yarnley, 'Philaretos – Armenian bandit of Byzantine general?', *REArm 9* (1972): 331–54, at 332.
9 Garsoian is one of many historians who have held such a view.
10 George Ostrogorsky, *A History of the Byzantine State*, trans. J. Hussey (Oxford: Blackwell Publishing, 1968), 237; similar sentiments can be found with the previous cited work from: Nina Garsoïan, 'The Byzantine Annexation of the Armenian Kingdoms in the Eleventh Century', in *The Armenian People: from Ancient to Modern Times, vol.1, from Antiquity to the Fourteenth Century*, ed. R. Hovannisian (Basingstoke: Macmillan, 1997), 188.
11 Jonathan Shepard, 'Constantine VII, Caucasian Openings and the Road to Aleppo', in *Eastern Approaches to Byzantium*, ed. A. Eastmond (Aldershot: Ashgate Publishing, 2001), 19.
12 *DAI*, 46, 214–23; for in-depth analysis on this episode see Nicolas Evans, 'Kastron, Rabaḍ and Arḍūn: the Case of Artanuji', in *From Constantinople to the Frontier: The City and the Cities*, ed. N. Matheou, T. Kampianaki, and L. Bondioli (Leiden: Brill, 2016), 343–64.
13 *DAI*, 46, 216–17.
14 *DAI*, 46, 220–1.
15 *DAI*, 46, 222–3; Shephard, 'Constantine VII, Caucasian Openings and the Road to Aleppo', 27.
16 *DAI*, 44, 204–5.
17 Shephard, 'Constantine VII, Caucasian Openings and the Road to Aleppo', 25.
18 Taron being the exception, which was annexed in 966.
19 Matthew of Edessa, *Armenia and the Crusades*, I, 19–21, 27–33; Warren Treadgold, *A History of Byzantine State and Society* (Stanford, CA: Stanford University Press, 1997), 511, n. 24; Treadgold quotes the work of: René Grousset, *Histoire de l'Arménie, des origines à 1071* (Paris: Payot, 1947), 497.
20 A city that lies slightly to the east of the ruins from the ancient Armenian capital called Tigranakert, Matthew of Edessa, *Armenia and the Crusades*, I, 16, n.4, 288. For further information on Melias see Chapter 1.
21 Shephard, 'Constantine VII, Caucasian Openings and the Road to Aleppo', 28.
22 Karen Yuzbashian, 'Les titres byzantins en Arménie', in *L'Arménie et Byzance: Histoire et culture*, Byzantina Sorbonesia 12, ed. N. Garsoïan (Paris: Publications de la Sorbonne, 1996), 213–21.
23 Constantine VII Porphyrogennetos, *De Ceremoniis*, 48, 687.
24 Aristakes, I, 7; indeed if one is to acknowledge the inscription at Ošk'i, David's title was originally *magistros*: Eastmond, *Royal Imagery in Medieval Georgia*, 28; Wachtang Djobadze, *Early Medieval Georgian Monasteries in Historic Tao, Klarrjet'i, and Šavšet'i* (Stuttgart: Steiner, 1992), 108, 117.
25 *DAI*, 43, 195.
26 An excellent study of the political/military structures on the eastern frontier is: Catherine Holmes, 'Byzantium's Eastern Frontier in the Tenth and Eleventh Centuries,' in *Medieval Frontiers: Concepts and Practices*, ed. D. Abulafia and N. Berend (Aldershot: Ashgate Publishing, 2002), 83–104.
27 There is some confusion regarding the persistence of this title; see note below on the disagreements in our sources for when David was awarded the title.

28 Eastmond, *Royal Imagery in Medieval Georgia*, 21; for Ošk'i see Djobadze, *Early Medieval Georgian Monasteries*, 89–131. Detailed description of Byzantine style for the 'Donor Figures' see 116–19.
29 All of the families were tied together through marriage, though some bonds seemed stronger than others.
30 Skylitzes, *Synopsis Historiarum*, ed. 284, trans. 271; Leo the Deacon, *Leonis Diaconi Caloënsis Historiae Libri Decem*, ed. 95–6, trans. 144–5, details the replacement of important officials within the capital.
31 Skylitzes, *Synopsis Historiarum*, ed. 290–1, trans. 278–9; Leo the Deacon, *Leonis Diaconi Caloënsis Historiae Libri Decem*, ed. 112–13, trans. 162; Caesarea had been the city which first heralded Nikephoros II Phokas as emperor; the city and its environs were the heartlands of the Phokades' power.
32 For further details on Skleros' career under Tzimiskes see Chapter 1. An excellent modern account of John I Tzimiskes can be found in Kaldellis, *Streams of Gold, Rivers of Blood*, 65–80.
33 This Basil was in fact a Lekapenos. Surviving the downfall of this family on account of his eunuch status, Basil was able to gain considerable influence in the court at the expense of his arch-rival Joseph Bringas.
34 Skylitzes, *Synopsis Historiarum*, ed. 314, trans. 299.
35 Interestingly Skleros seems to have had significant support from the Armenians settled in the eastern themes. Skylitzes reports that in a skirmish near Oxylithos Roman forces slaughtered every Armenian they could find. Skylitzes, *Synopsis Historiarum*, ed. 321, trans. 305.
36 Skylitzes, *Synopsis Historiarum*, ed. 326, trans. 309, has Phokas personally requesting aid from David.
37 'Life of Our Blessed Fathers John and Euthymios', in *Georgian Monks on Mount Athos: Two Eleventh-Century Lives of the Hegoumenoi of Iviron*, trans. T. Grdzelidze (London: Bennett and Bloom, 2009), 4–6, 57–9. The book of K'art'li does not mention the revolt of Skleros, although a later addition to the book details it in full: *Georgian Royal Annals: Rewriting Caucasian History: The Medieval Armenian Adaption of the Georgian Chronicles*, trans. R. Thomson (Oxford: Clarendon Press, 1996), 373, n. 24; Skylitzes, *Synopsis Historiarum*, ed. 326, trans. 309; Matthew of Edessa, *Armenia and the Crusades*, I, 28, 36–7; Stephen of Taron, *Patmut'iwn tiezerakan*, III, XV, ed. 192, trans. 244. Stephen's account does not tell us when David received the title but does acknowledge the territories he gained for assisting Basil during the rebellion of Skleros. Skylitzes makes no reference as to when David became a *Kouropalates*, while Yahya informs us this may have come about after David agreed to cede his lands to Basil in 990: Yahya of Antioch, *PO* 23, 429. For debates on ownership of border territories see Nicholas Adontz, 'Tornik le moine', *Byzantion* 11 (1936): 143–64; John Forsyth, 'The Chronicle of Yahya ibn Sa'id al-Antaki' (Ph.D. Thesis, Unpublished: University of Michigan, 1977), 389, n. 47.
38 Holmes, *Basil II*, 245–6, offers a minimalistic and readable sweep of events; a far more detailed account can be found in: Forsyth, 'The Chronicle of Yahya ibn Sa'id al-Antaki', 370–462.
39 Leo the Deacon, *Leonis Diaconi Caloënsis Historiae Libri Decem*, X.viii, ed. 171, trans. 213; Skylitzes, *Synopsis Historiarum*, ed. 330, trans. 313.
40 Skylitzes, *Synopsis Historiarum*, ed. 326, trans. 309; Yahya of Antioch, *PO* 23, 424–5.
41 This happened either in early 988 or 989: Leo the Deacon, *Leonis Diaconi Caloënsis Historiae Libri Decem*, X.ix, ed. 174, trans. 216, n. 88; Skylitzes, *Synopsis Historiarum*, ed. 336, trans. 318–19; Yahya of Antioch, *PO* 23, 425.

42 Yahya of Antioch, *PO* 23, 429.
43 Skylitzes, *Synopsis Historiarum*, ed. 339, trans. 321–2, offers a confused narrative that muddles the events of 990 with the expedition of Basil in 1000/1. For David's legacy on the development of royal imagery see Eastmond, *Royal Imagery in Medieval Georgia*, 20–39.
44 ազատ – literal translation is 'free' but commonly used to describe the entire Armenian noble class.
45 Aristakes, I, 7.
46 Matthew of Edessa, *Armenia and the Crusades*, I, 33, 39.
47 Skylitzes, *Synopsis Historiarum*, ed. 279, trans. 268.
48 Stephen of Taron, *Patmut'iwn tiezerakan*, III, XLIII, ed. 278, trans. 310. Sadly, our Byzantine sources provide no further illumination on this either.
49 Yahya of Antioch, *PO* 23, 430.
50 For further exploration on the dating issues in Matthew, see Andrews, 'The Chronology of the Chronicle: An Explanation of the Dating errors within Book 1 of the Chronicle of Matthew of Edessa', *REArm* 32 (2010): 141–64.
51 See earlier for Basil's portrayal in both Georgian and Armenian sources which is surprisingly positive.
52 Aristakes, I, 7; Stephen of Taron, *Patmut'iwn tiezerakan*, III, XLIII, ed. 277, trans. 309 and XLIV, ed. 278, trans. 310.
53 *Royal Georgian Chronicle*, 374, n. 25.
54 Stephen of Taron, *Patmut'iwn tiezerakan*, III, XLIV, ed. 279, trans. 310–11; Yahya of Antioch, *PO* 23, 460; Holmes, *Basil II*, 481.
55 Aristakes, I, 11.
56 Aristakes, I, 11.
57 Aristakes, I, 11.
58 Skylitzes, *Synopsis Historiarum*, ed. 366, trans. 346. The book of K'art'li omits any transgression on the part of Giorgi.
59 This date is corroborated in both the Georgian and Armenian version of the K'art'li: *Royal Georgian Chronicle*, 280 (Arm), 281–2 (Geo).
60 Aristakes, II, 19.
61 Yahya of Antioch, *PO* 47, 461.
62 A specific reference to the meeting can only be found in the Armenian version; the Georgian simply states: '[Basil stayed] in the vicinity of Trebizond. And there passed between them (the Georgians) envoys for peace and friendship.' *Royal Georgian Chronicle*, 282–3.
63 Matthew of Edessa, *Armenia and the Crusades*, I, 50, 46; Aristakes, II, 27; *Royal Georgian Chronicle*, 285.
64 Matthew of Edessa, *Armenia and the Crusades*, I, 50, 46. Dostourian notes that Paghakdziak was probably a monastery in the Amanus Mountains; Romanos III has an episode involving monks in these monasteries during his reign which will be touched on in section 'Religious Antagonism' in Chapter 3.
65 This may be a characteristic example of Matthew utilizing the eleventh-century chronicle of Yakob Sanahnec'i, which would explain the unusual occurrence of an amicable tone in Matthew's account when discussing the Byzantines in the early eleventh century. The questions surrounding Basil's religious convictions and his image in the Armenian chronicles will be expanded upon further in the chapter.
66 Aristakes, II, 29. As mentioned previously a point of fact that Bourtnoutian confuses with Senek'erim of Vaspurakan.
67 Matthew of Edessa, *Armenia and the Crusades*, I, 50, 46.

68 Skylitzes, *Synopsis Historiarum*, ed. 435, trans. 409.
69 Matthew of Edessa, *Armenia and the Crusades*, I, 9, 22. It should be noted that Matthew's account of this event is chronologically out of sequence. Aristakes has similar descriptions for the two brothers; see Aristakes, II, 15.
70 Matthew of Edessa, *Armenia and the Crusades*, I, 10, 23.
71 Aristakes, II, 15–16.
72 Aristakes, II, 15–16.
73 Aristakes, II, 15–16.
74 Despite other occurrences of Iberian-Armenian military cooperation in the late tenth century, there is no reference in the book of K'art'li that Giorgi had assistance from Ani.
75 Skylitzes, *Synopsis Historiarum*, ed. 435, trans. 409.
76 Aristakes places the transfer 'only two- or three-years previous' to the revolt of 1022: Aristakes, III, 35. This date corroborates with Matthew of Edessa. While Yahya of Antioch's account is uncharacteristically vague, mentioning that Vaspurakan was handed over at around the same time as Basil's eastern campaign against Giorgi: Yahya of Antioch, *PO* 47, 463.
77 This date is hard to justify as Garsoïan does not provide footnotes in her article, though it might arise from the dating variants from the manuscripts: Garsoïan, 'Byzantine Annexation', 190; Dostourian mentions the dating issue in his notes where he states that the text gives the year 465, which would make it the year 1016–17, though four variants and the Jerusalem manuscript give 467. The later date Dostourian feels is the more accurate as this corroborates with the arrival of the Seljuks in Armenia; see Matthew of Edessa, *Armenia and the Crusades*, 295, 47, n. 1.
78 Garsoïan, 'Byzantine Annexation', 190.
79 Skylitzes, *A Synopsis of Byzantine History*, trans. 336, n. 211.
80 Matthew of Edessa, *Armenia and the Crusades*, I, 49, 45. This was most likely a spiritual adoption as it occurred in Hagia Sophia. The religious connotations of this will be expanded later.
81 Yahya of Antioch, *PO* 47, 463. Events covering this revolt will be discussed later.
82 Garsoïan, 'Byzantine Annexation', 190; Matthew of Edessa, *Armenia and the Crusades*, I, 49, 46, n. 3, at 296.
83 Skylitzes, *A Synopsis of Byzantine History*, trans. 316, n. 211.
84 Holmes, *Basil II*, 485; Mahé, 'Basile II et byzance vus par Grigor Narekac'i', 555–72.
85 Zapranik became a member of the palace guard; see Mahé, 'Basile II et byzance vus par Grigor Narekac'i', 557–8, 560, 565–7.
86 Aristakes, III, 35. It is likely that Aristakes is confusing the name David with that of Senek'erim's son who had an important role to play in the rebellion of 1022.
87 Matthew of Edessa, *Armenia and the Crusades*, I, 48–9, 44–5.
88 Skylitzes, *Synopsis Historiarum*, ed. 336, trans. 355.
89 The revolt and the impact it had on the Armenian settlement in Sebasteia will be explored later.
90 Aristakes, VII, 63.
91 The woman in question was the widow of Salman's rival called 'Utair.
92 Matthew of Edessa, *Armenia and the Crusades*, I, 58, 52.
93 Skylitzes, *Synopsis Historiarum*, ed. 387, trans. 365.
94 Skylitzes, *Synopsis Historiarum*, ed. 387, trans. 365; *DO* 58.106. 3689.
95 Michael Psellos, *Fourteen Byzantine Rulers*, trans. E. Sewter (Harmondsworth: Penguin Publishing, 1966), VI, 193. The depiction of an ambitious Maniakes fits into

the later narrative of his rebellion in 1042–3, and both Psellos and Skylitzes were writing with this knowledge in mind.
96   Matthew of Edessa, *Armenia and the Crusades*, I, 58, 53. Annexation of Artsruni unpacked later.
97   Stephen of Taron, *Patmut'iwn tiezerakan*, III, VIII, ed. 180, trans. 231.
98   Matthew of Edessa, *Armenia and the Crusades*, II, 23, 104.
99   Ostrogorsky, *A History of the Byzantine State*, 313–14; Michael Angold, *The Byzantine Empire, 1025–1204: A Political History* (Harlow: Pearson Education Limited, 1997), 34.
100   Holmes, *Basil II*, 539.
101   This is specifically talking about the military families that had dominated the military command structures in the tenth century; see section 'Acceptance and Adoption of "Roman Customs"' in Chapter 1 for a detailed analysis on the main protagonists. James Howard-Johnston, 'Crown Lands and the Defence of Imperial Authority in the Tenth and Eleventh Centuries', *Byzantinische Forschungen* 21 (1995): 97–8; Whittow, *Making of Orthodox Byzantium*, 379; Holmes, *Basil II*, 518.
102   Howard-Johnston, 'Crown Lands', 97.
103   This Nikephoros was the son of the rebel Bardas Phokas, the rebel who launched a coup attempt in 987–989. Nikephoros was also a first cousin of the Empress Theophanu, the wife of Otto II of Germany.
104   Matthew of Edessa's account follows Aristakes' version very closely.
105   Aristakes, III, 35.
106   Xiphias was a distinguished veteran of the Bulgarian wars. His exemplary service was one acknowledged in the leniency of his punishment for participating in the rebellion, serving out his exile on the island as a monk: Yahya of Antioch, *PO* 47, 469; Skylitzes, *Synopsis Historiarum*, ed. 366–7, trans. 346.
107   Yahya of Antioch, *PO* 47, 463–9.
108   Skylitzes, *A Synopsis of Byzantine History*, trans. 346, n. 264; Matthew of Edessa, *Armenia and the Crusades*, I, 51, 47.
109   Michael the Syrian, *Chronique*, 301; Matthew of Edessa, *Armenia and the Crusades*, I, 51, 47; Cowe, 'Armenian Immigration to the Sebastia Region', 120. These settlements are in the vicinity of the modern city of Kayseri in Turkey.
110   At least three years before the revolt in 1022: Holmes, *Basil II*, 519.
111   Yahya of Antioch, *PO* 47, 469.
112   Howard-Johnston, 'Crown Lands', 97.
113   Cheynet, 'Basil II and Asia Minor', in *Byzantium in the Year 1000*, ed. P. Magdalino (Leiden: Brill, 2003), 71–108, at 94.
114   For examination of the status of the Armenian migrants of the eleventh century, see Chapter 4.
115   See section 'The Acceptance and Adoption of "Roman Customs"' in Chapter 1.
116   Cheynet is of the opinion that internal and external policies were indistinguishable from one another in Byzantium. Cheynet, 'Basil II and Asia Minor', 105.
117   For full details see later in the text.
118   Cheynet, 'Basil II and Asia Minor', 94.
119   See section 'The Royal Armenians in the Empire' in Chapter 3.
120   Aristakes, X, 97–9.
121   Matthew of Edessa, *Armenia and the Crusades*, I, 70, 63 and 74, 66; Aristakes X, 93. Skylitzes account has 1045, but this is identifying the annexation rather than

the deaths of Ashot and Yovhannes: Skylitzes, *Synopsis Historiarum*, ed. 435, trans. 409.
122 Matthew of Edessa, *Armenia and the Crusades*, I, 74–6, 66–7; Aristakes X, 103.
123 Skylitzes, *Synopsis Historiarum*, ed. 423, trans. 398.
124 For the rebellion of Maniakes see Skylitzes, *Synopsis Historiarum*, ed. 428, trans. 402–3. For the Rus' attack on Constantinople see Skylitzes, *Synopsis Historiarum*, ed. 430, trans. 404.
125 Psellos, *Fourteen Byzantine Rulers*, VI, 199–203.
126 Skylitzes, *Synopsis Historiarum*, ed. 435, trans. 410, τοῦ δὲ δοῦλον μὲν ἑαυτὸν ἀνομολογοῦντος Ῥωμαίων.
127 Aristakes, X, 99–101.
128 Matthew of Edessa, *Armenia and the Crusades*, I, 84, 71.
129 Aristakes, X, 109–11.
130 Matthew of Edessa, *Armenia and the Crusades*, I, 84, 72.
131 See section 'Ani (I)' in this chapter.

Chapter 3

1 The Jacobite Syrians will also come under increasing pressure to conform to imperial policies in this period. Despite living in proximity to the lands of the exiled royals, the Syrians were not settled in such numbers nor with their political loyalty structures intact, this latter point being the most crucial point of difference.
2 Kekaumenos and the events in Armenia will only be touched on lightly in this book, namely in a focus on the life and career of Grigor *Magistros*. For a study of the Byzantine administration of Armenia see Viada Arutjunova-Fidajan, 'Some Aspects of the Military-Administrative Districts and of Byzantine Administration in Armenia during the 11th Century', *REArm* 20 (1986–7): 309–20.
3 Jonathan Shephard, 'A Suspected Source of Scylitzes' Synopsis Historian: The Great Catacalon Cecaumenus', *Byzantine and Modern Greek Studies* 16 (1992): 176–9; Treadgold, *Middle Byzantine Historians*, 263–7.
4 See Chapter 4.
5 Speros Vryonis, Jr, *The Decline of Medieval Hellenism in Asia Minor: And the Process of Islamization from the Eleventh through the Fifteenth Century*, (Berkeley: University of California Press, 1986), 42.
6 These topics were covered in detail in section 'Acceptance and Adoption of "Roman Customs"' of Chapter 1.
7 Cheynet, *Pouvoir et Contestations*, 396; and see section 'The Rebellion of 1022' in Chapter 2.
8 Abara had been the stronghold of the Paulician Karbeas in *c.*843 and later destroyed by Basil I in 871 with the destruction of the Paulician enclave. Larissa had been a fort attested to the reign of Leo VI. It was to be later given to Gagik-Abas of Kars in 1064. See Jean-Michel Thierry, 'Données archéologiques sur les principautés armèniennes de cappadoce orientale au XIe siècle', *REArm* 26 (1996–7): 119–72, at 159–61; Skylitzes, *Synopsis Historiarum*, ed. 354–5, trans. 336; Matthew of Edessa, *Armenia and the Crusades*, I, 48–9, 44–6; Aristakes III, 35; Michael the Syrian, *Chronique*, iii, XIII.v, 133.

9   The second city, Larissa, was originally the home of a *tourmarches* under the control of Sebasteia, as attested by a seal from the ninth century: Nesbitt, Oikonomides and McGeer, *Catalogue*, iv, no. 52.1. It later became the headquarters of its own *strategos* in the eleventh century; see Cheynet's commentary in: Skylitzes, *A Synopsis of Byzantine History*, trans. 336, n. 212. A seal attests the presence of Aronios, who was the *strategos* from *c*.1015: it is possible that he was replaced by the arrival of the Artsruni: Vitalien Laurent, *La Collection C. Orghidan: documents de sigillographie byzantine* (Paris: Presses universitaires de France, 1952), no. 231. A certain Pherses Tzotzikios is the more likely holder of the title; see Nesbitt, Oikonomides and McGeer, *Catalogue*, iv, no. 43.13.
10 The man identified as Ibn al-Dayrani by Yahya has been shown to have been Derenik Artsruni, the nephew of Senek'erim: Yahya of Antioch, *PO* 47, 463, n. 52.
11 Michael the Syrian, *Chronique*, iii, XVII.xiii, 301; Matthew of Edessa, *Armenia and the Crusades*, I, 51, 47. Gérard Dédéyan, 'L'immigration arménienne en Cappadoce au XIe siècle', *Byzantion* 45, no. 1 (1975): 41–115, at 79, n. 226. The discussions surrounding which characters were involved can be found in section 'The Rebellion of 1022' in Chapter 2. Xawatanēk was situated some 40 kilometres south of Caesarea and later offered by Constantine X to Gagik-Abas of Kars in 1064. Thierry, 'Données archéologiques sur les principautés armèniennes de cappadoce orientale au XIe siècle', 163.
12 Thomas Artsruni, *History of the House of Artsrunik*, trans. R. Thomson (Detroit: Wayne State University Press, 1985), 370–1.
13 Matthew of Edessa, *Armenia and the Crusades*, I, 49, 45–6.
14 Speros Vryonis, 'The Will of a Provincial Magnate, Eustathius Boilas (1059)', *DOP* 11 (1957): 263–77, at 264–6; Paul Lemerle, 'Le testament d'Eustathios Boïlas (Avril 1059)', in *Cinq études sur le XIe siècle byzantin* (Paris: du centre national de la recherche scientifique, 1977), 15–63.
15 As argued in Chapter 2, Basil used the Artsruni to alter the power balance in the very regions that the Skleroi and Phokades had built their own areas of support.
16 Jean-Michel Thierry, 'Monastères arméniens du Vaspurakan', *REArm* 6 (1969): 141–80, at 154. The location of the burial in the Monastery of the Holy Cross is corroborated in: Matthew of Edessa, *Armenia and the Crusades*, I, 54, 50.
17 *The Georgian Royal Annals*, 285.
18 Matthew of Edessa, *Armenia and the Crusades*, I, 62, 55.
19 Matthew of Edessa, *Armenia and the Crusades*, I, 84, 72. They are estimated to have been located east of Caesarea, either in Charsianon or Lykandos. Thierry, 'Données archéologiques sur les principautés armèniennes de cappadoce orientale au XIe siècle', 162. Despite the interpretations of some recent research, we cannot dismiss out of hand the feeling of betrayal behind Gagik's surrender of Ani: Kaldellis, *Streams of Gold, Rivers of Blood*, 191.
20 Aristakes, X, 111.
21 Aristakes, X, 113.
22 Skylitzes, *Synopsis Historiarum*, ed. 437, trans. 411.
23 Werner Seibt, 'War Gagik II. von Grossarmenien ca.1072-1073 Μέγας δοὺξ Χαρσιανοῦ?', in *Τὸ Ἑλληνικόν: Studies in Honor of Speros Vryonis*, 2 vols (New Rochelle, 1993), 159–68.
24 For authoritative analysis on this topic see Claude Cahen, 'La Première penetration turque en Asie Mineure', *Byzantion* 18 (1948): 5–67.

25 Vardan, 'The Historical Compilation of Vardan Arewelc'i', trans. and ed. R. Thomson, *DOP* 43 (1989): 193; Aristakes, X, 111.
26 Aristakes, X, 115.
27 Aristakes, X, 113.
28 Nesbitt, Oikonomides and McGeer, *Catalogue*, iv, no. 76.2.; Cheynet, 'Les Arméniens', 72-3, n. 32.
29 Note the similarities with the series of commands that Gagik II of Ani may have been entrusted with by the early 1070s. For development of larger commands on the eastern frontier in the late tenth and eleventh centuries see Holmes, *Basil II*, 313-67.
30 Matthew of Edessa, *Armenia and the Crusades*, II, 23, 104.
31 Tzamandos was situated in the theme of Lykandos. It later became the partial residence of the two *Katholikoi* Grigor II and Barsegh of Cilicia. Note that Comana Pontica is different to Comana in Cappadocia. Thierry, 'Données archéologiques sur les principautés arméniennes de cappadoce orientale au XIe siècle', 162-3.
32 Dédéyan, 'L'immigration arménienne', 105; Garsoïan, 'Armenian Integration', 111.
33 Michael the Syrian, *The Chronicle of Michael the Great*, 292; this event is not corroborated by the Syriac version; as Garsoïan notes this is also highly dubious as the cathedral of Kars was made of stone (consecrated in 937) and is still standing: Garsoïan, 'Armenian Integration', 77, n. 97.
34 Matthew of Edessa, *Armenia and the Crusades*, II, 30, 110; with possible extension of this policy into the Komnenian era see Garsoïan, 'Armenian Integration', 72-3.
35 Michael the Syrian, *Chronique*, iii, XV.iii, 169; Vryonis, *The Decline of Medieval Hellenism*, 103. Both Cheynet and Dédéyan reject the claim by Michael the Syrian; see 'Les Arméniens', 68-71; Dédéyan, 'L'immigration arménienne', 114-15.
36 Bartikian, 'The Religious Diplomacy of Byzantium in Armenia', 55; Speros Vryonis, Jr., 'Byzantium: The Social Basis of Decline in the Eleventh Century', in *Byzantium: Its Internal History and Relations with the Muslim World*, ed. S. Vryonis (London: Variorum Reprints, 1971), 173.
37 Thierry, 'Données archéologiques sur les principautés arméniennes de cappadoce orientale au XIe siècle', 124-9.
38 Thierry, 'Données archéologiques sur les principautés arméniennes de cappadoce orientale au XIe siècle', 135-9.
39 Matthew of Edessa, *Armenia and the Crusades*, II, 46, 124.
40 Matthew of Edessa, *Armenia and the Crusades*, II, 74, 145. A story we will return to in Chapter 4.
41 The allegations against Romanos III and his drafting of monks into military service cannot truly be viewed as imperially sanctioned persecution.
42 Cowe, 'Armenian Immigration to the Sebastia Region', 113.
43 Cowe, 'Armenian Immigration to the Sebastia Region', 112-15.
44 Cowe, 'Armenian Immigration to the Sebastia Region', 112.
45 Similar logic has been employed to suggest that Basil II annexed the Armenian kingdoms because of a long-standing foreign policy sought out by the Macedonian emperors. See Chapter 2 for arguments against this theory.
46 Matthew of Edessa, *Armenia and the Crusades*, I, 93, 77-8; Aristakes, 14, ed. 82, trans. 89-90.
47 Aristakes, XIV, 163.
48 See later for discussion on the particular episode.
49 Aristakes, XIV, 163; Matthew of Edessa, *Armenia and the Crusades*, I, 93, 77-8.

50 Aristakes, XIV, 163; Matthew of Edessa, *Armenia and the Crusades*, I, 93, 77–8.
51 Constantine X Doukas ascended to the throne in late 1059, so this has to be the earliest date from which Khachik was summoned to the capital.
52 Aristakes, XIV, 163–5; Matthew of Edessa, *Armenia and the Crusades*, II, 14, 97.
53 Matthew of Edessa, *Armenia and the Crusades*, II, 13, 96.
54 For an excellent summary on this issue see Andrews, 'The Chronology of the Chronicle', 141–64.
55 Aristakes, VI, 59. The location of this monastery seems to be somewhere in the Taurus Mountains, though the exact location is matter of debate.
56 Matthew of Edessa, *Armenia and the Crusades*, II, 14, 97; Aristakes, XIV, 163.
57 Matthew of Edessa, *Armenia and the Crusades*, II, 14, 97; it is possible that Matthew was confusing this episode, largely revolving around the issue of money, with that of 1065 where theological differences were the main concern.
58 Matthew of Edessa, *Armenia and the Crusades*, II, 25–6, 106–7.
59 Matthew of Edessa, *Armenia and the Crusades*, II, 30, 110.
60 Matthew of Edessa, *Armenia and the Crusades*, II, 30, 110.
61 Matthew of Edessa, *Armenia and the Crusades*, II, 30, 110.
62 Matthew of Edessa, *Armenia and the Crusades*, II, 30, 111.
63 Matthew of Edessa, *Armenia and the Crusades*, II, 30, 111.
64 I personally see this 'document' as a later construction, perhaps in the early twelfth century. But this does not discount some of the important themes here, Gagik's character, the defence of the Armenian faith and perhaps even the desire by some Armenian churchmen to see a union with Constantinople through the later eleventh century.
65 Matthew of Edessa, *Armenia and the Crusades*, II, 42, 121.
66 Matthew of Edessa, *Armenia and the Crusades*, II, 43, 121–2.
67 Matthew of Edessa, *Armenia and the Crusades*, II, 43, 121–2.
68 Matthew of Edessa, *Armenia and the Crusades*, II, 43, 123.
69 Matthew of Edessa, *Armenia and the Crusades*, II, 43, 121.
70 Arguably this is the use by Matthew of standardized polemical language when used in describing the religious animosity of his own day: Matthew of Edessa, *Armenia and the Crusades*, II, 43, 121.
71 Matthew of Edessa, *Armenia and the Crusades*, II, 43, 122.
72 The full story of this peculiar episode can be found at: Matthew of Edessa, *Armenia and the Crusades*, II, 43, 121–3; see also; Christopher MacEvitt, 'The King, the Bishop, and the Dog Who Killed Him: Canine Cultural Encounters and Medieval Armenian Identity', in *Old Worlds, New Worlds: European Cultural Encounters, c.1100 – c.1750*, ed. L. Bailey, L. Diggelman, and K. Phillips (Turnhout: Brepols, 2009), 31–51.
73 Holmes, *Basil II*, 390–1; Holmes, 'How the East was Won in the Reign of Basil II', in *Eastern Approaches to Byzantium*, ed. A. Eastmond (Aldershot: Ashgate Publishing, 2001), 45. J.-C. Cheynet, 'Les limites du pouvoir à Byzance: Une forme de tolérance?' in *Toleration and Repression in the Middles Ages. In Memory of Lenos Mavromatis*, ed. K. Nikolaou (Athens: The National Hellenic Research Foundation, 2002), 15–28, at 28.
74 Dagron, 'Minorités ethniques et religieuses', 200. There is a further issue with Byzantine perceptions of the Miaphysite Christians. The label of 'heretic' seems too strong as used by Garsoïan, clearly toleration was the only way of control: Garsoïan, 'Armenian Integration', 68.

75 Anna Komnene, *Alexias*, IX, 6, ed. 272, trans. 250; Garsoïan, 'Armenian Integration', 95; Kazhdan, 'The Armenians in the Byzantine Ruling Class', 446.
76 Matthew of Edessa, *Armenia and the Crusades*, II, 60, 137; Garsoïan, 'Armenian Integration', 66, n. 59.
77 Colophon translated and included in: Garsoïan, *Armenian Integration*, 86, n. 131 and 57, n. 14.
78 Garsoïan, 'Armenian Integration', 111.
79 Viada Arutjunova-Fidajan, 'L'image de l'Empire byzantine dans l'historiographie arménienne médiévale (Xe-XIe s.)', in *L'Arménie et Byzance: Histoire et culture*, ed. N. Garsoïan, Byzantina Sorbonesia 12 (Paris: Publications de la Sorbonne, 1996), 15.
80 Matthew of Edessa, *Armenia and the Crusades*, II, 43, 122.
81 Garsoïan, 'Armenian Integration', 79.
82 Skylitzes, *Synopsis Historiarum*, ed. 354–5; trans. 336.
83 Cheynet, *Pouvoir et Contestations*, 396.
84 Matthew of Edessa, *Armenia and the Crusades*, I, 51, 47.
85 Garsoïan, 'Armenian Integration', 66.
86 This is the only source that mentions this episode.
87 ἀκόλουθος – the captain of the Varangian Guard.
88 Shapuh was a general who had served the Artsruni in Vaspurakan and migrated with the ruling house in *c*.1020. He appears in Matthew's account of the first encounter with the Turkomans in *c*.1016: Matthew of Edessa, *Armenia and the Crusades*, I, 48, 44–5. Shapuh does not appear in other accounts.
89 Matthew of Edessa, *Armenia and the Crusades*, I, 72–3, 65.
90 Information on this rebellion is relatively scant, although presumed to have occurred: Garsoïan, 'Armenian Integration', 115.
91 Aristakes, X, 113.
92 See Weller, *Imagining pre-Modern Imperialism*, 167, n. 411.
93 Aristakes, XIII, 157. For an extensive investigation into the events in Armenia during 1048 and the sources for it see Shepard, 'Scylitzes on Armenia', 269–311.
94 Aaron is later named as the *doux* of Mesopotamia in 1059, which corresponds with the death of Grigor (had he ever held the office). See Lemerle, 'Le testament d'Eustathios Boïlas (Avril 1059)', 39.
95 Weller, *Imagining pre-Modern Imperialism*, 159.
96 The term 'Hellenism' is problematic here. The Byzantine historiographical tradition would recognize no such term, but the point still stands that the educational heritage that was preserved in the classics was something that Grigor would have had a close relationship with: Weller, *Imagining pre-Modern Imperialism*, 161.
97 C. Yarnley, 'The Armenian Philhellenes: A Study of the Spread of Byzantine Religious and Cultural Ideas among the Armenians in the Tenth and Eleventh Centuries A.D.', *Eastern Churches Review* 8, no. 1 (1976): 45–53, at 50–1.
98 Skylitzes, *Synopsis Historiarum*, ed. 437, trans. 411.
99 David Artsruni seems to have died in *c*.1035/6; he was clearly not alive at the time of the rebellion of 1040 as highlighted earlier: Matthew of Edessa, *Armenia and the Crusades*, I, 62, 55.
100 Aristakes, X, 113.
101 Matthew of Edessa, *Armenia and the Crusades*, I, 62, 55.
102 Matthew of Edessa, *Armenia and the Crusades*, II, 30, 110.
103 Nina Garsoïan, 'The Independent Kingdoms of Medieval Armenia', in *The Armenian People: from Ancient to Modern Times, vol.1, from Antiquity to the*

Fourteenth Century, ed. R. Hovannisian (Basingstoke: Macmillan, 1997), 143–85, at 156–7.
104 Matthew of Edessa, *Armenia and the Crusades*, II, 30, 111. Such a statement reinforces how Gagik's position was remembered by Matthew's generation. Whether Matthew had access to oral testimony by a witness or if this is a rendering of what the author imagined Gagik to have said, we will never know.
105 Matthew of Edessa, *Armenia and the Crusades*, II, 30, 110–11.
106 Matthew of Edessa, *Armenia and the Crusades*, II, 43, 122.
107 The translator of Matthew, Ara Dostourian, notes that the original Turkish name cannot be ascertained and so it has been left in the nearest Armenian form, Nikephoros Bryennios calls Ktrich' *Chrysoskoulos*; see 318, 54, n. 1.
108 Matthew of Edessa, *Armenia and the Crusades*, II, 54, 129.
109 Matthew of Edessa, *Armenia and the Crusades*, II, 57, 132.
110 Matthew of Edessa, *Armenia and the Crusades*, II, 57, 132.
111 Michael Attaleiates, *The History*, trans. A. Kaldellis and D. Krallis (Cambridge, MA: Harvard University Press, 2012), 18.17, 247.
112 Matthew of Edessa, *Armenia and the Crusades*, II, 57, 133.
113 Matthew of Edessa, *Armenia and the Crusades*, II, 57, 133. Or indeed polemical spin on the part of the author.
114 Attaleiates, *The History*, 16.7, 177.
115 The choice of 'strategic' has been carefully chosen to avoid comparison with Friendly's interpretation of the battle. See first line of introduction: Alfred Friendly, *The Dreadful Day: Battle of Manzikert, 1071* (London: Hutchinson, 1981), 17.
116 Garsoïan, 'Armenian Integration', 62.
117 Skylitzes, *Synopsis Historiarum*, ed. 437, trans. 411.
118 Attaleiates, *The History*, 17.12, 207.
119 Attaleiates, *The History*, 17.15, 213.
120 Attaleiates, *The History*, 18.19, 249.
121 Attaleiates, *The History*, 20.14, 277.
122 Michael the Syrian, *Chronique*, iii, XV.iii, 169; Vryonis, *The Decline of Medieval Hellenism*, 103.
123 Aristakes, XXV, 319.

Chapter 4

1 For thorough analysis of this crucial period see Alexander Beihammer, *Byzantium and the Emergence of Muslim-Turkish Anatolia, ca. 1040-1130* (London: Taylor & Francis Group, 2017), ch. 5, 198–243; Kaldellis, *Streams of Gold, Rivers of Blood*, 248–70.
2 For discussions as to why Skylitzes finished his first edition in 1057, see Treadgold, *Middle Byzantine Historians*, 331–2.
3 Beihammer, *Byzantium and the Emergence of Muslim-Turkish Anatolia*, 33; for broader discussion on the earliest texts from the Seljuk tradition see Andrew Peacock, *Early Seljuk History: A New Interpretation* (London and New York: Routledge, 2010), 6–12.
4 *Annals of the Seljuk Turks*, trans. D. Richards, 1–10; Beihammer, *Byzantium and the Emergence of Muslim-Turkish Anatolia*, 34; Andrew Peacock, *The Great Seljuk Empire* (Edinburgh: Edinburgh University Press, 2015), 15–16.

5   To name a few (though not comprehensive list): Friendly, *The Dreadful Day*, John Haldon, *The Byzantine Wars* (Stroud: The History Press, 2008), 109–27; Kaldellis, *Streams of Gold, Rivers of Blood*, 241–8.
6   In truth the Diogenes family had only risen to their position a few generations earlier under Basil II, but their role in the army reinforced their thorough Roman credentials.
7   Attaleiates, *The History*, 20.26, 301.
8   Attaleiates, *The History*, 20.23, 293.
9   Attaleiates, *The History*, 21.3, 307.
10 Ibn al-Athir, *The Annals of the Saljuq Turks: Selections from Al-Kāmil fī al-tārīkh*, trans. D. Richards (London: Routledge, 2002), 170. Attaleiates mentions conversations regarding marriage between the respective families which was almost unheard of for a Byzantine prince/princess, particularly with a potential conversion to Islam by a member of the imperial family: Attaleiates, *The History*, XX, 26, 301.
11 Zahir al-Din Nishapuri, *The History of the Seljuq Turks: From the Jami al-Tawarikh: An Ilkhanid Adaption of the Saljuq-nama of Zahir al-Din Nishapuri*, trans. K. Luther, ed. C. Bosworth (Richmond, Surrey: Curzon Press, 2001), 52.
12 Skylitzes Continuatus, Ἡ Συνέχεια τῆς χρονογραφίας τοῦ Ἰωάννου Σκυλίτςη, ed. E. T. Tsolakes (Thessaloniki, 1968), 156–7. The failure of the Byzantines to uphold their end of the treaty is seen by our Muslim sources as the decisive factor that led to Alp-Arslan ordering his emirs to invade and settle on Byzantine territory: Beihammer, *Byzantium and the Emergence of Muslim-Turkish Anatolia*, 201–2.
13 Attaleiates, *The History*, 21.8, 315.
14 Ibn al-Athir, *The Annals of the Saljuq Turks*, 172.
15 Sibṭ ibn al-Jawzi, *Mirāt al-Zamān fī Ta'rikh al-Ayān (Mirror of Time Concerning the History of Notables)*; Beihammer, *Byzantium and the Emergence of Muslim-Turkish Anatolia*, 201.
16 Attaleiates, *The History*, 18.19, 249.
17 Matthew of Edessa, *Armenia and the Crusades*, II, 27, 108.
18 Cf. with the personal relationship between Bardas Phokas and David of Tao (see Chapter 2).
19 Beihammer refers to an element of separatism under Chatatourios during the civil strife between Romanos IV and the Doukas. This is arguably premature. While Chataourios supported Romanos over the new regime in Constantinople, allying oneself with a 'deposed' emperor was far more common practice within the Byzantine political landscape than is generally assumed. It can certainly be argued that a precedent was set for those who survived the conflict, that is, Philaretos: Beihammer, *Byzantium and the Emergence of Muslim-Turkish Anatolia*, 285.
20 Attaleiates, *The History*, 21.8, 317.
21 Psellos, *Chronographia*, VII, 364.
22 On the development of the position through late tenth to mid-eleventh century of *doux/katepano* of Antioch see Holmes, *Basil II*, 330–60; Philaretos' first formal title comes later in 1078.
23 Warren Treadgold, *Byzantium and Its Army, 284-1081* (Stanford: Stanford University Press, 1995), 41, n. 58.
24 Matthew of Edessa, *Armenia and the Crusades*, II, 60, 137.
25 Attaleiates, *The History*, 22.2, 329, n. 231, 604; Nikephoros Bryennios, *Material for History*, ed. and trans. P. Gautier, CFHB 9 (Brussels: Byzantion, 1975), II, 1, 142.
26 Attaleiates, *The History*, 22.3, 329–31.

27 Attaleiates, *The History*, 16.13, 185.
28 Vitalien Laurent, 'La chronologie des gouverneurs d'Antioche sous la second domination byzantine', *Mélanges de l'Université Saint-Joseph* 38 (1962): 219–54, at 246–7.
29 Joespeh Tarchaniotes had been part of the army that split before Manzikert. Our sources from the Muslim perspective claim that this force was decisively defeated by Alp-Arslan before Manzikert, whereas our Byzantine sources seem to suggest Joespeh had fled back to Melitene and played no further part in the debacle at Manzikert. Bryennios, *Material for History*, II, 28, 200.
30 Bryennios, *Material for History*, II, 28, n. 6, 7, 201; Laurent, 'La chronologie des gouverneurs d'Antioche sous la seconde domination byzantine', 249–50.
31 Vitalien Laurent dated Vasak's tenure to 1078, based on the Armenian year 527, which he claims Matthew stated. However, the year actually stated by Matthew was 525, which Dostourian puts at 1076–7: Matthew of Edessa, *Armenia and the Crusades*, II, 66, 141; Vardan, 'The Historical Compilation of Vardan Arewelc'i', 104.
32 Bryennios, *Material for History*, II, 28, 202.
33 Matthew of Edessa, *Armenia and the Crusades*, II, 66, 141.
34 Matthew of Edessa, *Armenia and the Crusades*, II, 66, 141.
35 Krallis, *Michael Attaleiates*, 126–34.
36 Zahir al-Din Nishapuri, *The History of the Seljuq Turks*, 52.
37 Zahir al-Din Nishapuri, *The History of the Seljuq Turks*, 53.
38 Beihammer, *Byzantium and the Emergence of Muslim-Turkish Anatolia*, 201–2.
39 For consistency's sake it is important to remind the reader that these stories come from Matthew of Edessa, whose account is not always concrete in fact.
40 Michael the Syrian, *Chronique*, iii, XV.iv, 173; Beihammer, *Byzantium and the Emergence of Muslim-Turkish Anatolia*, 203.
41 Matthew of Edessa, *Armenia and the Crusades*, II, 74, 144; T. S. R. Boase, *The Cilician Kingdom of Armenia* (Edinburgh: Scottish Academic Press, 1978), 3.
42 Matthew of Edessa, *Armenia and the Crusades*, II, 74, 144; *Les Sceaux Byzantins de La Collection Henri Seyrig*, eds. J.-C. Cheynet, C. Morrisson, and W. Seibt (Paris: Bibliothèque nationale, 1991), No. 40, 43–4. It was claimed by Boase that he received the position under Constantine IX in 1042, though no primary evidence was cited, and this would be an extraordinarily long tenure as governor which leads to the conclusion that this is untrue: Boase, *The Cilician Kingdom*, 2; Yarnley, 'Philaretos', 333; see Garsoïan, 'Armenian Integration', 57, n. 14 for issues on Ablgharib's installation date. John Pryor and Michael Jeffreys, 'Alexios, Bohemond, and Byzantium's Euphrates Frontier: A Tale of Two Cretans', *Crusades* 11 (2012): 31–86, at 68.
43 For the continuing practice of marriage alliances between Armenians and the participants of the First Crusade see Natasha Hodgson, 'Conflict and Cohabitation: Marriage and Diplomacy between Latins and Cilician Armenians, c.1097-1253', in *The Crusades and the Near East*, ed. C. Kostick (Abingdon: Routledge, 2011).
44 See earlier in the text for Seibt's identification of a seal belonging to Gagik which named him as *strategos* of Charsianon.
45 This seems to be referring to Gagik's journey during the reign of Constantine X Doukas and therefore is most likely apocryphal.
46 Matthew offers a different lineage: Matthew of Edessa, *Armenia and the Crusades*, II, 74, 144.

47 Vardan, 'The Historical Compilation of Vardan Arewelc'i', 105–6. Vardan also narrates a bizarre story of Yohanes (the elder son of Gagik) being killed in Constantinople. Some secondary debates: Boase, *The Cilician Kingdom*, 3; Yarnley, 'Philaretos', 337, n. 32.
48 Matthew of Edessa, *Armenia and the Crusades*, II, 74, 144; n. 4, 323; The same men are cited by Frankopan as evidence of Byzantine resistance to the invading Turks: Peter Frankopan, *The First Crusade: The Call from the East* (London: The Bodley Head, 2012), 43.
49 Matthew of Edessa, *Armenia and the Crusades*, II, 74, 145.
50 More on this development across the south-eastern frontier can be found in: Asa Ager, *The Islamic-Byzantine Frontier: Interaction and Exchange Among Muslim and Christian Communities* (London: I.B. Tauris, 2016), 273–6.
51 Samuel of Ani, 'Tables Chronologiques', trans. M.-C. Brosset, *Collection d'historiens arméniens*, 2 vols (St Petersburg: Imprimerie de académie impériale des sciences, 1876), ii, 339–483 at 453; For further discussion of evidence for a sudden migration after Gagik's death see Gérard Dédéyan, *Les arméniens entre grecs, musulmans, et croisés: Étude sur les pouvoirs arméniens dans le Proche-Orient méditerranean (1068-1150)*, 2 vols (Lisbon: Fundação Calouste Gulbenkian, 2003), I, 376–82.
52 Matthew of Edessa, *Armenia and the Crusades*, II, 74, 145; Yarnley, 'Philaretos', 337–8.
53 Matthew of Edessa, *Armenia and the Crusades*, II, 74, 145, who dates the king's death to 528/1079–80; for an earlier date, see Samuel of Ani, 'Tables Chronologiques', 449. For range of dates from secondary sources see Yarnley, 'Philaretos', 337–8; Boase, *The Cilician Kingdom*, 3; Dédéyan, *Les arméniens*, I, 375–6; Pryor and Jeffreys, 'Alexios, Bohemond, and Byzantium's Euphrates Frontier', 67.
54 Pryor and Jeffreys, 'Alexios, Bohemond, and Byzantium's Euphrates Frontier', 68; Beihammer, *Byzantium and the Emergence of Muslim-Turkish Anatolia*, 290.
55 Samuel of Ani, 'Tables Chronologiques', 453.
56 Matthew of Edessa, *Armenia and the Crusades*, II, 43, 123; II, 57, 133.
57 Attaleiates, *The History*, 16.4, 173; Matthew of Edessa, *Armenia and the Crusades*, II, 12, 94–6.
58 See section 'Religious Antagonism' in Chapter 3.
59 Yarnley, 'Philaretos', 337.
60 Yarnley, 'Philaretos', 337.
61 Matthew of Edessa, *Armenia and the Crusades*, II, 74, 144–5.
62 Attaleiates, *The History*, 35.10, 549.
63 This is most prominent in Anna Komnene's account: *Alexiad*, VI, 9, ed. 186, trans. 169.
64 Matthew of Edessa, *Armenia and the Crusades*, II, 60, 137.
65 Dédéyan, *Les Arméniens*, I, 32.
66 He is referred to as Ursinus in Albert of Aachen, *Historia Iherosolimitana*, ed. and trans. S. B. Edgington (Oxford: Oxford University Press, 2007), XI. 40, 816–17, and Ralph of Caen, *The Gesta Tancredi of Ralph of Caen: A History of the Normans on the Frist Crusade*, trans. B. and D. Bachrach, Crusade Texts in Translation 12 (Aldershot: Ashgate, 2005), XL, 63, but translated by Edgington to Oshin. J. Laurent argues that these three individuals were different people while MacEvitt finds the similarities between Oshin and Ursinus convincing. See J. Laurent, 'Arméniens de Cilicie: Aspiétès, Oschin, Ursinus', in *Études d'histoire arménienne* (Louvain: Éditions Peeters, 1971), 51–60; Christopher MacEvitt, *The Crusades and the Christian World*

of the East: Rough Tolerance (Philadelphia: University of Pennsylvania Press, 2008), 57.
67 Samuel of Ani, 'Tables Chronologiques', 453.
68 David of Sassoun is the hero of an Armenian epic poem *Daredevils of Sassoun* which recounts the resistance against the Muslim Arabs in the eight through tenth centuries.
69 Der Nersessian points to colophons for valuable information: Garegin I. Hovsepian, *Colophons of Manuscripts* (Antilias, 1951), col. 542, 552; these valuable resources are expanded in full: Dédéyan, *Les arméniens*, I, 311.
70 Dédéyan, *Les arméniens*, I, 318.
71 For claims of Byzantine authority still existing see Pryor and Jeffreys, 'Alexios, Bohemond, and Byzantium's Euphrates Frontier', 38. While for the opposite view see Beihammer, *Byzantium and the Emergence of Muslim-Turkish Anatolia*, 286, n. 125.
72 An excellent overview of the seal evidence has been completed by Ioanna Koltsida-Makre, 'Philaretos Brachamios, Portrait of a Byzantine Official', *TM* 21, no. 1 (2017): 325–32.
73 Attaleiates, *The History*, 35.10, 549; Skylitzes Continuatus, Ἡ Συνέχεια τῆς χρονογραφίας τοῦ Ἰωάννου Σκυλίτςη, 136; Anna's portrayal of Philaretos' loyalty towards Romanos seems misplaced or at least ill-informed; see Anna Komnene, *Alexias*, VI, 9, ed. 186, trans. 169; Pryor and Jeffreys, 'Alexios, Bohemond, and Byzantium's Euphrates Frontier', 38.
74 J.-C. Cheynet, *La société byzantine: l'apport des sceaux*, 2 vols (Paris: Association des amis du Centre d'histoire et civilisation de Byzance, 2008), II, 392–3.
75 Cheynet, *La société byzantine*, II, 393–6.
76 Skylitzes Continuatus, Ἡ Συνέχεια τῆς χρονογραφίας τοῦ Ἰωάννου Σκυλίτςη, 136–7.
77 Attaleiates, *The History*, 35.10, 549–51.
78 For full breakdown of seals see Pryor and Jeffreys, 'Alexios, Bohemond, and Byzantium's Euphrates Frontier', 83 and Cheynet, *La société byzantine*, II, 391–405.
79 Pryor and Jeffreys, 'Alexios, Bohemond, and Byzantium's Euphrates Frontier', 38.
80 Attaleiates, *The History*, 35.10, 549; Yarnley, 'Philaretos', 337.
81 See Attaleiates, *The History*, 18.12, 241, for where Philaretos seems to have failed in his task set by the emperor in defence against the Turks.
82 Koltsida-Makre, 'Philaretos Brachamios', 327.
83 Matthew of Edessa, *Armenia and the Crusades*, II, 60, 137; Attaleiates, *The History*, 18.12, 241.
84 This is Basil Apokapes, the executor to Eustathios Boilas' will and former Byzantine general. Alexios Savvides, 'The Armenian-Georgian-Byzantine family of Apocapes/Abukab in the 11th c.', Δίπτυχα 5 (1991): 96–104.
85 Known more commonly as Apokapes.
86 Mathew of Edessa, *Armenia and the Crusades*, II, 71, 142–3.
87 Michael Grünbart, 'Die Familie Apokapes im Licht neuer Quellen', in *Studies in Byzantine sigillography* 5, ed. N. Oikonomides (Washington D.C.: Dumbarton Oaks Research Library and Collection, 1998), 29–41.
88 Matthew of Edessa, *Armenia and the Crusades*, II, 77, 147; MacEvitt, *The Crusades and the Christian World of the East*, 66.
89 The translation of 'Ishkhan' (Իշխան) is 'prince'; therefore, this could actually be a generic reference to an aristocratic uprising rather than an individual with an unusual name.
90 Matthew of Edessa, *Armenia and the Crusades*, II, 77, 147.

91 Michael the Syrian, *Chronique*, iii, XV.iv, 173.
92 Attaleiates, *The History*, 17.15, 211–13.
93 Beihammer, *Byzantium and the Emergence of Muslim-Turkish Anatolia*, 226–31; Frankopan, *The First Crusade*, 46–7.
94 Ibn al-Athir, *The Annals of the Saljuq Turks*, 217–18; Beihammer, *Byzantium and the Emergence of Muslim-Turkish Anatolia*, 231.
95 Beihammer, *Byzantium and the Emergence of Muslim-Turkish Anatolia*, 231.
96 The chronicler only mentions 'Romans' as the controlling party of Tarsus: Sibṭ ibn al-Jawzi, *Mir'at*, 217, 229 taken from Beihammer, *Byzantium and the Emergence of Muslim-Turkish Anatolia*, 291. The same chronicle reports that a maternal uncle of Sulayman conquered Melitene in 1084, although it is highly unlikely this actually occurred as Gabriel of Melitene preserved his rule up until the arrival of the First Crusade.
97 Michael the Syrian, *Chronique*, iii, XV.vi, 179; Beihammer, *Byzantium and the Emergence of Muslim-Turkish Anatolia*, 302, n. 160.
98 Anna Komnene, *Alexias*, VI, 9, ed. 186–7, trans. 198–9.
99 Ibn al-Athir, *The Annals of the Saljuq Turks*, 217–18; Jean-Michel Mouton, *Damas et sa principauté sous les Saljoukides et les Bourides 468-549/1076-1154* (Cairo: Institut Français d'Archéologie Orientale, 1994), 26–8.
100 Matthew of Edessa, *Armenia and the Crusades*, II, 85, 152–3.
101 Matthew of Edessa, *Armenia and the Crusades*, II, 85, 152–3.
102 Michael the Syrian, *Chronique*, iii, XV.iv, 173.
103 Matthew of Edessa, *Armenia and the Crusades*, II, 87–8, 154.
104 Beihammer, *Byzantium and the Emergence of Muslim-Turkish Anatolia*, 294; Dédéyan, *Les Armeniens*, II, 1059.
105 It must also be noted that not all of the Armenian lords followed the Apostolic Church, and that there is little evidence of religious discord between the varying princes in the period where they were battling for survival.
106 This traditional viewpoint can be found here: J. Laurent, 'Les origines médiévales de la question arménienne', *REArm* 1 (1920): 35–54; Charanis, 'Armenians and Greeks', 26–7. See n. 1, 2.
107 I have chosen to maintain the name 'Gregory' for ecclesiastical figures as they have commonly been referred to as the occupants to the chair of St Gregory the Illuminator, the patron saint of the Apostolic Church. The connection between the Apostolic Church and the Pahlavuni family was one of the many reasons why Grigor's descendants did not play a role in twelfth-century Byzantium. Matthew of Edessa, *Armenia and the Crusades*, II, 26, 107.
108 Matthew of Edessa, II, *Armenia and the Crusades*, 52, 127–8.
109 Matthew of Edessa, II, *Armenia and the Crusades*, 26, 107.
110 Matthew of Edessa, II, *Armenia and the Crusades*, 52, 128.
111 Matthew of Edessa, II, *Armenia and the Crusades*, 52, 128.
112 Matthew of Edessa, II, *Armenia and the Crusades*, 59, 137.
113 Matthew of Edessa, II, *Armenia and the Crusades*, 59, n. 2, 331.
114 Matthew of Edessa, II, *Armenia and the Crusades*, 62, 139.
115 Yarnley, 'Philaretos', 341.
116 Yarnley, 'Philaretos', 341.
117 Matthew of Edessa, II, *Armenia and the Crusades*, 60, 137.
118 Matthew of Edessa, II, *Armenia and the Crusades*, 70, 142.
119 Matthew of Edessa, II, *Armenia and the Crusades*, 70, 142; Yarnley, 'Philaretos', 342.

120 Matthew of Edessa, II, *Armenia and the Crusades*, 82, 150.
121 Matthew of Edessa, II, *Armenia and the Crusades*, 62, 140.
122 Matthew of Edessa, II, *Armenia and the Crusades*, 83, 150.
123 Matthew of Edessa, II, *Armenia and the Crusades*, 83, 150-1.
124 Matthew of Edessa, II, *Armenia and the Crusades*, 83, 150-1. Matthew claims later in the passage that the Armenian nation in fact had six *katholikoi* – two in Egypt and four in Armenia – but does not quantify how an extra two were included in his count from the previously mentioned split of four.
125 For an excellent overview on the disparate Turkic lordships in northern Syria at the time of the First Crusade see Michael Köhler, *Alliances and Treaties between Frankish and Muslim Rulers in the Middle East: Cross-Cultural Diplomacy in the Period of the Crusades*, trans. P. Holt, ed. K. Hirschler (Leiden and Boston, MA: Brill, 2013), 8-20; Carole Hillenbrand, *The Crusades: Islamic Perspectives* (Edinburgh: Edinburgh University Press, 1999), 33.
126 Michael the Syrian, *Chronique*, iii, XV.vi, 179; Matthew of Edessa, *Armenia and the Crusades*, II, 108, 163. This is Matthew's first reference to Gabriel, which is strangely late in his chronology despite the length of his rule in Melitene.
127 Michael the Syrian, *Chronique*, iii, XV.viii, 187; while Matthew first notes Basil in his chronology during 1102: Matthew of Edessa, *Armenia and the Crusades*, III, 14, 192; MacEvitt, *The Crusades and the Christian World of the East*, 42; Jacob Ghazarian, *The Armenian Kingdom in Cilicia during the Crusades: The Integration of Cilician Armenians with the Latins, 1080-1393* (Richmond: Curzon Press, 2000), 46-7.
128 Matthew of Edessa, *Armenia and the Crusades*, III, 57, 211.
129 MacEvitt, *The Crusades and the Christian World of the East*, 76.
130 Michael the Syrian, *Chronique*, iii, XV.vi, 179; Franz Tinnefeld, 'Die Stadt Melitene in ihrer späteren byzantinischen Epoche (934-1101)', *Acts of the 14th International Congress* 1971, 3 vols (Bucharest: Editura Academiei Republicii Socialiste România, 1974), ii, 435-43, at 439. For argument of Gabriel seizing Melitene after 1092 see Pryor and Jeffreys, 'Alexios, Bohemond, and Byzantium's Euphrates Frontier', 70.
131 Michael the Syrian, *Chronique*, iii, XV.vi, 179.
132 Nicolas Oikonomides, *A Collection of Dated Byzantine Lead Seals* (Washington D.C.: Harvard University Press, 1986), 104; Cheynet, *Sceaux de La Collection Zacos*, no. 41; MacEvitt, *The Crusades and the Christian World of the East*, 42.
133 Michael does not mention at this juncture whether Gabriel's 'Greekness' was through language, religion or political affiliation, though one can expect a churchman such as Michael to have such a lens: Michael the Syrian, *Chronique*, iii, XV.vi, 180. Later, Michael confirms that Gabriel was of the Chalcedonian confession: Michael the Syrian, *Chronique*, iii, XV.vii, 180, 186.
134 Albert of Aachen, *Historia Iherosolimitana*, 524-5; William of Tyre, *Chronique*, ed. R. Huygens, Corpus Christianorum, Continuatio Mediaevalis 63, 2 vols., I, X.xxiv, 482; English Translation: *A History of Deeds Done Beyond the Sea*, trans. E. Babcock and A. Krey, 2 vols., i, 450. Erat autem predictus Gabriel natione, lingua, et habitu Armenius, fide tamen Grecus.
135 MacEvitt, *The Crusades and the Christian World of the East*, 76.
136 For various events concerning Buzan and events in the wider Islamic world see Matthew of Edessa, *Armenia and the Crusades*, II, 96 (campaigns in Anatolia), 103 (plot against Ismail), 104 (death), 157-61; Ibn al-Athir, *The Annals of the Saljuq Turks*, 274.

137 Matthew of Edessa, *Armenia and the Crusades*, II, 104, 161; Ibn al-Athir, *The Annals of the Saljuq Turks*, 280.
138 Michael the Syrian, *Chronique*, iii, XV.vi, 179.
139 Michael the Syrian, *Chronique*, iii, XV.iv, 173-4.
140 Fulcher of Chartres, *Fulcheri Carnotensis Historia Hierosolymitana (1095-1127)*, ed. H. Hagenmeyer (Heidelberg: Carl Winters Universitätsbuchhandlung, 1913), XIV.vi, 210; English Translation: *A History of the Expedition to Jerusalem, 1095-1127*, trans. F. Ryan and H. Fink (Knoxville: University of Tennessee Press, 1969), 89; MacEvitt, *The Crusades and the Christian World of the East*, 67.
141 William Saunders, 'The Greek Inscription on the Harran Gate at Edessa: Some Further Evidence', *Byzantinische Forschungen* 21 (1995): 301-4.
142 Matthew of Edessa, *Armenia and the Crusades*, II, 104, 161.
143 For example, see Matthew of Edessa, *Armenia and the Crusades*, II, 105, 162; for tenuous use of a similar term in our Muslim sources see Ibn al-Athir, *The Annals of the Saljuq Turks*, 280, n. 158.
144 See the Appendix for full inscription.
145 Cheynet, *Sceaux de La Collection Zacos*, 67-8.
146 Matthew of Edessa, *Armenia and the Crusades*, II, 117-18, 168-70.
147 Pryor and Jeffreys, 'Alexios, Bohemond, and Byzantium's Euphrates Frontier', 70, n. 158.
148 Matthew of Edessa, *Armenia and the Crusades*, II, 117, 169. The chronicle of Michael the Syrian simply reports T'oros' death: Michael the Syrian, *Chronique*, iv, XV.viii, 187; Albert of Aachen, *Historia Iherosolimitana*, III, 19-24, 168-77.
149 Matthew's first mention of Kogh Vasil is very clear on this point: Matthew of Edessa, *Armenia and the Crusades*, III, 14, 192.
150 Matthew of Edessa, *Armenia and the Crusades*, III, 25, 196.
151 Dédéyan, *Les arméniens*, II, 1057-60.
152 This seal can be found in the Khoury collection in the Antioch Museum; see Pryor and Jeffreys, 'Alexios, Bohemond, and Byzantium's Euphrates Frontier', 82; MacEvitt, *The Crusades and the Christian World of the East*, 84; Garsoïan, *Armenian Integration*, 123, n. 250.
153 Michael the Syrian, *Chronique*, iv, XV.viii, 187.
154 Matthew of Edessa, *Armenia and the Crusades*, III, 211.
155 Ralph of Caen, *The Gesta Tancredi of Ralph of Caen*, 58: Ea namque tempestate Turcis dominari contigerat, Graecis famulari, Armenis montium arduitate tueri libertatem.
156 In Hermenirorum intrauerunt terram – they entered the Armenian lands: *Gesta Francorum et aliorum Hierosolimitanorum*, ed. and trans. R. Hill (London: Thomas Nelson and Sons Ltd, 1962), IV, xi, 25.
157 Albert of Aachen, *Historia Iherosolimitana*, III, 3, 141; *Gesta Francorum*, IV, x, 24.
158 Thomas Asbridge, *The Creation of the Principality of Antioch 1098-1130* (Woodbridge: Boydell, 2000), 16-17.
159 Fulcher of Chartres, *Fulcheri Carnotensis Historia Hierosolymitana*, ed. 213-14, trans. 91; Matthew of Edessa, *Armenia and the Crusades*, II, 118, 168-9.
160 *Alexiad*, XI, 4, ed. XI, 4, trans. 306; Ralph of Caen, *The Gesta Tancredi of Ralph of Caen*, 87-8. Other sources identify the betrayer as a Muslim: Rebecca Slitt, 'Justifying Cross-Cultural Friendship: Bohemond, Firūz, and the Fall of Antioch', *Viator* 38, no. 2 (2007): 339-49.
161 Kaldellis, *Streams of Gold, Rivers of Blood*, 268.
162 A proponent of this view is can be found in: Frankopan, *The First Crusade*.

Closing remarks

1 See section 'Acceptance and Adoption of "Roman Customs"' in Chapter 1.
2 See section 'Religious Conversion and Conformity' in Chapter 1.
3 See section 'Unforeseen Circumstances' in Chapter 3.
4 Matthew of Edessa, Armenia and the Crusades, I, 84, n. 5, at 304.
5 Der Nersessian, *The Armenians*, 39.
6 See section 'The First Steps to Separatism' in Chapter 3.

Appendix I

1 Transcription of von Gaertringen provided by Saunders, 'The Greek Inscription on the Harran Gate', 302.
2 Anno Mundi starts 1 September, so the inscription can be dated to early to mid-1094.

BIBLIOGRAPHY

Primary sources

Acta et Diplomata Graeca Medii Aevi Sacra et Profana, 6 vols, ed. F. Miklosich and J. Muller, Aalen: Scientia Verlag, 1968.
Albert of Aachen. *Historia Iherosolimitana*, ed. and trans. S. B. Edgington, Oxford: Oxford University Press, 2007.
Arewelc'i, Vardan. 'The Historical Compilation of Vardan Arewelc'i', ed. and trans. R. Thomson, *Dumbarton Oaks Papers* 43 (1989): 125–226.
Aristides, Aelius. *Roman Oration*, trans. in Oliver, J., 'The Ruling Power: A Study of the Roman Empire in the Second Century after Christ through the Roman Oration of Aelius Aristides', *Transactions of the American Philological Association* 43 (1953): 871–1003.
Artsruni, Thomas. *History of the House of Artsrunik*, trans. R. Thomson, Detroit, MI: Wayne State University Press, 1985.
Attaleiates, Michael. *The History*, trans. A. Kaldellis and D. Krallis, Cambridge, MA: Harvard University Press, 2012.
Bryennios, Nikephoros. *Material for History*, ed. and trans. P. Gautier, CFHB 9, Brussels: Byzantion, 1975.
Choniates, Niketas. *Nicetae Choniatae Historia*, ed. J.-L. van Dieten, CFHB 3, Berlin and New York: Walter de Gruyter, 1973. English translation: *O City of Byzantium, Annals of Niketas Choniates*, trans. H. Magoulias, Detroit, MI: Wayne State University Press, 1984.
Constantine VII Porphyrogennetos. *De Administrando Imperio*, ed. G. Moravcsik, trans. R. Jenkins, Budapest: Pazmany Peter Tudomanyegyetemi Gorog Filologiaai Intezet, 1949.
Constantine VII Porphyrogennetos. *De Thematibus*, ed. A. Pertusi, Vatican City: Biblioteca Apostolica Vaticana, 1952.
Constantine VII Porphyrogennetos. *The Book of Ceremonies (De Ceremoniis)*, trans. A. Moffatt and M. Tall, 2 vols, Canberra: Australian Association for Byzantine Studies, 2012.
David, Niketas. *The Life of Patriarch Ignatius*, trans. A. Smithies, CFHB 51, Washington D.C.: Dumbarton Oaks Texts 13, 2013.
Fulcher of Chartres. *Fulcheri Carnotensis Historia Hierosolymitana (1095–1127)*, ed. H. Hagenmeyer, Heidelberg: Carl Winters Universitätsbuchhandlung, 1913. English Translation: *A History of the Expedition to Jerusalem, 1095–1127*, trans. F. Ryan and H. Fink, Knoxville: University of Tennessee Press, 1969.
Genesios, Joseph. *Iosephi Genesii Regum Libri Quattuor*, ed. A. Lesmüller-Werner and I. Thurn, CFHB 14, Berlin and New York: Walter de Gruyter, 1978. English Translation: *Genesios on the Reign of the Emperors*, trans. A. Kaldellis, Canberra: Australian Association for Byzantine Studies, 1998.

Georgian Royal Annals: Rewriting Caucasian History: The Medieval Armenian Adaption of the Georgian Chronicles, trans. R. Thomson, Oxford: Clarendon Press, 1996.
Gesta Francorum et aliorum Hierosolimitanorum, ed. and trans. R. Hill, London: Thomas Nelson and Sons Ltd, 1962.
Gregory of Narek. *The Festal Works of St. Gregory of Narek: Annotated Translation of the Odes, Litanies, and Encomia*, trans. A. Terian, Collegeville, MN: Liturgical Press, 2016.
Ibn al-Athir. *The Annals of the Saljuq Turks: Selections from Al-Kāmil fī al-tārīkh*, trans. D. Richards, London: Routledge, 2002.
John Catholicus. *Yovhannes Drasxanakertc'i, History of Armenia*, trans. K. Maksoudian, Atlanta, GA: Scholars Press, 1987.
Jus graecoromanum, ed. I. and P. Zepos, 8 vols, Athens, 1931.
Kartlis Tskhovreba. A History of Georgia, trans. R. Met'reveli and S. Jones, Tblisi: Georgian National Academy of Sciences, 2014.
Kinnamos, John. *Epitome*, ed. A. Meineke, CSHB, Bonn: Weber, 1836; English translation: *The Deeds of John and Manuel Comnenus, by John Kinnamos*, trans. C. Brand, New York: Columbia University Press, 1976.
Komnene, Anna. *Alexias*, ed. Diether R. Reinsch and Athanasios Kambylis, 2 vols, CFHB 40, Berlin and New York: Walter de Gruyter, 2001. English Translation: *The Alexiad*, trans. E. Sewter, London: Penguin Publishing, 2009.
Lastivertc'i, Aristakes. *Matenagrut'yan banasirakan k'nnut'yun*, trans. G. Manukyan, Yerevan: Erevani Hamalsarani Hratarakch'ut'yun, 1977. English Translation: *History*, trans. R. Bedrosian, Sophene, 2020.
Le Traité sur la guerrilla (De velitatione) de l'empereur Nicéphore Phocas, ed. and trans. G. Dagron and H. Mihăescu, Paris: Editions du Centre national de la recherche scientifique, 1986.
Leo the Deacon. *Leonis Diaconi Caloënsis Historiae Libri Decem*, ed. C. Hasii, CSHB, Bonn: Weberi, 1828. English translation: *The History of Leo the Deacon: Byzantine Military Expansion on the Tenth Century*, trans. A.-M. Talbot and D. Sullivan, Washington D.C.: Dumbarton Oaks Research Library and Collection, 2005.
Les Sceaux Byzantins de La Collection Henri Seyrig, ed. J.-C. Cheynet, C. Morrisson and W. Seibt, Paris: Bibliothèque nationale, 1991.
Life of John and Euthymios. 'La Vie de Jean et Euthyme: Le statut du monastère des Ibères sur l'Athos', trans. B. Martin-Hisard, *Revue des études byzantines* 49 (1991): 67–142. English translation: *Georgian Monks on Mount Athos: Two Eleventh-Century Lives of the Hegoumenoi of Iviron*, trans. T. Grdzelidze, London: Bennett and Bloom, 2009.
Matthew of Edessa. *Armenia and the Crusades*, trans. E. Dostourian, Lanham, MD: University Press of America, 1993.
Michael the Syrian. *The Chronicle of Michael the Great*, trans. V. Langlois, Venice: San Lazzaro degli Armeni, 1868.
Michael the Syrian. *Chronique*, trans. J. Chabot, 4 vols, Paris: Ernest Leroux, 1906.
Nicholas I, Patriarch of Constantinople. *Letters*, ed. and trans. R. Jenkins and L. Westerink, CFHB 6, Washington D.C.: Dumbarton Oaks Center for Byzantine Studies, 1973.
Nicholas I, Patriarch of Constantinople. *Miscellaneous Writings*, ed. and trans. L. Westerink, CFHB 20, Washington D.C.: Dumbarton Oaks Center for Byzantine Studies, 1981.
Ouranos Taktika, E. McGeer. *Sowing the Dragon's Teeth: Byzantine Warfare in the Tenth Century*, 88–163, Washington D.C.: Dumbarton Oaks, 2008.
Pakourianos, Gregory. 'Le typikon du sébaste Gregoire Pakourianos', trans. P. Gautier, *Revue des Études Byzantines* 42 (1984): 5–145.

Phokas, Nikephoros. 'Nikephoros Phokas Rules on the Land Claims and Homicide in the Armenian Themes', in *The Land Legislation of the Macedonian Emperors*, trans. E. McGeer, 86–9, Medieval Sources in Translation 38, Winnipeg: Hignell Printing, 2000.

Praecepta militaria, E. McGeer. *Sowing the Dragon's Teeth: Byzantine Warfare in the Tenth Century*, 12–59, Washington D.C.: Dumbarton Oaks, 2008.

Psellos, Michael. *Michele Psello Imperatori di Bisanzio (Cronografia)*, ed. S. Impellizzeri and trans. S. Ronchey, 2 vols, Milan: A. Mondadori, 1984. English translation: *Fourteen Byzantine Rulers*, trans. E. Sewter, Harmondsworth: Penguin Publishing, 1966.

Psellos, Michael. *Michaelis Pselli Orationes Hagiographicae*, ed. E. Fisher, Stuttgart and Leipzig: Teubner, 1994.

Ralph of Caen. *The Gesta Tancredi of Ralph of Caen: A History of the Normans on the Frist Crusade*, trans. B. and D. Bachrach, Crusade Texts in Translation 12, Aldershot: Ashgate, 2005.

Samuel of Ani. 'Tables Chronologiques', trans. M.-C. Brosset, *Collection d'historiens arméniens*, 2 vols, vol. II, 339–483, St Petersburg: Imprimerie de académie impériale des sciences, 1876.

Sebeos. *The Armenian History attributed to Sebeos*, vol. I, trans. R. Thomson, Liverpool: Liverpool University Press, 1999.

Skylitzes, John. *Synopsis Historiarum*, ed. J. Thurn, CFHB 5, Berlin and New York: Walter de Gruyter, 1973. English translation: *A Synopsis of Byzantine History 811-1057*, trans. J. Wortley, Cambridge: Cambridge University Press, 2010.

Skylitzes Continuatus. *Ἡ Συνέχεια τῆς χρονογραφίας τοῦ Ἰωάννου Σκυλίτζη*, ed. E. T. Tsolakes, Thessaloniki, 1968.

Stephen of Taron. *Patmut'iwn tiezerakan*, ed. S. Malxaseanc, St Petersburg: publisher unknown, 1885. English translation: *History of Step'anos Tarōnec'i*, trans. T. Greenwood, Oxford Studies in Byzantium, Oxford: Oxford University Press, 2017.

Sylloge Tacticorum. *A Tenth-Century Byzantine Military Manual: The Sylloge Tacticorum*, trans. Georgios Chatzelis and Jonathan Harris, Birmingham Byzantine and Ottoman Monographs, Abingdon and New York: Routledge, 2017.

Symeon the Logothete. *Symeonis Magistri et Logothetae Chronicon*, ed. Staffan Wahlgren, CFHB 44, Berlin and New York: Walter de Gruyter, 2006.

Tacitus, Cornelius. *Annals*, trans. M. Grant, London: Penguin Classics, 2003.

Tacitus, Cornelius. *Agricola*, trans. H. Mattingly, London: Penguin Classics, 2010.

Theophanes Continuatus. *Theophanes Continuatus, Ioannes Cameniata, Symeon Magister, Georgius Monachus*, ed. I. Bekker, CSHB, Bonn: Weber, 1838.

Theophanes Continuatus. *Chronographiae quae Theophanis Continuati nomine fertur Liber quo Vita Basilii Imperatoris amplectitur*, ed. I. Ševčenko, CFHB 42, Berlin and Boston, MA: Walter de Gruyter, 2011.

Theophanes Continuatus. *Chronographiae quae Theophanis Continuati nomine fertur Libri I–IV*, ed. M. Featherstone and J. Signes-Codoñer, CFHB 53/1, Berlin and Boston, MA: Walter de Gruyter, 2015.

Theophanes the Confessor. *Chronographia*, ed. C. de Boor, 2 vols, Hildesheim and New York: G. Olms, 1980. English translation: *The Chronicle of Theophanes Confessor*, trans. C. Mango and R. Scott, Oxford: Clarendon Press, 1997.

Three Byzantine Military Treatises, ed. and trans. G. Dennis, CFHB 25, Washington D.C.: Dumbarton Oaks, 1985.

Vasiliev, Alexander and Marius Canard. *Byzance et les Arabes*, 3 vols, Brussels: Institut de philologie et d'histoire orientales, 1935–68.

Yahya Ibn Saʻid d'Antioche. 'Histoire', ed. and trans. I. Kratchkovsky and A. Vasiliev, *PO* 18 (1924): 699–832 and *PO* 23 (1932): 349–520; 'Histoire de Yaḥyā ibn Saʻīd d'Antioche', trans. F. Micheau and G. Troupeau, *PO* 47 (1997): 373–559; *Yahya al-Antaki Cronache dell'Egitto fatimide e dell'impero Bizantino 937–1033*, trans. B. Pirone, Milan: Jaca Book, 1998.

Zahir al-Din Nishapuri. *The History of the Seljuq Turks: From the Jami al-Tawarikh: An Ilkhanid Adaption of the Saljuq-nama of Zahir al-Din Nishapuri*, trans. K. Luther, ed. C. Bosworth, Richmond, Surrey: Curzon Press, 2001.

Secondary Sources

Adontz, Nicholas. 'Les Taronites en Arménie et à Byzance', *Byzantion* 9 (1934): 715–38.
Adontz, Nicholas. 'Tornik le moine', *Byzantion* 11 (1936): 143–64.
Ahrweiler, Hélène. *L'idéologie politique de l'Empire byzantine*, Paris: Presses universitaires de France, 1975.
Ando, Clifford. *Imperial Ideology and Provincial Loyalty in the Roman Empire*, London: University of California Press, 2000.
Ando, Clifford. *Law, Language, and Empire in the Roman Tradition*, Philadelphia, PA: University of Pennsylvania Press, 2011.
Andrews, Tara. *Mattʻēos Uṙhayecʻi and His Chronicle*, Leiden and Boston, MA: Brill, 2017.
Andrews, Tara. 'The Chronology of the Chronicle: An Explanation of the Dating Errors within Book 1 of the Chronicle of Matthew of Edessa', *REArm* 32 (2010): 141–64.
Andriollo, Luisa. 'Les Kourkouas (IXe-XIe siècle)', *Studies in Byzantine Sigillography* 11 (2012): 57–87.
Angold, Michael. 'Byzantine "Nationalism" and the Nicaean Empire', *Byzantine and Modern Greek Studies* 1 (1975): 49–70.
Angold, Michael. 'The Byzantine State on the Eve of the Battle of Manzikert', *Byzantinische Forschungen* 16 (1991): 9–34.
Angold, Michael. *The Byzantine Empire, 1025–1204: A Political History*, Harlow: Pearson Education Limited, 1997.
Angold, Michael. 'Autobiography and Identity: The Case of the Later Roman Empire', *Byzantinoslavica* 60 (1999): 36–59.
Angold, Michael and Michael Whitby. 'Historiography', in *The Oxford Handbook of Byzantine Studies*, ed. E. Jeffreys, J. Haldon and R. Cormack, 838–52, Oxford: Oxford University Press, 2008.
Arnakis, George. 'Byzantium and Greece. A Review Article à Propos of Romilly Jenkins, Byzantium and Byzantinism', *Balkan Studies* 4 (1963): 379–400.
Arutjunova-Fidajan, Viada. 'Some Aspects of the Military-Administrative Districts and of Byzantine Administration in Armenia during the 11th Century', *REArm* 20 (1986–7): 309–20.
Arutjunova-Fidajan, Viada. 'The Ethno-Confessional Self-Awareness of Armenian Chalcedonians', *REArm* 21 (1988–9): 345–63.
Arutjunova-Fidajan, Viada. 'L'image de l'Empire byzantine dans l'historiographie arménienne médiévale (Xe-XIe s.)', in *L'Arménie et Byzance: Histoire et culture*, ed. N. Garsoïan, 7–18, Byzantina Sorbonesia 12, Paris: Publications de la Sorbonne, 1996.
Asbridge, Thomas. *The Creation of the Principality of Antioch 1098–1130*, Woodbridge: Boydell, 2000.
Asbridge, Thomas. *The First Crusade: A New History*, London: The Free Press, 2004.

Augé, Isabelle. 'Les Arméniens et l'Empire byzantine, 1025-1118', *TM* 21, no. 2 (2017): 789-808.
Barker, Ernest. *Social and Political Thought in Byzantium from Justinian I to the Last Palaeologus*, Oxford: Oxford University Press, 1957.
Bartikian, Hratch. 'The Religious Diplomacy of Byzantium in Armenia during the Tenth and Eleventh Centuries', in *Armenian Studies: In Memoriam Haïg Berbérian*, ed. D. Kouymjian, 55-62, Lisbon: Calouste Gulbenkian Foundation, 1986.
Bartikian, Hratch. 'Concerning the Byzantine Aristocratic Family of the Gavras', *Patma-Banasirakan Handes* 3 (1987): 181-93.
Beihammer, Alexander. *Byzantium and the Emergence of Muslim-Turkish Anatolia, ca. 1040-1130*, London: Taylor & Francis Group, 2017.
Boase, T. S. R. *The Cilician Kingdom of Armenia*, Edinburgh: Scottish Academic Press, 1978.
Bournoutian, George. *A Concise History of the Armenian People: From Ancient Times to the Present*, Costa Mesa, CA: Mazda Publishers, 2006.
Brice, William. 'The Turkish Colonization of Anatolia', *Bulletin of the John Rylands Library* 38 (1955-6): 18-44.
Brouselle, Isabelle. 'L'intégration des Arméniens dans l'aristocratie byzantine au IXe siècle', in *L'Arménie et Byzance: Histoire et culture*, ed. N. Garsoïan, 43-54, Byzantina Sorbonesia 12, Paris: Publications de la Sorbonne, 1996.
Browning, Robert. *Greece – Ancient and Medieval*, London: Ruddock and Sons Ltd, 1966.
Bryer, Anthony. 'The Armenian Dilemma', *History Today* 19, no. 5 (1969): 345-52.
Bryer, Anthony. 'The Late Byzantine Identity: An Abstract', in *Byzantium: Identity, Image, Influence*, Papers from the XIX International Congress of Byzantine Studies, ed. K. Fledelius, 49-50, Copenhagen: Danish National Committee for Byzantine Studies Eventus Publishers, 1996.
Cahan, Claude. 'La Première penetration turque en Asie Mineure', *Byzantion* 18 (1948): 5-67.
Cahan, Claude. 'The Turkish Invasion: The Selchükids', in *A History of the Crusades*, ed. K. Sutton, vol. 1, 2nd edn, 135-76, Madison, WI: The University of Wisconsin Press, 1969.
Cameron, Averil. *Byzantine Matters*, Princeton, NJ: Princeton University Press, 2014.
Charanis, Peter. 'Ethnic Changes in Seventh-Century Byzantium', *DOP* 13 (1959): 23-44.
Charanis, Peter. *The Armenians in the Byzantine Empire*, Lisbon: Fundação Calouste Gulbenkian, 1963.
Charanis, Peter. 'Observations on the Demography of the Byzantine Empire', in *Proceedings of the XIIIth International Congress of Byzantine Studies*, 445-63, Oxford: Oxford University Press, 1967.
Charanis, Peter. 'The Transfer of Population as a Policy in the Byzantine Empire', in *Studies on the Demography of the Byzantine Empire*, ed. P. Charanis, No. III, 140-54, London: Variorum Reprints, 1972, in *Social, Economic and Political Life in the Byzantine Empire*, ed. P. Charanis, No. VIII, 25-32, London: Variorum Reprints, 1973.
Charanis, Peter. 'Cultural Diversity and the Breakdown of Byzantine Power in Asia Minor', *DOP* 29 (1975): 1-20.
Charanis, Peter. 'The Formation of the Greek People', in *The "Past" in Medieval and Modern Greek Culture*, ed. S. Vryonis, 87-102, Malibu, CA: Undena Publications, 1978.
Cheynet, Jean-Claude. 'Manzikert: un désastre militaire', *Byzantion* 50 (1980): 410-38.

Cheynet, Jean-Claude. 'Les Phocas', in *Le Traité sur la guerrilla (De velitatione) de l'empereur Nicéphore Phocas*, ed. and trans. G. Dagron and H. Mihăescu, 289–315, Paris: Editions du Centre national de la recherche scientifique, 1986.

Cheynet, Jean-Claude. 'Notes Arabo-Byzantines', in *Mélanges Svoronos*, ed Chryssa Maltézou and Nikolaos Panagiotakes, 145–52, Rethymnon: Panepistēmio Krētēs, 1986.

Cheynet, Jean-Claude. 'Les Arméniens de l'Empire en Orient de Constantin X à Alexis Comnène (1059–1081)', in *L'Arménie et Byzance: Histoire et culture*, ed. N. Garsoïan, 67–78, Byzantina Sorbonesia 12, Paris: Publications de la Sorbonne, 1996.

Cheynet, Jean-Claude. *Pouvoir et Contestations à Byzance (963–1210)*, Byzantina Sorbonensia 9, Paris: Publications de le Sorbonne, 1996.

Cheynet, Jean-Claude. *Sceaux de La Collection Zacos (Bibliothèque Nationale de France), se rapportant aux provinces orientales de L'Empire byzantin*, Paris: Bibliothèque nationale, 2001.

Cheynet, Jean-Claude. 'Les limites du pouvoir à Byzance: Une forme de tolérance?' in *Toleration and Repression in the Middles Ages. In Memory of Lenos Mavromatis*, ed. K. Nikolaou, 15–28, Athens: The National Hellenic Research Foundation, 2002.

Cheynet, Jean-Claude. 'Basil II and Asia Minor', in *Byzantium in the Year 1000*, ed. P. Magdalino, 71–108, Leiden: Brill, 2003.

Cheynet, Jean-Claude. *La société byzantine: l'apport des sceaux*, 2 vols, Paris: Association des amis du Centre d'histoire et civilisation de Byzance, 2008.

Cheynet, Jean-Claude. 'Les arméniens dans l'armée byzantine au Xe siècle', *TM* 18 (2014): 175–92.

Cheynet, Jean-Claude and Jean-François Vannier. *Études prosopographiques*. Paris: Éditions de la Sorbonne, 1986.

Chitwood, Zachary. *Byzantine Legal Culture and the Roman Legal Tradition, 867–1056*, Cambridge: Cambridge University Press, 2017.

Chléirigh, Léan Ní. 'The Impact of the First Crusade on Western Opinion toward the Byzantine Empire: The *Gesta Dei per Francos* of Guibert of Nogent and the *Historia Hierosolymitana* of Fulcher of Chartres', in *The Crusades and the Near East: Cultural Histories*, ed. C. Kostick, 161–88, Abingdon: Routledge, 2011.

Chrysos, Evangelos. 'The Roman Political Identity in Late Antiquity and Early Byzantium', in *Byzantium: Identity, Image, Influence*, ed. K. Fledelius, 7–16, XIXth International Congress of Byzantine Studies, Major Papers, Copenhagen: Danish National Committee for Byzantine Studies Eventus Publishers, 1996.

Cowe, S. Peter. 'Relations between the Kingdoms of Vaspurakan and Ani', in *Armenian Van/Vaspurakan*, ed. R. Hovannisian, 73–86, Costa Mesa, CA: Mazda Publishers, 2000.

Cowe, S. Peter. 'Armenian Immigration to the Sebastia Region, Tenth–Eleventh Centuries', in *Armenian Sebastia/Sivas and Lesser Armenia*, ed. R. Hovannisian, 111–36, UCLA Armenian History and Culture Series: Historic Armenian Cities and Provinces, 5. Costa Mesa, CA: Mazda Publishers, 2004.

Curta, Florin. *Borders, Barriers and Ethnogenesis. Frontiers in Late Antiquity and the Middle Ages*, Studies in the Early Middle Ages, 12, Turnhout: Brepols, 2005.

Curta, Florin. *The Edinburgh History of the Greeks, c.500 to 1050, The Early Middle Ages*, Edinburgh: Edinburgh University Press, 2011.

Dagron, Gilbert. 'Minorités ethniques et religieuses dans l'orient byzantin à la fin du Xe et au XIe siècle: l'immigration syrienne', *TM* 6 (1976): 177–216.

Dagron, Gilbert. 'Formes et fonctions du pluralisme linguistique à Byzance (IXe -XIIe siècle)', *TM* 12 (1994): 219–40.

Dagron, Gilbert. *Emperor and Priest: The Imperial Office in Byzantium*, trans. J. Birrell, Cambridge: Cambridge University Press, 2003.

Dédéyan, Gérard. 'L'immigration arménienne en Cappadoce au XIe siècle', *Byzantion* 45, no. 1 (1975): 41–115.

Dédéyan, Gérard. 'Mleh le grand, stratège de Lykandos', *REArm* 15 (1981): 73–102.

Dédéyan, Gérard. 'Les princes arméniens de l'Euphratèse et l'Empire byzantin (fin XIe-milieu XIIe s.)', in *L'Arménie et Byzance: Histoire et culture*, ed. N. Garsoïan, 79–88, Byzantina Sorbonesia 12, Paris: Publications de la Sorbonne, 1996.

Dédéyan, Gérard. *Les arméniens entre grecs, musulmans, et croisés: Étude sur les pouvoirs arméniens dans le Proche-Orient méditerranean (1068–1150)*, 2 vols, Lisbon: Fundação Calouste Gulbenkian, 2003.

Der Nersessian, Sirarpie. *Armenia and the Byzantine Empire: A Brief Study of Armenian Art and Civilization*, Cambridge, MA: Harvard University Press, 1947.

Der Nersessian, Sirarpie. 'Armenia in the Tenth and Eleventh Centuries', in *Proceedings of the Thirteenth International Congress of Byzantine Studies*, ed. Joan M. Hussey, Dimitri Obolensky and Steven Runciman, 427–31, Oxford: Oxford University Press, 1967.

Der Nersessian, Sirarpie. *The Armenians*, London: Thames and Hudson, 1969.

Djobadze, Wachtang. *Early Medieval Georgian Monasteries in Historic Tao, Klarrjet'i, and Šavšet'i*, Stuttgart: Steiner, 1992.

Duri, Abd Al-Aziz. *The Rise of Historical Writing among the Arabs*, Princeton, NJ: Princeton Legacy Library, 1983.

Eastmond, Antony. *Royal Imagery in Medieval Georgia*, University Park, PA: The Pennsylvania State University Press, 1998.

Eger, Asa. '(Re)Mapping Medieval Antioch: Urban Transformations from the Early Islamic to the Middle Byzantine Periods', *DOP* 67 (2013): 95–135.

Eger, Asa. *The Islamic-Byzantine Frontier: Interaction and Exchange Among Muslim and Christian Communities*, London and New York: I.B. Tauris, 2015.

Ellenblum, Ronnie. *The Collapse of the Eastern Mediterranean: Climate Change and the Decline of the East, 950–1072*, Cambridge: Cambridge University Press, 2012.

Evans, Nicolas. 'Kastron, Rabaḍ and Arḍūn: The Case of Artanuji', in *From Constantinople to the Frontier: The City and the Cities*, ed. N. Matheou, T. Kampianaki and L. Bondioli, 343–64, Leiden: Brill, 2016.

Forse, James. 'Armenians and the First Crusade', *Journal of Medieval History* 17, no. 1 (1991): 13–22.

Forsyth, John. 'The Chronicle of Yahya ibn Sa'id al-Antaki', Ph.D. Thesis, Unpublished: University of Michigan, 1977.

Franklin, Simon. 'The Invention of Rus(sia)(s): Some Remarks on Medieval and Modern Perceptions of Continuity and Discontinuity', in *Medieval Europeans: Studies in Ethnic Identity and National Perspectives in Medieval Europe*, ed. A. Smyth, 180–95, Basingstoke: Macmillan Press, 1998.

Frankopan, Peter. *The First Crusade: The Call from the East*, London: The Bodley Head, 2012.

Friendly, Alfred. *The Dreadful Day: The Battle of Manzikert, 1071*, London: Hutchinson, 1981.

Garsoïan, Nina. *The Paulician Heresy: A Study of the Origin and Development of Paulicianism in Armenia and the Eastern Provinces of the Byzantine Empire*, The Hague: Mouton, 1967.

Garsoïan, Nina. 'Quelques précisions préliminaires sur le schisme entre les églises byzantine et arménienne au sujet du concile de Chalcédoine', in *L'Arménie et*

Byzance: Histoire et culture, ed. N. Garsoïan, 99–112, Byzantina Sorbonesia 12, Paris: Publications de la Sorbonne, 1996.

Garsoïan, Nina. 'The Byzantine Annexation of the Armenian Kingdoms in the Eleventh Century', in *The Armenian People: from Ancient to Modern Times, vol.1, from Antiquity to the Fourteenth Century*, ed. R. Hovannisian, 188–97, Basingstoke: Macmillan, 1997.

Garsoïan, Nina. 'The Independent Kingdoms of Medieval Armenia', in *The Armenian People: from Ancient to Modern Times, vol.1, from Antiquity to the Fourteenth Century*, ed. R. Hovannisian, 143–85, Basingstoke: Macmillan, 1997.

Garsoïan, Nina. 'The Problem of Armenian Integration into the Byzantine Empire', in *Studies on the Internal Diaspora of the Byzantine Empire*, ed. H. Ahrweiler and A. Laiou, 53–124, Washington D.C.: Dumbarton Oaks Research Library and Collection, 1998.

Garsoïan, Nina. *De Vita Sua*, Costa Mesa, CA: Mazda Publishers, 2011.

Geanakoplos, Deno. *Byzantium: Church, Society, and Civilization Seen through Contemporary Eyes*, Chicago, IL: University of Chicago Press, 1984.

Ghazarian, Jacob. *The Armenian Kingdom in Cilicia during the Crusades: The Integration of Cilician Armenians with the Latins, 1080–1393*, Richmond: Curzon Press, 2000.

Gooch, George. *History and Historians in the Nineteenth Century*, London: Longmans, Green and Co, 1952.

Greenwood, Timothy. 'Armenian Sources', in *Byzantines and Crusaders in Non-Greek Sources*, ed. M. Whitby, 221–52, Proceedings of the British Academy 132, Oxford: Oxford University Press, 2007.

Greenwood, Timothy. 'Armenian Neighbours (600–1045)', in *The Cambridge History of the Byzantine Empire c. 500–1492*, ed. J. Shepard, 333–64, Cambridge: Cambridge University Press, 2008.

Greenwood, Timothy. 'Patterns of Contact and Communication: Constantinople and Armenia, 860–976', in *Armenian Constantinople*, ed. R. Hovannisian and S. Payaslian, 73–100, UCLA Armenian History and Culture Series: Historic Armenian Cities and Provinces, 9, Costa Mesa, CA: Mazda Publishers, 2010.

Greenwood, Timothy. 'Aristakes Lastivertc'i and Armenian Urban Consciousness', in *Byzantium in the Eleventh Century: Being in Between*, ed. M. Lauxtermann and M. Whittow, 88–105, Society for the Promotion of Byzantine Studies 19, London and New York: Routledge, 2017.

Grousset, René. *Histoire de l'Arménie, des origines à 1071*, Paris: Payot, 1947.

Grünbart, Michael. 'Die Familie Apokapes im Licht neuer Quellen', in *Studies in Byzantine sigillography 5*, ed. N. Oikonomides, 29–41, Washington D.C.: Dumbarton Oaks Research Library and Collection, 1998.

Haldon, John. *Warfare, State, and Society in the Byzantine World, 565–1204*, London: UCL Press, 1999.

Haldon, John. 'Chapters II, 44 and 45 of the Book of Ceremonies: Theory and Practice in Tenth-Century Military Administration', *TM* 13 (2000): 201–352.

Haldon, John. *A Critical Commentary on the Taktika of Leo VI*, Dumbarton Oaks studies 44, Washington D.C.: Dumbarton Oaks Research Library and Collection, 2014.

Haldon, John. *The Byzantine Wars*, Stroud: The History Press, 2008.

Haldon, John. 'Res publica Byzantina? State Formation and Issues of Identity in Medieval East ROME', *Byzantine and Modern Greek Studies* 40, no. 1 (2016): 4–16.

Haldon, John and Hugh Kennedy. 'The Arab-Byzantine Frontier in the Eighth and Ninth Centuries: Military and Society in the Borderlands', *ZRVI* 19 (1980): 79–116.

Hamilton, Bernard and Janet Hamilton. *Christian Dualist Heresies in the Byzantine World c.650-c.1405*, Manchester: Manchester University Press, 1998.

Harris, Jonathan. 'Common Language and the Common Good: Aspects of Identity among Byzantine Emigres in Renaissance Italy', in *Crossing Boundaries: Issues of Cultural and Individual Identity in the Middle Ages and the Renaissance*, ed. S. Mckee, 189–202, Turnhout: Brepols, 1999.

Harris, Jonathan. *Byzantium and the Crusades*, 2nd edn, London: Bloomsbury Academic, 2014.

Hillenbrand, Carole. *The Crusades: Islamic Perspectives*, Edinburgh: Edinburgh University Press, 1999.

Hillenbrand, Carole. 'Sources in Arabic', in *Byzantines and Crusaders in Non-Greek Sources*, ed. M. Whitby, 283–340, Proceedings of the British Academy 132, Oxford: Oxford University Press, 2007.

Hillenbrand, Carole. *Turkish Myth and Muslim Symbol: The Battle of Manzikert*, Edinburgh: Edinburgh University Press, 2007.

Hodgson, Natasha. 'Conflict and Cohabitation: Marriage and Diplomacy between Latins and Cilician Armenians, c.1097-1253', in *The Crusades and the Near East*, ed. C. Kostick, 83–106, Abingdon: Routledge, 2011.

Holmes, Catherine. 'How the East was Won in the Reign of Basil II', in *Eastern Approaches to Byzantium*, ed. A. Eastmond, 41–56, Aldershot: Ashgate Publishing, 2001.

Holmes, Catherine. 'Byzantium's Eastern Frontier in the Tenth and Eleventh Centuries', in *Medieval Frontiers: Concepts and Practices*, ed. D. Abulafia and N. Berend, 83–104, Aldershot: Ashgate Publishing, 2002.

Holmes, Catherine. *Basil II and the Governance of Empire 976–1025*, Oxford: Oxford University Press, 2005.

Hovsepian, Garegin I. *Colophons of Manuscripts*, Antilias, 1951.

Howard Johnston, James. 'Crown Lands and the Defence of Imperial Authority in the Tenth and Eleventh Centuries', *Byzantinische Forschungen* 21 (1995): 76–99.

Howard Johnston, James. 'Anna Komnene and the Alexiad', in *Alexios I Komnenos*, ed. M. Mullett and D. Smythe, vol. 1, 260–302, Belfast: Byzantine Enterprises, 1996.

Huxley, George. 'Aspects of Modern Greek Historiography of Byzantium', in *Byzantium and Modern Greek Identity*, ed. D. Ricks and P. Magdalino, 15–23, Aldershot: Ashgate Publishing, 1998.

Inglis, Fred. *Clifford Geertz: Culture, Customs, and Ethnics*, Oxford: Polity Press, 2000.

Jenkins, Romilly. *Byzantium and Byzantinism* (papers presented at the University of Cincinnati for the Lectures in memory of Louise Taft Semple, November 5 and 6, 1962), Offprint From: Lectures in Memory of Louise Taft Semple, University of Cincinnati Press, 1963.

Jones, Lynn. 'The Visual Expression of Power and Piety in Medieval Armenia: The Palace and Palace Church at Aghtamar', in *Eastern Approaches to Byzantium*, ed. A. Eastmond, 221–41, Aldershot: Ashgate, 2001.

Kaldellis, Anthony. *Hellenism in Byzantium: The Transformations of Greek Identity and the Reception of the Classical Tradition*, Cambridge: Cambridge University Press, 2007.

Kaldellis, Anthony. 'From Rome to New Rome, from Empire to Nation-State: Reopening the Question of Byzantium's Roman Identity', in *Two Romes: Rome and Constantinople in Late Antiquity*, ed. L. Grig, 387–404, Oxford: Oxford University Press, 2012.

Kaldellis, Anthony. *The Byzantine Republic: People and Power in New Rome*, Cambridge, MA and London: Harvard University Press, 2015.

Kaldellis, Anthony. *Streams of Gold, Rivers of Blood: The Rise and Fall of Byzantium, 955 A.D. to the First Crusade*, Oxford: Oxford University Press, 2017.
Kaldellis, Anthony. 'The Social Scope of Roman Identity in Byzantium: An Evidence-Based Approach', *Byzantina Symmeikta* 27 (2017): 173–210.
Kaldellis, Anthony. *Romanland: Ethnicity and Empire in Byzantium*, Cambridge, MA: Harvard University Press, 2019.
Kazhdan, Alexander. 'The Armenians in the Byzantine Ruling Class Predominantly in the Ninth Through Twelfth Centuries', in *Medieval Armenian Culture*, ed. Thomas Samuelian and Michael Stone, 438–51, Chico, CA: Scholars Press, 1983.
Kazhdan, Alexander and Giles Constable. *People and Power in Byzantium: An Introduction to Modern Byzantine Studies*, Washington D.C.: Dumbarton Oaks, 1982.
Kazhdan, Alexander and Ann Epstein. *Change in Byzantine Culture in the Eleventh and Twelfth Centuries*, Berkeley, CA: University of California Press, 1985.
Kitromilides, Paschalis. 'On the Intellectual Content of Greek Nationalism: Paparrigopoulos, Byzantium and the Great Idea', in *Byzantium and Modern Greek Identity*, ed. D. Ricks and P. Magdalino, 25–33, Aldershot: Ashgate Publishing, 1998.
Koder, Johannes. 'Byzantium as Seen by Itself: Images and Mechanisms at Work', in *Proceedings of the 22nd International Congress of Byzantine Studies*, vol. 1, 69–82, Sofia: Bulgarian Historical Heritage Foundation, 2011.
Köhler, Michael. *Alliances and Treaties between Frankish and Muslim Rulers in the Middle East: Cross-Cultural Diplomacy in the Period of the Crusades*, trans. P. Holt, ed. K. Hirschler, Leiden and Boston, MA: Brill, 2013.
Koltsida-Makre, Ioanna. 'Philaretos Brachamios, Portrait of a Byzantine Official', *TM* 21, no. 1 (2017): 325–32.
Krallis, Dimitris. *Michael Attaleiates and the Politics of Imperial Decline in Eleventh-Century Byzantium*, Tempe, AZ: Arizona Center for Medieval and Renaissance Studies, 2012.
Kurkjian, Vahan. *A History of Armenia*, New York: Armenian General Benevolent Union of America, 1958.
Laiou, Angeliki. 'Peter Charanis', *DOP* 39 (1985): xii–xv.
Laiou, Angeliki. 'Institutional Mechanisms of Integration', in *Byzantium and the Other: Relations and Exchanges – Angeliki E. Laiou*, ed. C. Morrisson and R. Dorin, vol. III, 161–81, Farnham: Ashgate Publishing, 2012.
Laiou, Angeliki. 'L'étranger de passage et l'étranger privilégié à byzance, XIe – XIIe siècles', in *Byzantium and the Other: Relations and Exchanges – Angeliki E. Laiou*, ed. C. Morrisson and R. Dorin, vol. II, 69–88, Farnham: Ashgate Publishing, 2012.
Laiou, Angeliki. 'The Foreigner and the Stranger in 12th Century Byzantium: Means of Propitiation and Acculturation', in *Byzantium and the Other: Relations and Exchanges – Angeliki E. Laiou*, ed. C. Morrisson and R. Dorin, vol. I, 71–97, Farnham: Ashgate Publishing, 2012.
Lang, David. *Armenia: Cradle of Civilization*, London: George Allen & Unwin, 1970.
Lang, David. *The Armenians: A People in Exile*, London: George Allen & Unwin, 1981.
Laurent, J. 'Les origines médiévales de la question arménienne', *REArm* 1 (1920): 35–54.
Laurent, J. 'Arméniens de Cilicie: Aspiétès, Oschin, Ursinus', in *Études d'histoire arménienne*, ed. J. Laurent, 51–60, Louvain: Éditions Peeters, 1971.
Laurent, Vitalien. *La Collection C. Orghidan: Documents de sigillographie Byzantine*, Paris: Presses universitaires de France, 1952.
Laurent, Vitalien. 'La chronologie des gouverneurs d'Antioche sous la seconde domination byzantine', *Mélanges de l'Université Saint-Joseph* 38 (1962): 219–54.

Lemerle, Paul. 'Le testament d'Eustathios Boïlas (Avril 1059)', in *Cinq études sur le XIe siècle byzantin*, 15–63, Paris: Du centre national de la recherche scientifique, 1977.

MacEvitt, Christopher. 'The Chronicle of Matthew of Edessa: Apocalypse, the First Crusade and the Armenian Diaspora', *DOP* 61 (2007): 157–81.

MacEvitt, Christopher. *The Crusades and the Christian World of the East: Rough Tolerance*, Philadelphia, PA: University of Pennsylvania Press, 2008.

MacEvitt, Christopher. 'The King, the Bishop, and the Dog Who Killed Him: Canine Cultural Encounters and Medieval Armenian Identity', in *Old Worlds, New Worlds: European Cultural Encounters, c.1100 – c.1750*, ed. L. Bailey, L. Diggelman and K. Phillips, 31–51, Turnhout: Brepols, 2009.

Mackridge, Peter. 'Byzantium and the Greek Language Question in the Nineteenth Century', in *Byzantium and the Modern Greek Identity*, ed. D. Ricks and P. Magdalino, 49–61, Aldershot: Ashgate, 1998.

Macrides, Ruth. 'The Pen and the Sword: Who wrote the Alexiad?', in *Anna Komnene and Her Times*, ed. T. Gouma-Peterson, 63–81, New York and London: Garland Publishing, 2000.

Magdalino, Paul. 'Hellenism and Nationalism in Byzantium', in *Tradition and Transformation in Medieval Byzantium*, ed. P. Magdalino, XIV, Aldershot: Variorum, 1991.

Magdalino, Paul. *The Byzantine Background to the First Crusade*, Toronto: Canadian Institute of Balkan Studies, 1996.

Mahé, Jean-Pierre. 'Basile II et byzance vus par Grigor Narekac'i', *TM* 11 (1991): 555–73.

Mango, Cyril. 'Byzantinism and Romantic Hellenism', *Journal of Warburg and Courtauld Institutes* 28 (1965): 29–43.

Mango, Cyril. *Byzantine Literature as a Distorting Mirror. Inaugural Lecture, University of Oxford, May 1974*, Oxford: Clarendon Press, 1975.

Mango, Cyril. *Byzantium: The Empire of New Rome*, London: Phoenix, 1994.

Manuk-Khaloyan, Armen. 'In the Cemetery of their Ancestors: The Royal Burial Tombs of the Bagratuni Kings of Greater Armenia (890-1073/0)', *REArm* 35 (2013): 132–202.

Manz, Beatrice. 'Multi-ethnic Empires and the Formulation of Identity', *Ethnic and Racial Studies* 26, no. 1 (2003): 70–101.

McGeer, Eric. *Sowing the Dragon's Teeth: Byzantine Warfare in the Tenth Century*, Washington D.C.: Dumbarton Oaks, 2008.

Millas, Hercules. 'History Writing among the Greeks and Turks: Imagining the Self and the Other', in *The Contested Nation: Ethnicity, Class, Religion and Gender in National Histories*, ed. S. Berger and C. Lorenz, 490–511, Basingstoke: Palgrave Macmillan, 2008.

Morton, Nicholas. 'Encountering the Turks: The First Crusaders' Foreknowledge of their Enemy; Some Preliminary Findings', in *Crusading and Warfare in the Middle Ages: Realities and Representations: Essays in Honour of John France*, ed. S. John and N. Morton, 47–68, Aldershot: Ashgate, 2014.

Morton, Nicholas. *Encountering Islam on the First Crusade*, Cambridge: Cambridge University Press, 2016.

Mouton, Jean-Michel. *Damas et sa principauté sous les Saljoukides et les Bourides 468-549/1076-1154*, Cairo: Institut Français d'Archéologie Orientale, 1994.

Nesbitt, John, Nicolas Oikonomides and Eric McGeer. *Catalogue of Byzantine Seals at Dumbarton Oaks and in the Fogg Museum of Art*, 5 vols, Washington D.C.: Dumbarton Oaks, 1991–2005.

Neville, Leonora. *Heroes and Romans in Twelfth-Century Byzantium: The Material for History of Nikephoros Bryennios*, Cambridge: Cambridge University Press, 2012.

Nichanian, Mikaël. 'Byzantine Emperor Philippikos-Vardanes: Monothelite Policy and Caucasian Diplomacy', in *Armenian Constantinople*, ed. R. Hovannisian and S. Payaslian, 39–52, UCLA Armenian History and Culture Series: Historic Armenian Cities and Provinces, 9. Costa Mesa, CA: Mazda Publishers, 2010.

Nicol, Donald. *Byzantium and Greece* (paper presented at University of London, King's College for the Inaugural Lecture in the Koraës Chair of Modern Greek and Byzantine History, Language and Literature, October 26th, 1971), Hertford: Bowman Press Ltd, 1972.

Nicol, Donald. *Church and Society in the Last Centuries of Byzantium: The Birkbeck Lectures, 1977*, Cambridge: Cambridge University Press, 1979.

Nicol, Donald. 'Byzantine Political Thought', in *The Cambridge History of Medieval Political Thought c.350-c.1450*, ed. J. Burns, 51–79, Cambridge: Cambridge University Press, 1988.

Obolensky, Dimitri. *The Byzantine Commonwealth: Eastern Europe, 500–1453*, London: Weidenfeld & Nicholson Phoenix, 1971.

Oikonomides, Nicolas. 'L'évolution de L'organisation Administrative de L'Empire Byzantin Au XIe Siècle (1025–1118)', *TM* 6 (1976): 126–52.

Oikonomides, Nicolas. *A Collection of Dated Byzantine Lead Seals*, Washington D.C.: Harvard University Press, 1986.

Oikonomides, Nicolas. 'The "Peira" of Eustathios Romaios: An Abortive Attempt to Innovate in Byzantine Law', *Fontes Minores* 14 (1986): 169–92.

Ostrogorsky, George. *A History of the Byzantine State*, trans. J. Hussey, Oxford: Blackwell Publishing, 1968.

Panossian, Razmik. *The Armenians: From Kings and Priests to Merchants and Commissars*, London: Hurst & Company, 2006.

Paparrigopoulos, Constantinos. *Ἱστορία τοῦ Ἑλληνικοῦ Ἔθνους ἀπό τῶν ἀρχαιοτάτων χρόνων μέχρι τῶν καθ' ἡμᾶς*, Athens, 1886.

Payaslian, Simon. *The History of Armenia: From the Origins to the Present*, Basingstoke: Palgrave MacMillan, 2007.

Peacock, Andrew. *Early Seljūk History: A New Interpretation*, London and New York: Routledge, 2010.

Peacock, Andrew. *The Great Seljuk Empire*, Edinburgh: Edinburgh University Press, 2015.

Preiser-Kapeller, Johannes. 'Aristocrats, Mercenaries, Clergymen and Refugees: Deliberate and Forced Mobility of Armenians in the Early Medieval Mediterranean (6th to 11th Century A.D.)', in *Migration Histories of the Medieval Afroeurasian Transition Zone*, ed. J. Preiser-Kapeller, L. Reinfandt and Y. Stouraitis, 327–84, Leiden: Brill, 2020.

Pryor, John and Michael Jeffreys. 'Alexios, Bohemond, and Byzantium's Euphrates Frontier: A Tale of Two Cretans', *Crusades* 11 (2012): 31–86.

Redgate, Anne. *The Armenians*, Oxford: Blackwell Publishers, 1998.

Reynolds, Susan. *Kingdoms and Communities in Western Europe, 900–1300*, Oxford: Clarendon Press, 1997.

Rodley, Lynn. 'The Pigeon House Church at Cavusin', *Jahrbuch der Österreichischen Byzantinistik* 33 (1983): 301–39.

Rubenstein, Jay. 'Guibert of Nogent, Albert of Aachen and Fulcher of Chartres: Three crusade chronicles intersect', in *Writing the Early Crusades: Text, Transmission and Memory*, ed. M. Bull and D. Kempf, 24–37, Woodbridge: The Boydell Press, 2014.

Runciman, Stephen. *The Emperor Romanus Lecapenus and His Reign*, Cambridge: Cambridge University Press, 1963.
Sarkissian, Karekin. *The Council of Chalcedon and the Armenian Church*, The Karekin I Theological and Armenological Studies Series, New York: The Armenian Church Prelacy, 1975.
Saunders, William. 'The Greek Inscription on the Harran Gate at Edessa: Some Further Evidence', *Byzantinische Forschungen* 21 (1995): 301–4.
Savvides, Alexios. 'The Armenian-Georgian-Byzantine Family of Apocapes/Abukab in the 11th c.', *Δίπτυχα* 5 (1991): 96–104.
Scott, Roger. 'The Classical Tradition in Byzantine Historiography', in *Byzantium and the Classical Tradition*, ed. M. Mullett and R. Scott, 61–74, Birmingham: Centre for Byzantine Studies, University of Birmingham, 1981.
Seibt, Werner. *Die Skleroi*, Vienna: Verlag der Österreichischen Akademie der Wissenschaften, 1976.
Seibt, Werner. 'War Gagik II. von Grossarmenien ca.1072–1073 Μέγας δοὺξ Χαρσιανοῦ?', in *Τὸ Ἑλληνικόν: Studies in Honor of Speros Vryonis*, 2 vols, II, 159–68, New Rochelle, 1993.
Seton-Watson, Hugh. *Nations and States*, London: Methuen, 1977.
Shepard, Jonathan. 'Scylitzes on Armenia in the 1040s, and the Role of Catacalon Cecaumenus', *REArm* XI (1975–1976): 269–311.
Shepard, Jonathan. 'A Suspected Source of Scylitzes' *Synopsis Historian*: The Great Catacalon Cecaumenus', *Byzantine and Modern Greek Studies* 16 (1992): 171–81.
Shepard, Jonathan. 'Constantine VII, Caucasian Openings and the Road to Aleppo', in *Eastern Approaches to Byzantium*, ed. A. Eastmond, 19–40, Aldershot: Ashgate Publishing, 2001.
Shepard, Jonathan. 'Marriages towards the Millennium', in *Byzantium in the Year 1000*, ed. Paul Magdalino, Leiden and Boston, MA: Leiden, 2003.
Shirinian, Manea Erna. 'Armenian Elites in Constantinople: Emperor Basil and Patriarch Photius', in *Armenian Constantinople*, ed. R. Hovannisian and S. Payaslian, 53–72, UCLA Armenian History and Culture Series: Historic Armenian Cities and Provinces, 9. Costa Mesa, CA: Mazda Publishers, 2010.
Slitt, Rebecca. 'Justifying Cross-Cultural Friendship: Bohemond, Fīrūz, and the Fall of Antioch', *Viator* 38, no. 2 (2007): 339–49.
Smith, Anthony. *Nationalism and Modernism: A Critical Survey of Recent Theories of Nations and Nationalism*, London: Routledge, 1998.
Smith, Anthony. *The Nation in History: Historiographical Debates about Ethnicity and Nationalism*, Hanover, NH: University Press of New England, 2000.
Speck, Paul. 'Byzantium: Cultural Suicide?', in *Byzantium in the Ninth Century: Dead or Alive?*, ed. Leslie Brubaker, 73–84, Aldershot and Burlington, VT: Ashgate, 1998.
Stouraitis, Ioannis. 'Roman Identity in Byzantium: A Critical Approach', *Byzantinische Zeitschrift* 107, no. 1 (2014): 175–220.
Stouraitis, Ioannis. 'Reinventing Roman Ethnicity in High and Late Medieval Byzantium', *Medieval Worlds* 5 (2017): 70–94.
Stouraitis, Ioannis. 'Migrating in the Medieval East Roman World', in *Migration Histories of the Medieval Afroeurasian Transition Zone*, ed. J. Preiser-Kapeller, L. Reinfandt and Y. Stouraitis, 141–65, Leiden: Brill, 2020.
Tannous, Jack. 'Romanness in the Syriac East', in *Transformations of Romanness: Early Medieval Regions and Identities*, ed. W. Pohl, C. Gantner, C. Grifoni and M. Pollheimer-Mohaupt, 457–79, Berlin and Boston, MA: De Gruyter, 2018.

Thiery, Jean-Michel. 'Monastères arméniens du Vaspurakan', *REArm* 6 (1969): 141–80.
Thiery, Jean-Michel. 'Données archéologiques sur les principautés armèniennes de cappadoce orientale au XIe siècle', *REArm* 26 (1996–7): 119–72.
Thomson, Robert. 'The Influence of their Environment on the Armenians in Exile in the Eleventh Century', in *Proceedings of the Thirteenth International Congress of Byzantine Studies*, ed. Joan M. Hussey, Dimitri Obolensky and Steven Runciman, 432–8, Oxford: Oxford University Press, 1967.
Thomson, Robert. 'The Crusaders through Armenian Eyes', in *The Crusades from the Perspective of Byzantium and the Muslim World*, ed. A. Laiou and R. Mottahedeh, 71–82, Washington D.C.: Dumbarton Oaks, 2001.
Tinnefeld, Franz. 'Die Stadt Melitene in ihrer späteren byzantinischen Epoche (934–1101)', in *Acts of the 14th International Congress 1971*, 3 vols, ii, 435–43, Bucharest: Editura Academiei Republicii Socialiste România, 1974.
Tougher, Shaun. 'Michael III and Basil the Macedonian: Just Good Friends?', in *Desire and Denial in Byzantium*, ed. L. James, 149–58, Aldershot: Ashgate Publishing, 1999.
Toumanoff, Cyril. 'The Background to Manzikert', in *Proceedings of the Thirteenth International Congress of Byzantine Studies*, ed. Joan M. Hussey, Dimitri Obolensky and Steven Runciman, 411–26, Oxford: Oxford University Press, 1967.
Treadgold, Warren. *Byzantium and Its Army, 284–1081*, Stanford, CA: Stanford University Press, 1995.
Treadgold, Warren. *A History of Byzantine State and Society*, Stanford, CA: Stanford University Press, 1997.
Treadgold, Warren. *The Middle Byzantine Historians*, Basingstoke: Palgrave MacMillan, 2013.
Trypanis, Constantine. *Medieval and Modern Greek Poetry*, Oxford: Clarendon Press, 1951.
Vakalopoulos, Apostolos. 'Byzantinism and Hellenism: Remarks on the Racial Origin and the Intellectual Continuity of the Greek Nation', *Balkan Studies* 9 (1968): 101–26.
Vakalopoulos, Apostolos. *The Origins of the Greek Nation: The Byzantine Period, 1261–1461*, New Brunswick, NJ: Rutgers University Press, 1970.
Van Lint, Theo. 'From Reciting to Writing and Interpretation: Tendencies, Themes, and Demarcations of Armenian Historical Writing', in *The Oxford History of Historical Writing*, vol. 2, Oxford: Oxford University Press, 2012.
Vryonis Jr, Speros. 'The Will of a Provincial Magnate, Eustathius Boilas (1059)', *DOP* 11 (1957): 263–77.
Vryonis Jr, Speros. 'Byzantium: The Social Basis of Decline in the Eleventh Century', in *Byzantium: Its Internal History and Relations with the Muslim World*, ed. S. Vryonis, vol. II, London: Variorum Reprints, 1971.
Vryonis Jr, Speros. 'Recent Scholarship on Continuity and Discontinuity of Culture: Classical Greeks, Byzantines, Modern Greeks', in *The 'Past' in Medieval and Modern Greek Culture*, ed. S. Vryonis, 237–56, Malibu, CA: Undena Publications, 1978.
Vryonis Jr, Speros. *The Decline of Medieval Hellenism in Asia Minor: And the Process of Islamization from the Eleventh through the Fifteenth Century*, Berkeley, CA: University of California Press, 1986.
Vryonis Jr, Speros. 'The Vita Basilii of Constantine Porphyrogenitus and the Absorption of Armenians in Byzantine Society', in *Ευφρόσυνον· Αφιέρωμα στον Μανώλη Χατζηδάκη*, 2 vols, ii, 676–93, Athens: Ekdosē tou Tameiou Archaiologikōn Porōn kai Apallotriōseōn, 1992.
Vryonis Jr, Speros. 'Greek Identity in the Middle Ages', *Études balkaniques* 6 (1999): 19–36.

Weller, AnnaLinden. *Imagining Pre-Modern Imperialism: The Letters of Byzantine Imperials Agents outside the Metropole*, Unpublished Thesis, Rutgers, 2014.
Whittow, Mark. 'How the East was Lost: The Background to the Komnenian *reconquista*', in *Alexios I Komnenos, vol. 1: Papers*, ed. M. Mullett and D. Smythe, 55–67, Belfast: Belfast Byzantine Enterprises, 1996.
Whittow, Mark. *The Making of Orthodox Byzantium, 600–1025*, Basingstoke: Palgrave Macmillan, 1996.
Wilson, Nigel. *Scholars of Byzantium*, Cambridge, MA: Medieval Academy of America, 1996.
Witakowski, Witold. 'The Chronicle of Eusebius; Its Type and Continuation in Syriac Historiography', *Aram Periodical* 11–12 (1999–2000): 419–37.
Witakowski, Witold. 'Syriac Historiographical Sources', in *Byzantines and Crusaders in Non-Greek Sources*, ed. M. Whitby, 253–82, Proceedings of the British Academy 132, Oxford: Oxford University Press, 2007.
Yarnley, C. 'Philaretos – Armenian Bandit of Byzantine General?', *REArm* 9 (1972): 331–54.
Yarnley, C. 'The Armenian Philhellenes: A Study of the Spread of Byzantine Religious and Cultural Ideas among the Armenians in the Tenth and Eleventh Centuries A.D', *Eastern Churches Review* 8, no. 1 (1976): 45–53.
Young, Frances. *From Nicaea to Chalcedon: A Guide to the Literature and Its Background*, London: SCM Press Ltd, 1983.
Yuzbashian, Karen. 'Les titres byzantins en arménie', in *L'Arménie et Byzance: Histoire et Culture*, ed. N. Garsoïan, 213–21, Byzantina Sorbonesia 12, Paris: Publications de la Sorbonne, 1996.

INDEX

Abara 76
Abbasid Caliphate 4–5, 51
Abydos (battle of) 53
Adana 111
Adrianople 24, 26
Agapios of Kyminas 49
Aleppo 106, 117
Alexander 34
Alexios I Komnenos 39, 102, 108, 117, 126
al-Hakim (the mad) 56
alienation 52, 73, 80, 90
   loyalty 96, 101
   religious antagonism 73, 80–90, 95–6, 98
Alp Arslan 88, 97, 103–5, 109–10
Amasia 62, 79
Amida 50
Anazarbos 118
Anemas (of Crete) 15, 17
Angold, Michael 63
Ani
   Byzantine governance of 46
   sack by Seljuk Turks 90
annexations 48–62
   Ani 56–8, 61, 67–70, 77, 94
   Edessa 61–2
   Kars 62–3, 79
   Tao/Tayk 50, 51, 54, 59
   Taron 29, 35, 54
   Vaspurakan 59–60
Antioch 25, 40, 50, 57, 103, 108, 115, 117–18, 128
   doux 55, 105
   Nikephoros 107, 115
Aparank 60
Apokapes, Basil 115–16
Apokapes, Pharasmanios 117
Argyros, Eustathios 29
Aristakes Lastivertc'i 46, 48, 74
Aristides (*Roman Oration*) 9

Armenians 4
   Apostolic Church 5, 8, 15, 18, 36–7, 48, 73, 80–1
   army 31–6, 90, 98–9
   Chalcedonians 42
   in Constantinople 23
   elections of *katholikoi* 120–2
   expansion 84–6, 95, 117
   frontiers 21, 25, 29, 49, 99, 103
   identity 5, 17–19
   medieval Armenia 4
   nobility 5
   post-Manzikert 119–24
   settlement (eleventh century) 64–7, 73–5
   settlement (pre-eleventh century) 22–6
Arminius 12
Arsacids 4, 26
Artanuj 49
Artsruni 50, 59, 66, 73, 79, 85, 90, 123
   Ablgharib 89, 108, 110, 112, 114–15
   Abusahl 73, 77, 85–7, 92–3, 96–7, 111
   Atom 73, 77–8, 84–7, 92–3, 95–7, 111
   David (*see* David Artsruni)
   Derenik 76, 92
   Gagik I (of Vaspurakan) 5
   migration 47
   rebellion of 2, 91–3
   settlement in Cappadocia 63–5, 75–6, 81, 83
   Shapuh 92–3
Ashot (Asotios) Kiskasis 49
Ashot (the long armed) 29
Ashot I Bagratuni 4
Ashot II the Iron 39
Ashot III 39, 41, 50, 63
Ashot IV 57–8, 68–70, 93
Aspietes, *see* Oshin

Index

assimilation
  acceptance of Roman customs 26–31, 67, 100
  bonds of kinship 26–8
  ideology 28–31, 67, 80, 90
  law 43
  mechanics of 21
  model 21, 26
  religious 36–43, 80
  settlement 22–6
  titles 51, 54, 66, 73, 76–9, 94, 126
Attaleiates, Michael 74, 102
Augustus 10
Aurelian 12
azats 5, 54, 58, 64, 69, 92

Baghdad 52, 124–5
Bagrat of Iberia 50–1, 55
Baldwin of Boulogne 127–8
Bardas (Caesar) 27
Basil I 2, 4, 16, 32–4, 39, 44, 49
  events in Southern Italy 16
  origins 22, 24, 27–8
Basil II 2, 14, 50, 52–3, 59, 61, 63, 69
  Bulgarian wars 55
  conflict with Georgia 45, 47, 55, 59, 68
  image 46–8, 57, 90, 92
  policy in Caucasia 45, 51, 54–5, 58, 63–4, 67
  revolt of Bardas Phokas 30, 35, 51–3
  revolt of Bardas Skleros 29–30, 35, 51–3
  revolt of Nikephoros Phokas and Nikephoros Xiphias 59–60, 63–7, 76
  settlement policy 64–7, 71, 76–9, 83, 92
Basil Lekapenos (the Chamberlain) 53
Bertha of Provence 14
Bjni 78
Bohemond 108
Boilas, Eustathios 76
Brachamios, Philaretos 15–16, 89, 106–8, 110–11, 113–19, 126, 128
  interactions with the Armenian church 120–3
  titles 114–15
Brousselle, Isabelle 8

Bryennios, Nikephoros 102, 107
Bulgarophygon (battle of) 29
Buzan (emir) 119, 125
Byzantium
  collapse of eastern frontier 74, 106–8, 112–19, 129
  ideology of 48, 50
  legacy of Rome 3
  relationship with Armenians 1, 15, 43, 45, 47–8, 50–2, 67, 79–80, 90, 94, 97, 100–1, 110, 112, 129–30
Romaioi 3, 7

Caesarea 52, 65, 76–7, 111–12
Camndaw 65
Cappadocia 2, 32, 41, 47, 63–7, 70–1, 73, 75–8, 80, 83, 86, 93, 95–6, 101, 109, 112, 129
Cavuşin, Pigeon House Church 35, 40
Chalcedon, council of 3, 5, 37
Chaldia 34
Charanis, Peter 7
Charlemagne 15
Charpezikon 33
Charsianon 75, 77, 101, 109
Chatatourios 105–6
Cheynet, Jean-Claude 8, 59–60, 67
Choniates, Niketas 14, 16
Chrysopolis (battle of) 52
Cilicia 15, 21, 24–5, 33, 75, 102, 106, 109–10, 113–15, 117, 124, 128, 130, 135
Claudius 9
Claudius II Gothicus 12
Colmesol 112
Comana 62, 79
Commagene 15
Constantine (the Armenian) 27
Constantine I 11, 28
Constantine V 23
Constantine VI 15, 26
Constantine VII 13, 24, 32, 34–5, 39, 49–50
  Cretan expedition (949) 33
  De Administrando Imperio 13, 15–16
Constantine VIII 46, 68
Constantine IX Monomachos 57–8, 69, 71, 77–8, 82, 84–5, 94, 96

Constantine X Doukas   62, 80, 82, 85–6, 95, 104, 107
Constantine Leichoudes (Syriac patriarch)   74
Constantinople   15–16, 51
  Rus attack (1043)   69
Corbulo, Gnaeus Domitius   1
Cowe, S. Peter   8
crusaders   101, 128
custom (ἔθος)   2, 13 – 16, 19

Dagron, Gilbert   8
David III *Kouropalates* of Tao   38, 42, 46, 48, 50–1, 53, 57, 66, 68, 116
  murder of   53–5
David Artsruni (son of Senek'erim-Yovhannes)   59, 65, 77, 81, 86, 91, 95–6, 110
David of Sassoun   114
Dédéyan, Gérard   29, 80
Demetrius of Cyzicus   46
Diocletian   12
Djakrous (the patrician)   53
Dorostolon (battle of)   35
Dostourian, Ara   59–60
Doukas, Andronikos   29, 104–6
Doukas, John   104
Dyrrachium   30

Edessa   115–16, 118–19, 124–8
Elissaios (eunuch)   15
Ephesus, council of   37
Erytho/Rotrude   15, 17
Eudokia   103, 107

Fatimids   99, 103
First Crusade   103, 119, 124–5, 128–30, 136

Gabriel of Melitene   110, 119, 123–7, 136
  Morphia (daughter)   125
Gagik I   57
Gagik II   47, 63, 67–71, 73, 77–8, 80–2, 84–8, 90, 93, 95–8, 100–1, 105, 109–10, 120
  death   110–13, 129
  marriage alliances   110–11
  murder of Mark metropolitan of Caesarea   88–9, 110

Gagik-Abas II   62, 79, 90, 110–11
Garsoïan, Nina   7, 38, 42, 59, 80, 90
George Lorensis   120–1
Georgia (kingdom)
  creation   55
  sources   46
Germanicus   12
Giorgi I   46, 55–8, 68, 77
Greenwood, Timothy   18
Gregory II (katholikos)   86, 119–23, 127
Gregory III (katholikos)   122
Gregory the Illuminator   4
Grigor Narerkac'i   46, 60
Gurgen-Kvirike II (of Lori)   122
Gurgen of Iberia   50–1, 55

Harold Hardrada   69
Harran gate   126, 137
Hellas   31
Hierapolis   99, 107, 117
Hilarion   54–5
Holmes, Catherine   46, 60, 63, 65
Howard-Johnston   64, 66
Hugh of Provence   14

Iasites, Michael   79
Iberia   38, 49, 98, *see also* Georgia
Ibn al-Athīr   103
Iconoclasm   3
Ikonion
  sack (1069)   97
Irene   26
Islam   3–4, 14, 17, 118

John I Tzmiskes   24, 32, 34–6, 39, 41, 50, 52, 103
John II Komnenos   14–15
John V the Historian (katholikos)/Yovhannes Drasxanakertc'i   38–41
John VII Grammatikos (patriarch)   27
John VII Sarigta (Syrian patriarch)   41, 83
John the Monk (of Lydia)   46, 74
Julian II the Roman   12
Justinian
  Corpus Juris Civilis   2

Kaldellis, Anthony

Armenian Fallacy 6, 8
Kallipolis (Italy) 16
Kars 80
Kaycon 79
Kayean 78
Kazhdan, Alexander 8
Kekaumenos, Katakalon 46, 74, 94
Kelesine 97
Kesoun 119, 121, 124, 127, 128
Khachik I/Xač'ik I (katholikos) 40
Khachik II (katholikos) 83–6, 89
Khawatanēk 65
Khliat 104
Kiwrakos 68
Kizistra 111–12
Kogh Vasil 119, 127–8
Komnene, Anna 102
Komnenos, Isaac 107–8
Kourkouas (family) 34–5, 52
Kourkous, John 31, 49
Kourtikios 25, 35
 Manuel (son of) 35
Kozern, Yovhannes 74, 93
Krinites (interpreter) 35
Ktrich' 97–8

Laiou, Angeliki 8
Lakape 33
Lampron 111
Lapara 25
Larissa 62, 76, 79
Lekapenoi (family) 31, 33–4
Leo (the Armenian) 24, 26, 28
Leo IV 24
Leo VI (the Wise) 23, 25, 29, 31, 49
Lokana 25
Lombards 69
Lugdunum (Lyon) 9
Lykandos 25, 29, 75, 77, 98, 101, 109, 113

Maiktes 24, 26, 28
Malik-Shah 117–18, 124, 136
Mamistra 110–11, 113, 118
Maniakes, George 61–2, 69
Manuel of Tekis/Tephrike 23, 25
Manzikert 104
 battle of 2, 73, 90, 97, 99–101, 103–5, 112, 129

Marash (Msher) 113, 115, 116, 121–3, 128
Matthew of Edessa 15, 17–19, 46–7, 87, 102
Maurice 23
medieval Hellenism, *see* Charanis, Peter
medieval Syria
 Miaphysite (Jacobite) Church 8
Melias (the Great) 25, 29, 35
Melias (the younger) 35–6, 40, 50
Melissenos (family) 52
Melitene 25, 29, 33–4, 41, 49, 77, 83, 98, 105, 113, 115, 119, 121, 124–7, 136
Mesopotamia 34, 75, 79, 94, 98
Mesrop Mashtots 4
Miaphysite 5
Michael IV the Paphlagonian 68–9, 91–2
Michael V Kalaphates 69
Michael VII Doukas 14, 105, 110, 113–14, 117
Michael the Syrian 23, 39, 102
Missis, *see* Mamistra
Mushegh of Kars 62

Nero 1
Nicaea 117
 council of (325) 37
Nicholas I Mystikos (patriarch) 38, 40–1
Nikephoros II Phokas 23, 32–3, 41–2, 50, 52, 54
Nikephoros III Botaneiates 102, 105, 107–8, 115, 117
Nikephoros Ouranos 55
Normans 69

Oshin (Hetumid) 113–14, 117–18, 123–4
Ošk'i 52
Ostrogorsky, George 63

Paetus, Lucius Caesennius 1
Pahlavuni, Grigor (magistros) 78–9, 89, 93–5, 120
 Vahram (son) (*see* Gregory II)
 Vasak 108
Pahlavuni, Vahram 69, 79
Paparon 111
Parsegh of Cilicia 122

Paul of Varag   122–3
Paulicians   23–4
Peter I (Bulgaria)   13
Peter I (katholikos)   47, 56–7, 70, 83–6, 89, 123
Philomelion   56
Phokas (family)   32–3, 52, 64, 71
Photios (patriarch)   22, 39
Pizu   82
Plantanion   32
Prine   32
Prosuch   15, 17
Psellos, Michael   62, 69, 102

Robert Guiscard   14
Romaios, Eustathios (judge)   42
Roman I (of Bulgaria)   24
Romanization   4, 6, 9–17
    army   11–12
    Christianization   11
    Constitutio Antoniniana   10
    Imperial Cult   10–11
Romanopolis   115
Romanos I Lekapenos   13–14, 16, 33–5, 49
    Maria (daughter)   13
Romanos II   13–15, 32, 34
Romanos III Argyros   61, 80, 84
Romanos IV Diogenes   74–5, 80–1, 97–9, 101–6, 109–10, 112, 113, 117
Ruben   112
Rubenids   113

Salman of Edessa   61–2
Samonas (eunuch)   29
Samosata   33, 62
Samuel (of Bulgaria)   24, 30
Samuel of Ani   102, 111–12, 114
Sargis (of Ani)   70
Sarkis I (katholikos)   40
Sarkis of Edessa   115
Sarkis of Marash (nephew of Peter I)   121
Sebasteia   33, 41, 48, 70, 73, 75–9, 81, 84, 93, 95–7, 101, 109, 111–12, 123, 129
Seleukeia   99
Seljuk Turks   62–3, 90, 98, 104
    settlement of Anatolia   109
Senek'erim-Yovhannes (Artsruni)   59–60, 64–7, 76–7, 81, 91

separatism   96–9, 103, 109–18
    imperial agents   101, 109, 112, 113, 115, 135
    lordships   103, 112–18
Severus, Marcus Valerius   9
Sharaf al-Dawla Muslim ibn Quraysh   118
Shepard, Jonathan   51
Sibṭ b. al-Jawzī   103, 105
Sirmium   13
Skleroi (family)   29–32, 52, 71
Skylitzes, John   16, 45, 74, 102
St Gregory the Illuminator   4, 81
Stephen III (katholikos)   41
Stephen of Taron   17–18, 46
Sulayman b. Qutlumush   117–18
Svyatoslav   35
Syrian Church   41
Syrian migration   82–4

Tancred   128
Tanushman   110
Tao/Tayk   47, 51–2, 56
Tarchaniotes, Joseph   107–8
Tarchaniotes, Katakalon   107–8
Taron   23, 35, 42, 79, 94
Taronites, Ashot (Asotios)
    marriage to Miroslava (daughter of Samuel of Bulgaria)   30
Taronites, Bagrat   23, 29, 44, 51, 54, 67
Taronites, Grigor   23, 29, 44, 51, 54, 67
Taronites, Michael   89
Tarsus   25, 83, 110, 113, 115, 117–18, 121
Tephrike/Tekis   23, 33, 81
Theodora Porphyrogenita   69
Theodore Alakhosik (Honi)   122
Theodore of Sebasteia   46
Theodosioupolis   34, 49
Theophanes the Confessor   15
Theophilos   27
Thessalonica   30
Thrakesion   33
Tiddis   10
Tigranes VI   1
Tiridates I   1
Tiridates IV   4
T'ornik   53
Tornikios family   35
T'oros of Edessa   119, 124, 126–8, 136

Treadgold, Warren   46, 106
Trebizond   30, 47, 53, 56, 59
   treaty of   56–8, 67–8
Tutush of Damascus   125
Tzamandos   29, 62, 79

Urbicus, Quintus Lollius   9
Ursinus, *see* Oshin

Vahan (katholikos)   41
Varag   76, 81, 122
Varangians   14, 69
Vaspurakan   5, 41, 50, 59–60, 63–5, 75, 76, 79, 94

Venetians   15–16
Vladimir I Sviatoslavich   14
Vologases I   1
Volubilis   9

Xawatanēk   76

Yahya of Antioch   46, 74
Yovhannes-Smbat III   57–8, 60–1, 63, 68–70, 93

Zahir al-Din Nishapuri   104, 109
Zapranik of Mokk   60
Zoe Porphyrogenita   69